# From Herodotus

# to Columbus

## Randall S. Howarth

The Flügel Company

ISBN 978-0-9893991-0-4

First Edition published by
The Flügel Company
821 West Second Street
Erie PA 16507

Printed in the United States of America

Cover Art: author photos of the
Domitian Cancelleria reliefs
on display in the Vatican Museums

Cindy, cara mea

# Table of Contents

# Illustrations and Maps

# Caveat Legior[*]

*Why this volume?*

According to the conventions developed by Historians, Western Europe, defined here broadly as a triangle whose points lie in Greece, Spain and Britain, proceeded through three major historical phases—ancient, medieval,[†] and modern. This book looks at the first two of these. The book features twelve historical topics covering contexts from the ancient world up to the threshold of the modern era (circa 1500) and so resembles in outward structure a traditional Western Civilization textbook. But, while the volume does proceed in a more or less chronological fashion, it does not present a continuous narrative nor does it present a comprehensive treatment of any one civilization or moment in time. It is not therefore a *typical* Western Civilization textbook and there is a reason for this. At the scholarly level, it is nowadays a matter of some debate whether or not understanding patterns of western thought and social organization for periods before 1500 is useful to explain the present in any meaningful way. The chief proponents of that position are noticeably modern historians, that is, they are interested in and therefore study only the period since 1500, and more particularly that since the American and French Revolutions. Those scholarly assumptions inevitably filter down to the popular imagination where, although there has certainly been an increasing exposure

---

[*] *Caveat Legior:* Latin for *"let the reader beware."*

[†] *Medieval:* relating to the Middle Ages, the period between the fall of the Roman Empire in Italy (c. 500) and the Italian Renaissance (c. 1350). It also an idiomatic expression in English connoting *unenlightened, brutish,* or *cruel.* For example, there is a reference in the 1994 film *Pulp Fiction* where the character Marcellus Wallace promised "to get medieval" on someone. The connotation is clear; sadistic torture is about to happen.

of the ancient and medieval worlds, the cartoonish nature of that exposure and the lack of sophistication in the historical knowledge of many screenwriter teams threatens to relegate everything before Columbus to the realm of fantasy. This book is my attempt at a corrective.

Each people has a memory of its own past, usually an imperfect one, and that memory is a predictable element in a people's image of itself. Each succeeding phase of history constructs its own special version of the past, most predictably in a way that supports or justifies the present. In European history, we see this clearly in the zeitgeists* of the main periods we mentioned above (ancient, medieval and modern). In the Middle Ages, the shattered remnants of the Roman empire were everywhere. In both real and metaphorical fashion, medieval intellectuals and leaders quarried Roman building blocks to construct a universe that both embraced the pagan Romans and rejected them at the same time. The modern period begins in the Italian Renaissance during which Europeans embraced antiquity with new enthusiasm. From then through the Enlightenment† period western thinkers used Greek and Roman history and science to construct a cross upon which they crucified both medieval thinking and the excesses of religion and they used its literature as a source of archetypical heroes and villains. The writers of the American constitution were intimately familiar with this idiom and used it extensively in their construction of political theory. Now however, in our sophisticated "post-modern" view of things, we have again thrown aside the political idiom that inspired numerous statues depicting George Washington as a modern version of the Roman hero, Cincinnatus. However, in our vainglorious sophistication, we have perhaps thrown out the baby with the bath water and abandoned the ancient and medieval worlds to the specialists. Even if the distant past were not interesting—which thankfully is not at all true—

---

* *Zeitgeist:* the spirit of a time.

† *Enlightenment:* the period of European intellectual history (from about 1600 to about 1800) characterized by a fundamental confidence in human reason to make sense of the world.

there remains *far* too much to ignore in these periods that is directly or indirectly responsible for the way westerners think.

My goal here is not so much to relate in comprehensive manner everything of potential significance in the periods covered as it is to highlight some of the connections we have to this part of our heritage, some real and some imagined, and to provide opportunities for reflection and discussion. My method is to present a series of arguments with topical relevance to modern concerns and sensibilities. The relationship of religion, community, and the individual, represents a recurrent topic wending its way through the volume.

The various historical contexts and my choices for supporting detail reflect the emphases of my survey classes after twenty years of teaching at the university level. Although the volume proceeds in a chronological manner, it is occasionally necessary to take examples from different moments in time in order to illustrate major points. Each argument will provide an approach to a given moment in time upon which it is possible to build further according to the interests and curiosity of the reader. A careful reader with no background in these periods will derive a significant cultural vocabulary from reading this book and gain a sense of the sort of historical issues that continue to interest and beguile scholars. On the other hand, the relatively bare bones presentation reflects my expectation that readers can and will reach for more detailed treatments if they so choose.

I have long since given up trying to cover everything and some will undoubtedly regard my little volume with a jaundiced eye, especially when they discover what it leaves out. Instructors who decide they *do* like the volume will do so probably because it allows them extra space to create a more flexible course. For my own part, I augment the book with a primary sourcebook reader I have developed and I do stand-alone presentations on interesting topics. But all of these are adjuncts to the greater questions of ethics, the interaction between religion and politics, and the origins of our aesthetic preferences, all of which can best be developed using the kind of thematic approach to History that this book attempts to embody. I have accumulated many hundreds of images and video clips over the years. In my vanity, I have included a few of these in the form of sketches.

# Chapter One: Herodotus and the Invention of History

*Is History "just the facts ma'am," or is it something more?*[*]

What is History? The word comes from the ancient Greek and originally meant "research." Herodotus, a Greek living in the great city of Athens at the height of its power and glory, introduced it as a new genre of prose literature. Although word was imprecise when it was first used, ever since Herodotus, readers tend to understand "History" as a progress of political affairs set forth in narrative form. Those who *now* write history might say the same, except they would add that their main source of evidence is text as opposed to, for example, archaeology or anthropology, both of which emphasize physical remains and comparative observation. With the distant past, much of the textual evidence we have as sources are actually second hand bits of history written by people who lived in the past-Herodotus, for example. His famous book featuring the Greek and Persian Wars is the earliest European attempt to explain human affairs in prose form. The reason why we now associate "History" with politics and war is that these subjects were what the various Greek and Roman historical writers who followed Herodotus thought was most important. This has changed somewhat in our own time; modern researchers now tend to put more emphasis on "*Social* History." What were women doing? What were children doing? What were individual soldiers doing? What did they eat? How did they entertain themselves?

---

[*] "Just the facts ma'am" is a line often uttered by LAPD Sgt. Joe Friday in *Dragnet,* a police show that went through various iterations as a radio show, a TV series, and several movie versions. It has become an idiomatic expression for a presentation without editorial or interpretation.

Because Herodotus was the first historian in the western tradition there were no rules to break in the writing of history and much of what he wrote would actually fall into other categories if he only knew what they were. His book covers topics from anthropology to zoology. He tells us about gold digging ants in India and he tells us about ritual prostitution in Persia. He dabbles in political theory and he speculates on the formation of the Nile delta. But what he was always most interested in, and what ties his huge book together was answering the big question: *why?* For Herodotus, the biggest "why" was this: *why did the plans and schemes of so many great men fail?*

HERODOTUS' GOLD-DIGGING ANT

More specifically, he wanted to know how it could be that a handful of squabbling Greek city-states set aside their differences long enough to defeat an army sent by the mighty Persian Empire to conquer them. There is an important intellectual moment here. Herodotus is not just describing events, he is presenting a theory, an argument; he is presenting a series of historical events in a pattern in support of that argument.

We will talk about his argument below, but it is first important to note that the way Herodotus set about his task provides an important link in an intellectual tradition that has helped define the modern western mind. It also provides an object lesson in the problems of knowing the distant past. Unlike the modern world where one can visit city archives to look up birth and death records or read old newspapers for contemporary descriptions, the ancient world survives for us in an incomplete fashion. Sometimes the only surviving records we have left are writings of men like Herodotus. It gets gradually better over time, but there are huge swathes of time for which we have only the tiniest amount of contemporary evidence and frequently the evidence we do have is problematic. I mean... come on; gold-digging ants in India? Are you kidding me? Does this mean we throw everything he wrote out the window? Or do we excavate his text in search of reliable artifacts? How do we tell what is reliable and what is not? Where do we even start? *What was Herodotus' process*? Let us begin by considering our own process.

It is natural to think of history simply as a record of the past; a presentation of events and artifacts or, for non-fans of history, one damn thing after another. This is a perfectly reasonable but narrow definition of history. It implies that something is important *just because it happened.* By this logic, everything that has happened is equally important except that some things are just more interesting than other things. But let us be serious. If we put aside whether something is interesting, *the only real reason that anything in the past could ever matter is that it must somehow be relevant to the present.* Or the future. Remembering this gets us much closer to understanding process and understanding process prepares us to excavate ancient historical writing, including that of Herodotus.

Even those uninterested in History are familiar with some version of the dictum: "Those who ignore the mistakes of the past are doomed to repeat them." Let us not repeat *that* mistake--whatever it was. Here the theoretical impact of the past on the present is obvious and a potential *usefulness* emerges logically. But is *this* why the past matters? So we can *learn* from it? What *do* we learn exactly? I am not sure, but I *can* say that there is *something else* going on as well and it has much to do with the *direction* of history. What do I mean by this? When we think of the past, we are accustomed to thinking of it as moving *toward* us. It happened before us so it affected us. It made us who we are, blah, blah, blah. OK. That's the *past.* But is "the past" *History*? I would argue that *the past is only half of History*; the other half is the present and—the present changes the past. This seems counterintuitive and logically impossible; how can something that has already happened change because of something that happens afterwards? Obviously it can't *literally* change, but *what we know* about the past definitely changes. And, much more to the point, how we *feel* about the past changes and *what we think is important* most definitely changes as well. It is certainly true, for example, that the gender and racial politics of the last fifty years of US History has transformed the study of ancient Greece and Rome. Historians interested in the ancient past had little interest in women as a category of interest, and analyses of race and ethnic identity in ancient society were few and far between. Since the 1960s this had changed dramatically. Now some of the most interesting and provocative investigation of the ancient world is being done with these categories as featured elements. So why should the racial and gender politics of modern America have any impact on Ancient History? What has one to do with the other? The answer is simple: we grapple with the present in our study of the past. And since every generation has a new set of problems, this inevitably translates into a different history for every generation. Consequently, we must allow room for an understanding of history as an ongoing and *changeable* relationship between the past and the present; one might also argue that history *ought* to change, as we become better versions of ourselves. Part of understanding the development of the western mind involves plotting the moments where *we changed our minds* about things.

## Editorial Intention and Historical Theory

The original conception of the course for which this book is designed provides an obvious example of editorial intention. The first and most essential emphasis of all "Western Civilization" courses is an admiration for classical Greek and Roman political forms and their aesthetic principles as interpreted by post-medieval European artists and writers. The origins and evolution of Christianity represents a second and separate essential emphasis. The resulting narrative is a synthesis of these two streams of influence. The underlying assumption is that a studied balance between Greco-Roman political ideals and Christian ethical principles has engendered true human progress toward the greater good. This interpretation of Western Civilization resonates with the linear understanding of time that is so much a product of modern thinking. Called "Whiggish" history, it was first developed by Europeans and later adopted by Americans all of whom noticed that the west has dominated much of the planet for most of the last 500 years and sought a *scientific* explanation for it.* One can like the way things turned out or not like it; it really doesn't matter. But there ought to be some logical explanation for how western domination came to be. There are lots of good places to start, but the one that is most reflexive, the one that is most, let us say, chauvinistic,† is to begin with the assumption that there is something superior in western civilization because successful domination is evidence of success.

The course for which this book is intended is, at the university level, usually presented as part one of a two-course sequence conventionally entitled *Western Civilization*. Many schools designate one or both parts, or a combined version, as fulfilling a core requirement. Although other options now exist that "check the box" so to speak, *Western Civilization* has historically been regarded as an essential orientation to the idea of an emergent and successful West. It is not neutral. It is not "just the facts ma'am;" it is a polemic, which means that it is intended to advance a particular argument, and by extension the falsity of other arguments. The implicit argument is that Western Culture is the best and that its inherent superiority is responsible for the domination of the west. The alternate argument would be that the West has prevailed due to some combination of accidents of geography, personality, and climate. In order to understand the starting point for this argument, one need only recall that this conception of European history evolved in the eighteenth and nineteenth centuries, that is to say, in the context of active western domination of the entire planet. Add to this the rhetorical equation of westernization with modernization and the intended message of this category of history becomes even clearer: the west is dominant *because of its* history and will continue to be so as long as we remember how we got here. The ultimate extension of Whig history is the presumption that all other development paths are flawed and must be avoided.

For various reasons, some good and some bad, philosophers and historians over the last fifty years have distanced themselves from Whiggish narratives even as colleges and universities continue to offer the courses

---

* *Whig*: the word is first associated with British opponents of absolute monarchy in the late 1600s. The Whigs embraced ideas of political reform and technological progress as inevitable steps toward improving the human condition.

† *Chauvinism*: an exaggerated belief in one's superiority.

that were inspired by them. This divergence has two important results: a re-orientation of existing Western Civilization courses and the parallel development of an *alternative* course sequence: *World* History. As it is now, nearly all universities have World History courses and secondary school students are now more likely to take a World History course than a Western Civilization course. Triumphalist rhetoric in surviving Western Civilization courses is muted or deleted in favor of sidebars touting the contributions of non-elites. Narratives featuring kings and battles have been replaced with descriptions of peasants and beer making. We can live without some of that triumphalist rhetoric to be sure, and it is nice to know what someone besides the king is doing. But what is the *narrative?* Without a unifying *narrative*, history can devolve, alas, into one damn thing after another. And we have enough of that on the internet.

So if there is a difference between "just the facts ma'am" and "History," then it is found in the interpretive constructs that historical writers impose on the facts. Just as we see that the traditional notion of "Western Civilization" is essentially an interpretive construct useful to validate our socio-economic position in the world, so also can we see that the narrative construct it represents stands outside of and essentially precedes the facts that comprise it. And not only does a narrative bring life and order to collections of facts, it also determines which facts are relevant! Here's where we see a tension between history as science or history as literature. To see it as only one or the other is a strictly modern problem.[i] Truly, any history written before the present continues to survive as a form of literature and in its infancy the discipline was always intended as such. It is a vanity on our part to think of it strictly as a science. The real science in history is in seeing the malleable relationship of narrative and subject and understanding it as a record of two different things. So we first ask whether the details are reliable, representative, or at least plausible. Then we ask whether the narrative carrying the details is actually the point, as opposed to what happened. Once we make that distinction, we are in a position to

---

[i] One sees this tension in modern universities where the History department is sometimes located in the school of "Social Sciences" and in others where it is located in the school of "Humanities."

10

reassemble the details in a rubric more consonant with our own interests.

We do not read Herodotus' description of gold digging ants to gather insight on ancient insects. We do so because it tells us something about the way ancient Greeks viewed the world. We can do the same with all historical narratives.

WHAT CHERRY TREE?

Every culture looks into its past, celebrates certain moments, and claims ownership of certain things. In essence, this is a form of ancestor worship. Like any religiously tinged endeavor, adherence to strict rules of evidence and proof are not required. Who has not heard the "George Washington and the Cherry Tree" story? This kind of history is evident in every culture and is intended to resonate *within* those respective cultures and is, on that account, the least scientific. At one and the same time, every culture has a narrower and more practical interest in a scientific version of its own past, at the very least because the past is where law and custom come from. This is not to say that cultures are duty bound to know their past and to cite it honestly. But to claim the authority of the past presupposes *in the mind of the listener* the existence of a plausible understanding of that past. The purpose for which the past is adduced as an authority obviously defines what portion of the past is emphasized. This yields an essential observation concerning History: *it is a combination of what happened then*—whenever then was—*and how we feel now*. For example, I have begun to use an environmental history of the classical world as an assigned reading in some of my ancient world electives. Such a book could only be written now as we live in a period of anxiety about our own impact on the environment. Likewise one can interpret the explosion of historical treatments of pre-modern women, of ethnic identity, of the economy, of alternate political models, and of religion. We ask questions about the past that are relevant in our own present. Whether the answers we generate are actually useful to remedy the present is another matter, but we see that the past is at the very least useful, and safe in a sense, as a forum for working through our anxieties about the present. And since how we feel changes one can say that History also changes.

So History as a discipline can be defined as a process through which we consider our present through the lens of the past. The problem is that neither the past nor the present sit still. The past keeps getting farther away and there is always more of it accumulating. And the present is always new; this means that, practically speaking, every generation must look backward in time and see the past in terms of its own experience. Let me give you two examples: consider such men as Julius Caesar and Alexander the Great. History records them as successful and charismatic conquerors. Books lauding their preeminence in this category have existed from their day until our own and I dare say that history will never tire of them altogether. But a curious thing happened in the mid-1900s. Treatments of ancient conquerors in Greece and Rome began to exhibit signs of disapproval. And the why of it is entirely logical. The center stage of world history was occupied by charismatic conquerors: Hitler, Stalin, and the rest. These were all charismatic dictators who killed, enslaved, and destroyed cultures. So if you wrote a book about Julius Caesar in 1940, who were you, in a sense, *really* writing about? If we step back to the theoretical level, you can see that in this instance you began with an opinion, a premise, or a point of view: People who kill, enslave, and destroy are bad. Then you turned to your topic area, say perhaps Julius Caesar, and then emphasized that part of the record which seemed to exemplify your starting premise: People who kill, enslave, and destroy are bad.

In a more recent example, we notice a trend in war writing. What do Steven Ambrose's *Band of Brothers*, and the films *Saving Private Ryan* and *The Hurt Locker* have in common? They ignore the politics and the generals and any agonizing over the decisions that throw civilizations into conflict in favor of highlighting the valor and travails of ordinary citizens whose lists of priorities feature mere survival. The emphasis and appeal of these powerful stories comes from our own contemporary distrust of government. This is certainly not new as an idea. But whereas Joseph Heller's *Catch-22* and the Stanley Kubrick film *Dr. Strangelove* played on the absurdity and incompetence of government and bureaucracy, this later generation of war writing ignores those issues altogether. In all of these cases, the structures of the narratives are defined by feelings about what is happening in the "now," not the "then," whenever the "then" was. Much historical writing is inherently editorial and polemic by nature, and therefore controversial because whatever stand one takes, whatever interpretation one imposes, it is not inherently a function of *the facts*, it is a function of the *arrangement* of the facts.

It is certainly true that many modern writers write histories that seem narrowly focused and never get past the specifics of what actually happened. To some extent this is the result of professional backbiting and author timidity. All novel interpretations invite reaction. It is safer, especially for the beginner historian, to keep grand interpretations to a minimum. Even so, the best of these "micro-histories" rest on some underlying premise of a symbolic or emblematic importance. I'll give you an example. Just for fun, I recently read a book about the wreck of a merchant sailing ship in the early 1800s.* The author alternated between a first person narrative recounting his research process and a series of third person reconstructions of the events. The book was essentially a narrative of his process. He began with a theory about why this ship went down. As his research unfolded, he altered his reconstruction again and again, sometimes dramatically, each time in response to a newly discovered inconsistency in the evidence he turned up. Each surviving member of the crew of that ship so cruelly tossed had a different experience, each villager who witnessed the tragedy saw it in his or her own way, and each of the on-site investigators imagined it a bit differently. All of these problems made any objective understanding of the event seem an impossible dream. In this case, the "how we feel about what happened" was not the feature of the history. Instead, the author was lamenting the ephemeral quality of historical memory and, by extension, individual human experience.

The discussion so far has been intended to highlight the role of narrative in history writing. Narrative is not inherently neutral. We make up our mind about something and then arrange the narrative to support our conclusion. There is nothing inherently dishonest in this but it does present

---

* Jeremy Seal's *Treachery at Sharpnose Point* (2001).

a problem for the consumer of historical narrative. Does the reader recognize that a point is being made? And that the facts are arrayed to enhance that point? Are important facts not directly germane to that point left out? Again, this is not to suggest an inherent dishonesty in the arrangement of facts, though that may in fact be the case. It is merely to say that awareness of the point being carried in any piece of history writing will enable the reader both to make a distinction between facts and argument and critique the writer's efficacy in carrying his argument.

## Herodotus and Historical Theory

Herodotus shaped his historical treatment of Greek affairs around a basic premise. He believed that all significant human events could be understood in terms of the interaction of two forces, hubris and nemesis,* and he occasionally resorted to little allegories that try to cue the reader to this dynamic as he saw it. In the most famous of such allegories, Herodotus paints a picture for you. First you have to imagine that the King of Persia,

WAS HERODOTUS HIDING IN THE CLOSET? WHAT DO YOU THINK !?!

Xerxes, was in his conference room with all of his advisors, pacing back and forth, wondering aloud whether or not he should invade Greece. Keep in mind that Herodotus was writing this 40 or 50 years later—long after the invasion actually took place. What are the chances that Herodotus was in the room when this conversation took place? Think about it; absolutely none. Herodotus is making this up. But why? The hint is in the dialogue (in

---

* *Hubris and nemesis*: both from the Greek. Hubris is excessive pride and nemesis is the natural tendency of the universe to correct and check hubris. Much more on this below.

14

ancient narrative, the hint is *always* in the dialogue). According to Herodotus, Xerxes puts this question to his councilors: "should I invade Greece?" And then Herodotus gets to the point: Xerxes then says… "If I *do* invade Greece, the borders of my kingdom will be god's own sky." Imagine that you are among Xerxes' advisors and you are all afraid to answer because you really don't know what the right answer is. Xerxes is the most powerful man on planet Earth; no one wants to say the wrong thing. But Herodotus needs someone to make the moral of the story obvious.

Keep in mind that Xerxes' decision to invade was well known to Herodotus' audience because some of them were actually alive when the invasion happened. And the story was so well known that those too young to have survived the events were well acquainted with the basic narrative. It was a massive invasion and the Persians should have crushed the Greeks but that is not what happened. For those listening to Herodotus read his history out loud, the only question in their mind was *why did the Persians lose?* They outnumbered the Greeks substantially and were better organized. Herodotus' answer lies within Xerxes' connection of his own kingdom to that of god. Now it doesn't take a genius to figure out that gods, as a rule, frown on being compared to humans. And that is the point that Xerxes' uncle Artabanus now makes. "Nephew," Uncle Artie said (according to Herodotus)…

> have you ever noticed that god only strikes down the tall trees…? Does not god like to bring down that which exalts itself? Is it not obvious that god does not appreciate humans who hold themselves too high?

Artabanus is implicitly accusing Xerxes of comparing himself to god and reminds Xerxes that this is a crime against god, a kind of impiety. Hubris is the appropriate word in Greek and its definition in modern English— excessive pride—serves well enough for us to see the point. We even have a modern parallel for this sentiment: *pride goeth before a fall.* So according to Herodotus, the reason why the Persians lost was that Xerxes was guilty of excessive pride. The reaction by the forces of the universe, call them god if you like—the Greeks called this Nemesis—was to smack his army down. The point of all this is that Herodotus is *interpreting* history and not just telling a story. He is explaining *why* the Persians lost and not just that they did. Once we see that this is so, we have to wonder for whose benefit this morality tale was told. There is no way of knowing absolutely, but we do have a good candidate: the great city of Athens. Herodotus lived in Athens when he wrote his history and he did so during the period of Athens' greatest prosperity. It was also the period during which Athens had begun to routinely abuse her long-time allies and there were many who complained of it. If Herodotus did have this in mind when he wrote of the Persian defeat then he was essentially using the past as a way of understanding his own present, his own time. At the same time, he was using his present as a way of organizing his narrative of the past. Herodotus linked the past and the present in an active relationship. In this allegory you see that Herodotus's theory for what

HERODOTUS' THEORY OF HISTORY

happened to the Persians might have been intended as a warning to the Athenians (if it was a warning, the Athenians didn't notice). Even if it was not all pointed at Athens, Herodotus' theory provides a model explaining why unexpected things generally happen. All really good history writing connects the particular moment to some greater meaning. Herodotus succeeds in doing this. Moreover, his theory is portable in the sense that it can be imposed on other events in other places and be a generic explanation for everything: *men act contrary to what nature intended, and nature forces an adjustment.* This is a cyclical kind of historical theory in that it supposes that nothing is really supposed to change. Things get out of balance, out of synch with the universe so to speak, and the divine forces suffusing the universe put things back in their proper place. Pre-modern theories of history tend to adhere to this principle.

An Arab scholar named Ibn Khaldoun articulated another pre-modern cyclical theory. Khaldoun's theory of historical change has characteristics that you might recognize. But first, who was he? Khaldoun lived in the 1400s. He was especially interested in explaining why the Arab kingdoms had so obviously declined from their pre-eminence over the preceding centuries. In the century or so before Khaldoun wrote the Mongols had rocked the Arab world and the Turks were becoming the ascendant Mediterranean power. Baghdad had been the intellectual and cultural center of the west for centuries, but had long since fallen from that position. Just as they themselves had been a peripheral people who moved into the center of things and took over, now it was the turn of the Turks. As a scholar, Khaldoun wanted to understand the "why" of it and he created a theory in answer. Of course the beauty of his theory, and all historical theories actually, is that they can be used as a template to interpret all historical change and not merely the special episode with which they are first associated...just as with the model employed by Herodotus.

Khaldoun starts with a premise with which you are most likely familiar; the virtue of the ancestors. Most of us project into the past a positive endorsement of our ancestors. To some extent we are aware that our ancestors, even if we are only talking as far back as our grandparents, endured hardships that we in our own generation have not had to endure. This accounts at least in part for the respect we give them. They lived a tough life and yet here they are, good people, and we come from them. Of course, there is frequently a bit of generational tension at play because of an implicit comparison. Do not our seniors occasionally suggest that our lives are just a bit too...soft? Why should they begrudge us the comfort they did not have but we do? Are not our grandparents, at least some of them, suspicious that we are being coddled? You have undoubtedly heard some version of this story: "When I was your age, I had to walk uphill to school...and back..." It is all about two readily connected concepts: hardship and virtue. Today we are familiar in our contemporary culture with the expression "what doesn't kill you makes you stronger." What is the flip side? If hardship makes you stronger, logically, what coddles you makes you weaker.

And so these twin premises bolster Ibn Khaldoun's theory. Hardship engenders virtue; easy living makes you weak. If you are an Arab and you are envisioning your ancestors you would probably situate them in the desert. And the desert provides a ready metaphor for hardship and deprivation. And with that sort of hardship comes fierce competition for resources. And in the desert the oasis becomes the metaphor for resources, for survival even, and the competition for these resources is the struggle for

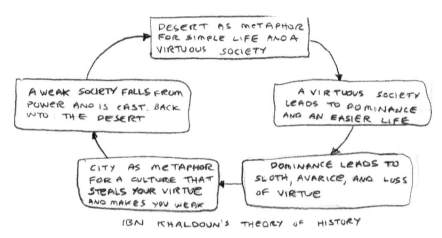

DESERT AS METAPHOR FOR SIMPLE LIFE AND A VIRTUOUS SOCIETY

A WEAK SOCIETY FALLS FROM POWER AND IS CAST BACK INTO THE DESERT

A VIRTUOUS SOCIETY LEADS TO DOMINANCE AND AN EASIER LIFE

CITY AS METAPHOR FOR A CULTURE THAT STEALS YOUR VIRTUE AND MAKES YOU WEAK

DOMINANCE LEADS TO SLOTH, AVARICE, AND LOSS OF VIRTUE

IBN KHALDOUN'S THEORY OF HISTORY

life. The competition for resources inevitably creates a requirement for a warrior ethos. We must fight to survive; we must fight to protect what is ours. Naturally, if you are virtuous enough, you will be successful in this competition and this success moves your ancestors to the next theoretical stage in the history of any successful culture: a life of ease. And what happens to all that virtue when you live a life of ease? The virtue disappears and here you see the explanation for the decline of the Arab world, at least as in so far as Ibn Khaldoun imagined it. The hardship and simplicity that conditioned their early success had been blunted and diluted by that very success. Implicitly, the greatness they once tasted was there to be regained, were that virtue recovered.

Variations on this theme—loss of virtue—were very common among the ancient writers. An example from the Roman period comes to mind.

Titus Livy lived and wrote during the dramatic civil conflict that destroyed the Roman Republic and replaced it with a monarchy under the Caesars. Livy blamed the whole crisis on a loss of virtue. Here is how he starts his monumental history covering the entire period of Roman history up to his own day:

> Let the reader consider how, with the relaxation of discipline, morals collapsed, sinking lower and lower until the present day in which we can neither endure our vices nor contemplate their remedy (Livy, *From the Foundation*; Introduction to Book One).

The remedy at which Livy here hints was the strong hand of the first true emperor, Augustus, nephew and adopted son of Julius Caesar. One implicit message of Livy's history is that the Romans caused their own difficulties by forgetting the virtues of the ancients. Another is that the monarchy represented in Augustus was necessary for Rome to recover and regain their former glory.

Other Roman historians alive in those decades also focused on what they regarded as key moments in the crisis. In all these instances, an ideal is retrojected into the past against which a flawed present could be unfavorably compared. For all the ancients, this literary and rhetorical trope was practically a reflex as ancient thinkers tended to conceive of any change as decay and was therefore inherently bad. And this impulse has not gone away; in modern America it is common to find politicians referring to an ideal past, usually as an indictment of social change or as a tool to attack political opponents: "Change is bad; let's go back to the good old days under [fill in the blank]" or "Let's take back America..." However weak these assertions are intellectually, they have a predictable and perennial appeal. It is no surprise that we should see it deployed as social criticism by the earliest generations of historians.

Another way in which to structure this sort of history is to say "we deserved what we got." In the case of all the examples noted thus far (Herodotus, Ibn Khaldoun, and Livy) explanations for historical change centered on virtue or the lack thereof. Other ancient writers chose a more "scientific" approach, even as they accepted the essential notion of decline. Polybius, a Greek writer who lived in Rome for decades, provides a great example. He was a witness to the critical period wherein Rome became for their own day what the United States has become for ours, the predominant political power in Europe and the Middle East. By the time Polybius wrote (around 140 BC, a century before the decline of which Livy complained) Rome had already seized control of the Greek homeland and this was for many Greeks a bitter pill to swallow. In his book about Roman success, Polybius went off on a substantial tangent in order to describe Rome's political institutions; he was convinced that the Romans won in large part because they had a better system of government. What really caught Polybius's attention was that Rome *seemed* to have broken a rule of history. All ancients believed that change was inherently bad and that all things good tend to decline. This goes especially for political systems. The basic idea was that all governments decline from an ideal form to a corrupted form. This was an idea that was first articulated by Aristotle but Polybius' version was more widely read in the American colonial period and had an important influence on the constitution of the United States.

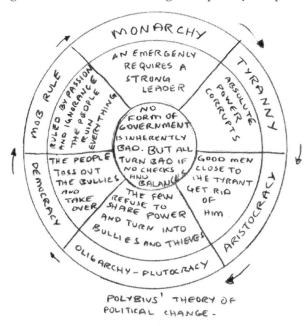

POLYBIUS' THEORY OF POLITICAL CHANGE.

Polybius' model is, for example, the reason why the founders decided to create a bicameral legislature (to balance aristocratic and democratic elements; the President provides, of course, the monarchial element) and why that same model was duplicated at the state level.

The Torah, or the first five books of the Christian Bible, provides another example of an analytical approach to history—albeit one that featured the hand of God. Modern scholars have concluded that these texts arrived at their current organization in and shortly after the period known in biblical history as the Babylonian captivity (597-538). First, the background to the story. The ancient Hebrew state coalesced in Jerusalem under the successive leaderships of David and Solomon in the 900s BC. In the centuries between, the Hebrews crafted a political religion from legends and tradition. A prominent element of that political religion was that a compact had been made between God and men, namely, that the land of milk and honey would belong to the Hebrews so long as they obeyed the laws delivered from God by Moses.

Now fast forward to the Babylonian captivity wherein we see that the Hebrews, or at least a large number of them, had been exiled to Babylon after a failed revolt against the Neo-Babylonian ruler, King Nebuchadnezzar. Decades passed and descendants of those exiled kept their culture intact by remembering and celebrating their original promise to obey the laws of Moses. Implicitly, the message was clear: God had withdrawn the Promised Land because the Hebrews had forgotten the bargain made with God. Nebuchadnezzar's decision to exile the Hebrews was the hand of God at work.

Just as implicit was the possibility of redemption, an obviously recurrent notion in the Judeo-Christian tradition. And so likewise was the Persian King Cyrus's decision to return the Hebrews to their land also excellent evidence of God's hand at work. For our purposes, the narrative point is that the Hebrews first deserved to lose their land, and they eventually earned it back. The *historiographical* point is that the Torah, organized in the time of the redemption, was constructed essentially to flesh out an interpretation of the past that existed outside of the evidence.

Imagine that you have decided that the reason for the predicament your culture is in is that God is mad at you. And you look back over all the

---

* *Historiography*: the history, methods, and principles of History writing.

religious prophecies and predictions collected over time and you discover some that said, "Hey! God is mad at you! Beware...", You will say, "Aha!", and say the evidence was here all along and you will naturally feature those elements in the history of the relationship of your people with God. Never mind all those other prophecies, the ones that never came true. So you see that interpretation, the theory underlying the historical narratives, existed before the historical narratives did. Historical theory gives shape to narratives and frankly, is what makes them interesting. Theories also govern what is relevant as far as evidence and what is not.

This is not just true of ancient historical narrative. As we have noticed here and there in the discussion above, humans have always been receptive to the idea that the past is a better place than the present. But this presents an essential and obvious contradiction for modern writers. Society is rapidly changing and it would seem, on the whole, that change is for the better. Standards of living seem to be going up, at least globally, and technology is making a real difference in the way we live. Face it, few of us would prefer to live in a world without toilet paper, antibiotics, or portable phones. And if the past wasn't so great after all, then we moderns have to think of new ways of imagining the flow of history and the "whys" of things. Instead of assuming the present to be a broken version of the past, the modern impulse is to think of the present as an incomplete version of the future. The present is still flawed, but no longer do we seek a remedy for this flawed present in a return to an ideal past.. Once that intellectual shift is made, then the historian revisits the past to see the degree to which rational progress can be discerned toward a putative future. This belief in a logical progression *toward* something *instead of away from* something is a product of the Enlightenment and the Industrial Revolution eras. The so-called Enlightenment era of European History (c. 1650-c. 1800) can be summed up as enshrining the belief that progress in the human condition was possible through the embrace of reason. The Industrial Revolution (c. 1750-1850) reinforced this basic presumption by stimulating the production of better and better tools along with the belief that everything can be known and understood scientifically, even human history. The whole idea of linear historical *progress* belongs in the modern mind; pre-modern thinkers were mostly cyclical thinkers.

The Whig theory we mentioned above is the most obvious example of linear thinking. Although we might be tempted to consider this theory proved because of the success of the West compared to the rest of the world, it still remains a theory. But if you *were* convinced it were true, and you found yourself charged with the mission of writing a Whig history, you would organize your history around pieces of evidence that seem to support the starting proposition. For example, what political principles do Westerners like to trumpet in comparison to other political systems? Democracy of course. We are not here to argue the proposition, but I think you will agree that we—that is, we in the West—tend to assume that democracy is superior to any alternative, and lo!, we—that is, we in the West —thought of it first, so the history of the origins of the success of the West would naturally feature Athens, the famous Greek laboratory for direct democracy, and the ancient Roman Republic, the laboratory for representative democracy. The presumption is that these historical developments had a determinative effect on the present—they did not merely precede it, they caused it. One might be tempted to say even that because the West invented democracy, the triumph of the west over the rest of the world was already inevitable 2500 years ago. But this would be wrong as it is clear that Chinese technological prowess and their economy were both further advanced as late as the European Renaissance.

One important implication of Whig history is that the history of one culture is potentially replicable in another. Logically, for another culture to achieve a comparable success, it must progress through the same steps as the model. Now we see an important ramification of modern linear theories of history, they have the potential of becoming foundations for political theory and supporting rationales for political action. It is not a coincidence that the birth of modern political theory begins as part and parcel of modern historical theories like Whiggish History.[*] Another modern thought system that embodies this logic is Marxism. This is not a political science book and there is little need to delay our discussion with an excursus on the

---

[*] One should also see Darwin's theory of evolution as part of this same intellectual shift.

principles underlying Marxist thought, but the most fundamental tenet of Marxism is the belief in an evolutionary progress of economic systems leading ever upward toward a more perfect world—at least according to the principles Marxists embrace. And so a Marxist history of any point in the past, or a Whig one too for that matter—begins with deciding where along the path to utopia a given culture is at some particular point in time.

So if I were asked whether History is what happened, I would obviously not have a short answer. History is *about* what happened in the past, but it is *also* about what is happening now and what is yet to be. The most interesting histories--I think anyway--are histories that argue something; histories whose meanings are derived from their arrangement into patterns. A practiced reader must always recognize however, that these patterns exist in the mind of the historian and other patterns remain possible. Is history writing then a hopelessly relativistic endeavor? Is there no enduring truth to be derived from its study? To both of the first of these the answer is a resounding "NO." The historian has an enduring duty to be true both to his evidence and to the context of that evidence. While it is not intellectually defensible to impose the standards of one historical context upon another, it is also not ethically responsible to stubbornly ignore the evidence of our human failings. Therein lies an enduring truth: the human past is a living tapestry of contradictions the contemplation of which can help us reach for our better selves.

# Chapter Two: Public Religion and the Ancient State

*What are the predictable functions of ancient religious practice?*

When we look to the ancient world, we can't help but notice how prominent are the symbols and monuments of ancient religion. It all seems a confusing collection of strange gods and mysterious practices. We resort to comfortable words like *polytheism* (believing in multiple gods) and *pagan* (oriented to folk religion). But neither of these words come with helpful meanings especially if we are prepared to admit that Christianity has space for more than one supernatural entity and that the word pagan is essentially a pejorative expression originally connoting 'rustic' (as in hillbilly). Nevertheless, we begin by counting gods and looking for odd belief systems instead of emphasizing the social functions of religion. We do this because modern ideals of religiosity provide our frame of reference. Secondly, our sensibilities about separating political and religious categories obscures the degree to which these categories actually overlapped in the ancient world. If, on the other hand, we try to emphasize the broad practices of ancient religion one begins to see that it all makes a lot more sense and even has a lot in common with modern religion.

The title of this chapter emphasizes the word public and this is not accidental. Most of what is visible and known to us about ancient religion took place in the public space. By clear implication, publicly displayed elements of religion have to serve social and/or political functions aside from any strictly devotional aspects. What functions are served are not always obvious. We scratch our heads, for example, when we consider the Lupercal, a Roman festival in mid-February that featured the twin sacrifices of a goat and a dog along with naked city officials running through the streets of Rome whacking passersby. These exceptions notwithstanding, I think it useful to emphasize the functional elements of ancient religion and look for modern parallels. If we are able to emphasize threads of continuity we will, I would argue, come a bit closer to understanding ancient religion, changes in religious practice, and, perhaps, store up some insights useful for the eventual transition to Christianity, a topic we will treat in chapter seven.

Let us begin with an essential. The word religion comes from the Latin, *religare*, to tie or to bind. Religion can be understood therefore as that set of things that binds us together; a sort of social glue. However many devotional practices or beliefs may be included or even prominent among that set of things that binds us together, it is the act of their gluing us together which lies at the heart of religion. This is an important distinction. It is certainly true, for example, that a shared belief in certain fundamental doctrines are what technically defines a Christian, but it is participation in the ritual of communion and the witnessing of the ritual that signifies that membership. Here I am pressing a distinction between what is believed and what is done. Let's take it a step further: what percentage of those who self-identify as Christians understand or even care about the intricacies of Christian dogma? That percentage may vary from denomination to denomination but I would not be too far wrong to suggest that percentage is small. For the rest, take away the dogma and it becomes a social club with nifty rituals whose origins have some obvious pre-Christian elements.* Like other sorts of social clubs, churches are, in practical terms, settings for social networking providing possibilities for suitable marriages, conduits for the distribution of alms to the poor, and contexts within which one celebrates the passages of life. These are not defining elements of religious belief; these are things that take place within the boundaries of a community that defines itself by participation in certain set of ritual events and only secondarily, I am now arguing, in a particular belief system.

---

* Eggs and rabbits and the Christian feast of the resurrection of Christ, for example. Eggs show up in many cultural contexts celebrating the spring equinox and fertility. The commonly used title for the feast is of course Easter, an obvious resonance of Eostre, a Celtic fertility goddess whose symbol was the rabbit. Other pre-Christian festivals feature resurrection elements in conjunction with springtime. Sumerian Inanna and Egyptian Osiris represent two very early examples.

26

This is a constructed community—as opposed to one defined by nature—and this sort of community can be defined in many different ways and the degree to which any given community has relevance changes over time. Where and how boldly we scribe the lines of our various group memberships is part of the process of creating an "identity." The perceived usefulness of membership within any given community determines the degree to which we are invested in that category of identity and governs the rules and rituals of admission. I would argue that no one willingly abandons a constructed category of identity that he or she finds to be actually useful. We can therefore interpret the demise or growth of any given community on the basis of its perceived usefulness and we can also see how any individual defines oneself can vary for the same reason. If identity is not inherently static, neither are the rituals associated with that identity. Rituals have a sort of inertia to them that can survive the extinct, archaic, or mooted community or context that originally generated them if they continue to serve a useful function. We might suppose, for example, that the Roman Lupercal we mentioned above, thought by most modern scholars to be a vestige of an archaic fertility ritual, remained popular in the big city of Rome because it accorded ordinary citizens an opportunity to see high status citizens literally stripped of their rank and privilege. Or maybe it was just plain fun, like the whole Easter egg thing.

Every level of society either generates a unique set of symbols and practices or it adapts those already in existence, or more often, a combination of both. As villages coalesce into cities and cities into empires, as empires dissolve and economies evolve, as political fortunes change and new peoples arrive, in each of these cases and others besides, symbols and practices are dragged from one context to another and end up serving different functions in different contexts. All of this is intended as at least a partial explanation for the confusion of religion that tumbles out in front of us every time we turn a corner in the ancient world. Nevertheless, all pre-modern societies feature elements of religion and ritual that perform some fairly predictable functions. In this chapter, we will concentrate on the common categories; four predictable functions emerge, though there be some overlap among them: claims of divine sanction, control over esoterica useful for community, celebration of community, and protection of the community.

## Claims of Divine Sanction

Every community that officially acknowledges the existence of gods uses them to justify political power. King Hammurabi of Babylon provides one vivid example. Hammurabi was king of Babylon for about 40 years until his death around 1750 BC. A successful ruler, he expanded the kingdom he inherited to include most of Mesopotamia. The most well know artifact associated with his reign is a stele* inscribed with Hammurabi's law code. Were it not for the survival of this stele, now on public view in the Louvre, we probably wouldn't care much about Hammurabi or his inscription, as this is certainly not the earliest known law code, and Hammurabi's kingdom was lost in the next generation. But the stele did survive and the text inscribed upon it offers us a wealth of insight into a long extinct culture. First we take particular note of the image carved atop the stone and the prologue and epilogue of the inscribed law code. In the image, Shamash, the Babylonian sun god, hands symbols of political authority to Hammurabi.† The scene is one familiar to us; we recall Moses in a similar moment. The message in this instance is clear: as the sun brings light to the earth, so Shamash brings justice to humans, and, of course, puts Hammurabi in charge. In the inscribed prologue to the laws, Hammurabi expands on the visual message by expressly claiming that his political authority in this matter came not only from Shamash but from a few other gods as well. In the epilogue of the inscription, Hammurabi threatens divine punishments on any future kings who might consider undermining his laws. All in all, the stele provides a solid example where religion is used to justify and reinforce political authority and one can be quite sure that devotional festivals featuring Shamash were not subtle in their reference to Hammurabi's authority.

---

* *Stele*: a stone tablet with an inscribed surface erected in the public space.
† Known to scholars of the period as "the rod and ring of kingship."

HAMMURABI
SHAMASH

HAMMURABI GETS THE MEMO
FROM SHAMASH

On the surface then, the main message of the monument is clear, but it also goes to something subtler, and I think perhaps universal. That is, Hammurabi was particularly concerned to associate his political authority with the idea of *justice*. This hints at something fundamental: that in the minds of those Hammurabi desired to influence, a featured function of civil authority, perhaps even the most important one, was the maintenance of justice. I would argue that *the citizens of any polity*, no matter its form, *will remain perfectly content so long as they perceive that justice prevails*, or is at least the norm. This may be an axiom useful for understanding political change as well as resistance to political change in modern contexts as well.* As a related observation, one notes that the custody of the law in any pre-modern society is intimately bound up with divine sanction. The most powerful priests in ancient Rome, for example, were the college of Pontiffs whose particular expertise was in fact the law. In primitive cultures we frequently observe shaman figures whose social pre-eminence is rooted both in the custody of the group's cultural norms—the law—and in a maintenance of an alliance with divine forces, however they be imagined.

---

* One can certainly see these dynamics at work in the ongoing Arab Spring.

# Control over Esoterica useful to the Community

DETAIL OF HAMMURABI'S CODE

Esoterica is information understood by only a few. We are all familiar with the expression that knowledge is power; if I know something you don't, and I can convince you that you need what I know, then I have a kind of power over you. The text of the laws inscribed on Hammurabi's stele is in fact a form of esoterica. Let's face it, it's not as if the average person could read it. To anyone interested in justice, the prominent display of mysterious script placed in the public space was a demonstration of the importance of the state, and by extension, its leader Hammurabi. That seems reasonable enough but, by itself, it doesn't seem like enough of a reason to answer this question: what was the point of writing the whole thing out? "For all to see," or some version of this, is the usual response. This remains an unsatisfactory response, at least to me. Something is missing. And then an answer came to me from an unexpected direction and from way, *way* back in human history.

Anyone who has taken an art history course is familiar with the tiny female figurines collectively known as Venus figures. The figures date to around 25,000 years ago, a time when Europeans were still mostly organized in hunter-gatherer bands and the global climate was much colder. Many of the figures are obese and they tend to feature exaggerated genitalia. The most well known example, Venus of Willendorf, is illustrated here. Notice that features ordinarily suggesting an individual identity or personality; eyes, details of faces, that sort of thing, are all notably absent. On that observation, scholars are inclined toward generic or abstract interpretations, and most agree that these figures have some connection with the idea of fertility. This seems a perfectly reasonable proposition, as fertility is essential for human survival on so many levels. Ok, now what? What do you DO with a fertility doll? Worship it? What does that mean, exactly? Let's break it down: 1) fertility is good, 2) let's make a representation of fertility, 3) (hopefully) fertility happens. We might suppose that somewhere between numbers two and three, we might do a dance, sing a song, beg perhaps, but the most logical endpoint of the process is to capture the essence, the soul perhaps, of the abstract notion of fertility and to put that to work for humans. We might define worship, at least in this context, as an attempt to control or manipulate superhuman forces rather than to offer them love and devotion.

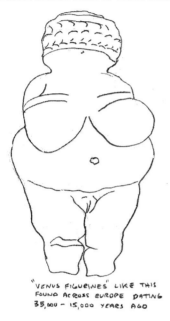

"VENUS FIGURINES" LIKE THIS FOUND ACROSS EUROPE DATING 35,000 – 15,000 YEARS AGO

We can apply the same theory to cave paintings. Cave paintings from as far back as 40,000 years ago have been found all over the world. Naturally, there are significant variations but the depictions in the vast majority tend to be wild creatures and, conversely, rarely of humans. Where human presence is depicted in the imagery it is intentionally schematic or might consist only of handprints. If we apply the same logic as with the Venus figures we get a complementary result: 1) Animals (food items) are good 2) let's make a representation of animals 3) (hopefully) animals appear and then we kill them. Do we have a pattern? One implication is that by making a representation of a thing one somehow gains control over it; it is a extension of power over the thing represented. The reverse logic might explain both the lack of individual features on the Venus figures and the reticence about depicting humans in cave painting. Humans would not intentionally choose to yield control to another.

Before we return to Hammurabi's code, let us note a parallel with regard to secret names. It was a recurrent practice in some cultures that secret names be assigned to men coming of age. Simply, if you regard a name as a representation, and a representation of a thing as a tool exerting control, then having a secret name is to be on guard against unwanted or unknown attempts at magical manipulation. Use of one' true name is a kind of possession for which one does not give permission. One certainly sees this at work in the Hebrew commandment against blasphemy and the related strictures concerning the name of God. To call *His* name is to summon *Him* and who is he that dares to manipulate God? What hubris is that?

So what does all of this have to do with the text of Hammurabi's code? If the items adduced above represent a real pattern, namely, that humans have predictably believed that making a representation of a thing is to gain control over it, then we are in a position to apply this logic to the text of the code. Each individual law that is inscribed is only a law, but considered collectively, one can think of it as a representation of something greater, an abstract, perhaps the *idea* of justice. The form in which it is displayed is indeed mysterious and inaccessible except to experts who can read. The total effect of the stele is to demonstrate not only that justice is a thing important to Hammurabi and that the gods have legitimized his control over it, but that Hammurabi also has the special knowledge to insure its application. He has demonstrated his literal control over an esoteric knowledge essential for civil society. The display of the text becomes a demonstration of Hammurabi's power. Long term stability in any political arrangement is dependent on an implied social contract, in this case a three-way contract between gods, kings, and the population at large. It is a predictable purpose of ancient religion to enshrine this contract in ritual and it explains the regular presence of religious experts in virtually all ancient political contexts.

Let us consider a different sort of example from ancient Rome. Everyone knows that the ancient Romans were good at conducting war and they acquired an impressive empire. The Romans liked to say they only fought just wars and we think, "oh yeah, right...wink, wink." Well, actually they *did* only fight just wars, at least during the Republican period. "Just,' however, means something other than what you might think it does. *We* think of the word 'just' as in 'justified' or perhaps 'fair,' as in, the Romans beat up their neighbors only when their neighbors deserved it. So long as one looks at it in that way, then it's hard to take the pronouncement, "the

Romans only fought just wars," very seriously. But the word 'just' also denotes 'according to law or custom,' and whether it be fair or deserved is a different kind of question. That is for the gods to decide once the war actually begins. So what *the Romans actually meant* is that they only fought *legal* wars. So the Romans had experts on staff to insure that all their wars were legal and this way the gods wouldn't be upset with the Romans for starting illegal wars. These Roman experts on legal war were priests called *fetiales*. While we never think of war as a religious issue, it *is* in fact a religious issue, at least as far as ancients were concerned. It helps to think of war as a legal proceeding in which a dispute is argued in front of divine judges. The *fetiales* are the lawyers. You may recall from the previous chapter that the ancients were sensitive to being punished by the gods for thinking too big (hubris). Making war for no good reason is certainly asking for the gods to intervene against you. Let's consider a specific example of how all of this works in practice.

The date was 282 BC. The Romans had by that time established colonies up and down the Italian peninsula and made alliances with numerous cities, especially in the south. They had already become the most dominant power in Italy. This made a lot of independent cities very nervous. One such city was Tarentum, a Greek city located in the instep of the Italian boot. It was originally a colony founded by Sparta hundreds of years earlier, but was now independent and had become prosperous through trade made possible by their excellent harbor facilities. Tarentum enjoyed a strategic position in the trade between mainland Greece, Italy and Sicily. To protect this position, Tarentum maintained a modest fleet of ships to deter pirates and established treaties with nearby rivals demarcating areas of influence. This included Rome.

In that year, a squadron of Roman ships appeared in Tarentine waters. The details are sketchy, but as far as Tarentum was concerned this was an illegal incursion and they determined to drive off the interlopers. There were casualties, prisoners were taken, and the Romans lost one or more ships. For reasons that will become clear in chapter five, the Romans were predisposed to provoke war with their neighbors and the whole episode may have been designed for that very purpose. Even so, it is important to note that the Romans tended not to rush directly to war. Instead, they stuck with the procedure for legal war and sent the *fetiales* to Tarentum to complain. The process was this: the priests travel to the offending city and made a series of announcements from a prepared script. First, at the frontier to no one in particular; secondly, to the first person they met along the road and, finally, in the agora or forum of the offending city. The script was archaic and the wording had to be read exactly right in order to insure that the gods would consider all of this to be valid. It worked in much the same way as a prayer might. You may note how careful modern priests are in their recitations of prayers and liturgies. The obvious implication is that if you don't get these exactly right, the gods are free to ignore them. The formulae of the prayers are key to holding the attention of the gods; if the prayer is done right, the gods *must* pay attention. This is a predicable part of all priestly imprecations, a careful attention to the form of the address and, on that basis, an argument for the state to maintain a monopoly over the appropriate experts. This is another example of official control of esoterica useful to a community.

This particular episode is famous because of what happened after the final announcement by the *fetiales* in the agora of Tarentum. It seems that a local citizen looking down from his position on the floor above where the priests were standing, perhaps amused by the appearance of foreigners speaking gibberish from a prepared script in the middle of town, made an unfortunate decision to urinate on one of the priests. We might be suspicious that the Romans exaggerated the insult later on in order to maximize the guilt of Tarentum in the Roman mind. Since official ambassadors between cities traveled under the protection of the gods, an insult of this sort would certainly be a form of impiety, an insult against the gods, and a way of influencing the gods' sympathy toward the Roman case. Conversely, the effort by the *fetiales* to seek redress for the attack on Roman ships, a process witnessed by the gods whose careful reading of the archaic script guaranteed their attention, presents Rome as a pious observant of religion. The gods would surely be pleased with the Romans. The sequel to this little drama will be related in chapter five but the end result was that Tarentum surrendered in 272. Meanwhile we can see that what is religious ritual in the Roman context is merely the deployment of special knowledge intended to guarantee divine support for Roman military endeavor.

The oracle of Delphi provides another example of ancient religion providing a cloak for special knowledge. Oracles are individuals who have access to divine advice. The principle, in general, is that a question put to an oracle—for a price of course—is referred to some god and the answer is then relayed back by the same route. Partly on the basis of deposits of votive objects, archaeologists and historians have identified numerous sites around the Mediterranean where pilgrims came in search of divine guidance. The most famous of these is Delphi, located west of Athens on the side of a mountain. The priestess of Delphi—the Pythia was her title—referred pilgrim inquiries to Apollo, a Greek god reputed to be sympathetic to human concerns, and returned Apollo's answers in the form of a kind of gibberish. Happily, attendants were on hand to render the gibberish back into Greek. Delphi had a great reputation and therefore fielded inquires of every conceivable sort from individuals, rulers, cities, you name it; visitors came from all over the Mediterranean. While many of the specific answers attributed to Delphi seem somewhat evasive, at least those concerning the politics of kings and war, it seems rather likely that much of the advice or information was in fact sound. The explanation for this lies most probably in the sheer volume of inquiries. Every visitor to Delphi brought information, all of which was undoubtedly noted and filed away for re-use. The modern cynic in us tempts us to regard it all as an elaborate fraud but the fact remains that Delphi really *was* the best place to gather information.

# Celebration of Community

Our third category of ancient public religion encompasses all the rituals designed to celebrate community identity, the ancient equivalents of the US Fourth of July, Canada Day, Bastille Day, etc. Ancient versions of these rituals and festivals tend to stress or reenact a critical moment in the distant and perhaps mythological past where the community either comes into existence or receives some sort of divine sanction. Festivals of this sort encourage participants to set aside competing categories of identity in favor of those that tend to unify the community as a whole. The first such example we cite is the Panathenaia, celebrated in Athens every summer since the mid-500s BC, as a recognition of the "coming together" of many tiny villages to make Athens a city in the sense of having a genuinely political meaning. As the Athenian democracy took its most advanced shape in the 400s BC, the festival became more and more elaborate. The leaders from each of the Ten Athenian voting districts managed the festival. There were contests of all sorts with generous prizes of money and wine; voice, instrument, and dance competitions, gymnastic and equestrian events; and the voting districts competed to provide leaders for the choruses.* The biggest event of the festival was a grand procession of choruses and citizens around an actual ship, towed through the streets of the city, carrying a woolen cloak for the giant statue of Athena that stood inside the Parthenon. The cloak was made fresh every four years by a special committee of high status women and embroidered with elaborate representations of the founding mythology of the city. The garment was hung from the yards of the ship as it was pushed back and forth through the streets of Athens until ultimately making its way to the foot of the acropolis upon which a grand sacrifice of 100 bulls was arranged.† The meat from the sacrificial victims was then distributed according to voting district and village. Now that's a serious barbeque!

The second most important festival in Athens was actually a series of local festivals called the *Dionysia.* that culminated in a centralized version in the city of Athen*s*. It began with a series of village level events spread out over a month or so. Like the Panathenaia, one can easily identify the emphasis on coming together into a converged center but one also sees more archaic elements resonating from a distant past. Many of the same types of entertainments and contests that took place in the Panathenaia also took place in the *Dionysia*, but the ritual elements of the *Dionysia* were

---

* All Greek festivals featured musical choruses of citizens arranged by age and gender. The funding to support these was provided by wealthier citizens and as such was a useful means of enhancing their personal and political prestige.

† The ship was almost certainly an addition of the 400s BC, during which the Athenians created a substantial navy. Yards are wooden cross-trees on the ships.

focused on fertility and agriculture. For example, though there were variations in the way the various villages shaped their versions of the festival, all featured processions in which young maidens carried phallus-shaped objects, including baskets of appropriately shaped bread, through the city. The political element was undoubtedly a later addition; children born since the previous year in the various villages were officially enrolled as citizens in Athens.

The patron goddess of Athens was Athena and her special connection to Athens accords us an opportunity to note how elastic were all the legends and myths surrounding the Greek gods. According to Athenian legend, Athena and Poseidon contended for the position of divine patron of the new city. Poseidon offered water, but that water was salty. Athena invented the olive tree and offered it. Mmm, which is the better choice? Salt water? Or the olive tree? The Athenians went with the olive tree, the perfect crop for a land too dry for many other crops. Although Athena and Poseidon show up in other cities' legends, this particular legend is peculiar to Athens. Given the close connections most Greeks felt to the sea, one is not surprised to see that many temples across the Greek world were dedicated to Poseidon, but each featured rituals celebrating legends specific to its own location.* The modern analogy would be this: imagine that every American city sponsored a major religious holiday celebrating a visit of Jesus. The net effect is that as one roams from city to city, one would meet a brand new version of Jesus at every stop. Imagine if you will, the Jesus you might meet in Chicago, rescuing the citizens from the Great Fire of 1871 and bringing the citizens Blues music from the Delta. Or perhaps imagine the Jesus you might meet in Pittsburgh, celebrated for guiding the football from Terry Bradshaw to the waiting hands of Franco Harris, forever to be known as the true patron of "the Immaculate Reception." Or imagine the Jesus of the Great Salt Lake, who guided his pilgrims to a new home in the far west. And all of these existing in parallel and without regard

---

* One might read Hesiod's *Theogony*, written around 700 BC, as indicating a coherent scheme tying together all the Greek mythology but this is largely an illusion. For most of the legends Hesiod recounts, there is at least one alternate version.

for each other. Christmas and Easter may be celebrated in any of these locations but they would be demoted to secondary level festivals. They might even ignore them altogether.

Among the Romans we also find festivals with clearly political overtones. One festival of this sort that we find frequently mentioned in the evidence was the "Latin Festival" celebrating an alliance of original Italian cities that became the backbone of Roman success early on in Rome's history. Every year, representatives of Rome and her allies would meet on Mount Alba (now a hill in the suburbs of Rome). Each city brought offerings of food to Jupiter and a grand feast took place. The representatives of the various cities would hang discs with images of local deities on a tree signifying the cooperation of all the local gods. Because the Latin Festival was repeated every year, this celebration is by definition a ritual. Because the ritual acts emphasize a political identity that supersedes local identities, it acts to reinforce a sort of federal political identity. Across all of these examples we see the same dynamic at work, community festival under divine patronage and the most practical benefit of participation in such community festival is civic unity. We also get an important hint as to why the Christians, when they show up in the Roman context, will be so clearly misunderstood. But that is a topic we will explore in more detail in chapter seven.

# Protection of the community

And finally we come to that set of practices centered on the protection of the community. All festivals to one degree or another have wrapped up within them an intent to guarantee the protection of the gods. With this intention in mind, the question then becomes whether the gifts and devotions made to the gods throughout the regular calendar are actually achieving the desired effect. Are the gods happy, unhappy, or at least neutral? So the ancients needed ways of finding this out and ancient cultures invented elaborate methods of what we call divination: the art of finding out what the gods are thinking. If the news is bad, recommendations were made to recover divine favor. So how does all of this work?

As a broad generalization, the ancients all looked to nature for clues as to the temperament of the gods. Unusual patterns in the weather or in the heavens, anomalies in the behavior of animals, the discovery of malformed creatures, not to mention the apparent suspension of the normal rules of physics: any of these would be sufficient to send experts scurrying to their records in search of divine significance. The Romans provide an entertaining example in their literature. First of

all, when the Romans went on campaign they, like all sensible peoples on the march, checked in with the gods on a regular basis—after all, it is best not to have a battle on a bad day. To accomplish this the Romans brought with them chickens to observe. Chickens are especially useful as they are relatively easy to round up after their use. The idea is to observe the chickens and watch for anomalous behavior. Now, if you have ever seen a chicken in his preferred environs, he or she was probably scratching the ground in search of a snack. So in the case of the sacred chickens, the idea would be to see whether the chickens would act normally, were they given an opportunity to do so. Well, it happens that in 249 BC a Roman general in command of a fleet of Roman warships eagerly sought battle with a Carthaginian fleet that had embarrassed him on several previous occasions. P. Claudius Pulcher (Claudius the Honorable), dutifully consulted his expert who reported that the chickens would not eat. Chickens refusing to eat was not a good sign. But according to the testimony given in the trial that took place a few months later, Claudius not only chose to ignore this clear omen of defeat, he compounded the mistake by tossing the chickens overboard.

Of course the Roman were defeated and Claudius' political career ended with a conviction of impiety. Aside from the obvious lesson this story was designed to give--Don't ignore the gods--you can also see that the Romans cleverly avoided taking responsibility for the military defeat by laying blame for the loss on a technicality. The Romans didn't lose because they faced a superior commander. *Noooo*. They lost because they ignored a warning from the gods! It was all Claudius' fault. From the standpoint of troop morale this is a really handy approach. It is always easier to get the troops fired up for another round of fighting if they believe that their previous defeat was not their fault.

Athenian history provides a fabulous example of a great disaster following upon a bad omen. Here the lesson is different. Whereas Claudius erred in ignoring the gods, in this case, the offending general is criticized for a bad interpretation. In the late 400s BC the Athenians took it into their heads to conquer Sicily and prepared an invasion fleet to accomplish this bold plan. Ancient Sicily featured a number of independent cities among which was Syracuse, the chief target of Athens. The Athenians believed they could take advantage of Sicilian disunity and turn a critical mass of other Sicilian cities against Syracuse. The plan failed miserably and the invasion turned out a bad decision on a truly epic scale. Despite early Athenian successes, it didn't take long for the Syracusans to start making life extremely difficult for the invaders. Each day that passed brought new difficulties until finally the Athenians were on the point of abandoning the whole proposition. It was almost too late. And then a full lunar eclipse took place. Nicias, the Athenien commander, consulted his experts who counseled a delay of a full cycle of the moon. And so the army, already in trouble, settled in and...waited. This fatal decision on Nicias' part gave Syracuse the time to mount an all-out assault. Nearly all the Athenians, including Nicias, were executed, killed on the run, or died horrible deaths as slaves working in the quarries.

When things are going wrong they really go wrong. But what can you do when the gods are mad at you, or are not protecting you? At various points in Roman history we see the Romans repeating entire festivals when the omens associated with their conclusion were not positive. We see them occasionally breaking their own rules against human sacrifice when their own experts counseled this, and even repeating the gathering of omens again and again until the desired response was achieved. It seems like a kind of cheating to keep asking the gods the same question until you get the right answer but this was actually OK, just as it was also OK to encourage the right answer by, for example, keeping the sacred chickens hungry before they were consulted. In addition, the Romans possessed a set of official books that listed, among other things, various responses previously employed to offset bad omens and a set of officials whose sole job was to consul them.

So far in this chapter we have emphasized public or community expressions or acts of religion. For each of these there is some private expression that corresponds. On a popular level this is very familiar to us now. Ladders, black cats, broken mirrors: these are all harbingers of bad luck; salt over the shoulder, rabbits' feet and knocking on wood all provide remedies. This would be just as true in the ancient world, and individuals with greater resources left behind more durable versions of these apotropaic* acts. A promise of a gift at a shrine as payment for divine intervention is as sensible a response now as it was two thousand years ago. And in an environment where there is no necessity for exclusive devotion to any one divine entity, you can see not only the possibility for covering multiple divine bases but more importantly a clear explanation for the profusion of temples and shrines all ancient cityscapes offered. In Rome for example, one walks through the remains of dozens of ancient temples vowed and dedicated to various gods as reminders of individual services to the community and incidentally to the assistance of the god in question.

For example, the temple dedicated by the emperor Augustus to the god Mars Ultor (Mars the Avenger) noted Augustus' victory over the assassins of his adopted father and of course underscored his legitimacy. The most famous surviving temple in Rome is the Pantheon, dedicated to "all the gods." When you visit, note the very prominent inscription on the front: "Marcus Agrippa, son of Lucius, built this in his third consulship." The

---

* *Apotropaic*: something intended to ward off evil.

political benefits of this are obvious. The clever benefactor will endow his temple or shrine with sufficient resources to celebrate in an annual festival the relationship of god and the dedicator. A by-product of this process is the confusion of temples and rituals we noted at the top of this chapter. Bit by bit you can see that the religious calendar became noisier and noisier as time went on.

We have been emphasizing public religion because it is the best place to start when looking at ancient religion. But nothing in public religion prevents the existence of private religious practice. We know of many cults offering mysterious insights into divine knowledge or providing special access to channels of divine influence. As the Roman world subsumed all the little worlds it conquered, it rolled up bits and pieces of the many foreign cults it encountered along the way. The Romans received some of these passively; synagogues, for example, are found in many ancient Roman cities. Others were Roman adaptations and adopted and adapted by the Romans and bear only cosmetic resemblance to their original versions. The cults of Mithra, Isis, and even Christianity fall into this category as these were adapted from earlier versions in Iran, Egypt, and Judea, respectively. Each of these as practiced in the Roman context took on a distinctly Roman character. In some cases, we see the authorities acting in a hostile manner to these importations from eastern provinces, most famously in the case of the Christians. We will get into this in much more detail in chapter seven, but when that reaction was hostile, it was always predicated on the impression that the offending cultic practice undermined or contradicted the state religion.

All of the expressions of piety we have looked at here have functional elements with some parallels in the modern world. What is most notable—and what constitutes the most significant difference between modern and ancient conceptions of religiosity—is the absence of canonical dogma. In the ancient world, it was much more clearly the case that gods and humans were bound together in a transactional relationship the overriding purpose of which was to maintain and protect a functional community.

A GENIE:
AN
ASSYRIAN
GUARDIAN FIGURE

# Chapter Three: War and Politics in Ancient Greece

*How did Greek ways of fighting affect Greek ways of governing?*

The political history of the west, at least as we imagine it, begins in ancient Greece. Everyone in the west associates democracy with the ancient city of Athens. The first great political theoreticians were Greek philosophers and Historians: Plato, Aristotle, Polybius are featured among these. We noted in chapter one that Polybius' political theories were an important inspiration for the US framers Glance at virtually any government building in America built before 1900 and more than likely you will find yourself looking at a modern version of a Greek temple. We are therefore very interested in examining the development of Greek ideas of governance.. Although we might imagine that all ancient Greeks stood around waiting to vote on something, it was never as simple as that. First, you have to realize that every city in ancient Greece acted like it was a separate country. Every city had its own form of government and democracy was only one possibility among several. And within the category of cities that *were* democracies, there were vast differences in how democracy actually worked in practice. In Athens, for example, one must realize that at its most generous point, eligibility to vote was restricted to free male residents whose parents were also citizens. Variations in political development flowed out of different experiences, different economies, not to mention different geographic situations. It turns out, however, that the most common factor dictating how Greek cities developed politically was how they organized themselves for war. And this is not surprising. Imagine a land, not particularly fertile, where hundreds of little villages compete for resources. The most compelling reason people have to form a government is to protect those resources. The chapter that follows will argue that the ways in which the

Greeks organized themselves to fight overshadowed all other factors in their political evolution. Or, put another way, in ancient Greece it is generally true that those who fought, or who were prepared to fight, were the only true citizens.

It is easy to downplay this fundamental because there is so much in classical Greek culture and history that appeals to, what is for us, a higher and more laudable set of values: keenly evolved ideas of beauty and proportion, an abiding interest in the idea of justice, and a consistently scientific approach to the unknown. The eventual triumph of Rome over the Greeks (and everybody else) helps us to forget how much the Greeks loved war and how much war actually defined them before the Romans took over. In the previous chapter, we talked a bit about elements of community identity and how ownership of that identity might shift in response to changing circumstances. The Roman take-over of the Greek world certainly stimulated a re-evaluation in the Greek mind of what it meant to be Greek. But until that time, all Greek ideas about the worth, value, and construction of a man were wrapped up in a life-long competition whose highest expression was war. The Greek word for virtue is *arete*. It is best understood as an indication of usefulness. If you are male, your value is determined by how useful you are as a warrior and as a friend; a woman's value flows from her reproductive capability, her proper submission to appropriate male authority, and her skills in managing the domestic economy.

Meanwhile, one should try to remember that the Greek world was never one political thing; it was always a *collection* of fractious city-states co-existing in a more or less constant state of conflict. There are of course other imperatives affecting how various Greek city-states organized themselves: economic conditions, land quality, persistent existential threats, etc.* No surprise then, that the political and military systems of Sparta, Athens, and Macedon, the main subjects of this chapter, each faced a

---

* *An existential threat*: a threat to someone's or something's existence. For example, Greek cities on the island of Sicily had constantly to be aware of the power of nearby Carthage. This was prudent as Carthage tried repeatedly to conquer the Greek cities of Sicily.

unique set of problems, limitations, and opportunities. The result for each was a different path, a different destiny, and a different political experiment. Each community saw things its own way, shaped its own diplomatic objectives, and followed its own political path. With respect to culture, much was shared in the Greek world, language, values, and religious sensibilities being chief among these. We will discuss some of these elements in the next chapter. But there was never any meaningful political connotation to the idea of "Greek" until the modern state of Greece emerged in the 1800's AD. Each city-state, or occasionally each league of cities, had its own destiny.

I will organize the presentation in four stages. The first of these is a prelude to a period of political experimentation that began in earnest after about 700 BC. Before that date all power was vested in a tiny elite whose power stemmed from control of the best land. After that date, regional economic changes, significant population growth, and the proliferation of new weapons and fighting styles stimulated political challenges to that entrenched elite. The second through fourth stages represent different stable political alternatives that coalesced in the period after 700. While these are presented in the order of their appearance, that should not be taken to suggest the necessity of an orderly transition through each successive stage.

# Pre-hoplite Greece (Greece before c. 700 BC)

From c. 1600 to 1200 BC, a warrior elite ruled Greek cities from great palaces we now call the Mycenaeans. The Mycenaeans were tied into trade and social networks that connected the entire eastern end of the Mediterranean Sea. The various Mycenaean warlords built their political dominance on the patronage of a chariot-borne warrior class. Fragments of their world survive in the legends adapted by Homer centuries later and the ruins of their palaces hint at the vast social distance that lay between themselves and the peasant class that fed them. The expense of maintaining the horses alone must have been sufficient to keep the peasant class in a state of crushing poverty, although we cannot really know for sure. We do know however that between 1200 and 1000 the Mycenaean warlords disappeared and their palaces were laid waste. Their fate, when considered in isolation, seems all rather mysterious. But the simultaneous collapse of New Kingdom Egypt and the Hittite kingdom in Anatolia suggest a regional phenomenon to which all three fell victim. Various theories have been advanced, none entirely satisfactory. The Egyptians blame a mysterious "Sea Peoples." Some moderns have suggested environmental issues and/or economic collapse. Others point to a period of earthquake activity. The most attractive theory emphasized something these three civilizations have in common: chariots. The armies of all three of these kingdoms featured chariot-borne elites. The best evidence we have indicates that chariots were deployed in conjunction with mercenary foot soldiers trained to disable enemy chariots. The natural result is the proliferation of the practical knowledge necessary for the mercenaries to turn on their paymasters. It is a very attractive proposition to see this as an explanation for the near-simultaneous collapse of all three civilizations.

It is not hard to imagine experienced raiders acting in concert with disaffected peasants to destroy the palaces and their occupants. The vast social distance we noted already would have made peasant support of the invaders a likely proposition. In any case, with the total destruction of the Mycenaean noble class its matrix of long distance trade connections disappeared almost overnight. Some Historians call this the Greek Dark Ages. The Greek world devolved into hundreds of micro-economies physically separated by rugged geography and loosely connected by the sea. We know very little about the next several hundred years in Greece except for what archaeology tells us and the oral legends eventually put down on paper by Homer, the greatest and most influential of all Greek writers, around the year 700.

And so, for the period between 1100 and 700, we have only a schematic idea of how Greeks organized themselves politically and the way they fought. Power was fragmented and vested in a land-owning elite whose local preeminence was enforced by the loyalty of personal entourages. Regional stability was managed by cooperation between powerful family patronage networks. Meanwhile, we see glimpses of a growing sea based economy combining elements of both piracy and trade. One might argue that these are merely two points on the same spectrum. There are "kings" everywhere, but not much in the way of kingdoms. There are no impressive ruins to see because no social or economic mechanism existed that might concentrate wealth sufficiently to build anything of any consequence. There are only two classes that really matter, the noble/warrior class and the peasant class and the social distance between them was relatively small compared to both earlier and later. Without a state apparatus to patronize it, there is no priestly elite either. What social stratification existed may have been defined as much by access to weapons and high quality tools as anything else. When we hear armor mentioned in Homeric epic, it is either because a hero has fallen—rendering his armor up for grabs—or we see it used as a gift. Both of these are indications of how rare and expensive was armor. In the long run, the descendants of this tiny warrior class will survive to become the *eupatrid*s* (the leading citizens) of the city-states in the periods to follow. The details are all rather fuzzy of course as we are relying to a large degree on legends written down long after the events they purport to describe. We have thousands of images surviving on Greek pottery but none reliably depict anything from the period they purport to illustrate. Those vase images attempting to depict the epic myths of the late Mycenaean and Dark Ages do so using armor and clothing current in the classic period, the period when the vases were actually made. The Greeks who painted the pottery were as blithely unaware of this as are, it seems, the producers of Hollywood depictions of Homeric epic.

---

* *Eupatridae*: from the Greek, meaning the *well-born*. The *eupatridae* claimed to be the oldest families and they controlled the best land.

# Hoplite Greece (Greece after about 700 BC)

Iron age technology became increasingly widespread after the year 1000 and with it came a new impetus for trade and technology exchange. When we see Greece emerging from the so-called Dark Ages we see two related phenomena: a period of colonization and the adoption of new kinds of warfare. These are both, in all probability, driven by the same dynamic: increased competition for resources in Greece. Think of it logically; if there is a limited amount of high quality land available, you have to defend what you have or find some more, or both. The period of Greek colonization was concentrated between the years 700 and 500 BC. In most cases,

ASSYRIAN SOLDIER

colonies began as trading entrepots and evolved into something more elaborate. Greek ruins from this period found under the modern cities of Syracuse in Sicily, Marseilles in France, Naples in Italy, Sinop in Turkey, and the ruins of Cyrene in Libya give some idea of the scope of this diaspora.

Meanwhile, a new form of warfare was emerging in the Greek world. The spectacular collapse of the Neo-Assyrian empire to the east may have played a role in the dispersion of a new simpler set of weapons and armor. The images above and opposite show clear similarities in the basic fighting kit of the Assyrian soldier and the new kit adopted by the Greeks. The new style of combat featured the use of a shield, jabbing spears, shin guards (greaves), a helmet and sometimes a breastplate. The amount of armor used in this kit is modest and iron is cheaper than bronze; in a world where everybody pays for their own gear, these factors allowed for more men to participate in battle. In addition, having less of the body being covered stimulated coordinated battle tactics. Men identically equipped fought in orderly ranks and not as individuals. The group was called a phalanx. Before the introduction of this innovation, Greek warfare must have been an endeavor limited in scope and tiny in scale, although there is much we do not know of this period. But it is clearly the case that hoplite warfare encouraged social cooperation. Some scholars believe that this facilitated political change.

In the pre-hoplite system, the line between the warrior class and the productive class was hardened by the expense of weapons and armor. Cheaper weapons meant more weapons and more soldiers. Theoretically, the effective social distance between the peasant and warrior classes shrank until these two categories actually overlapped. Given the necessity of group cooperation in the hoplite phalanx, this evolution worked to devalue the importance of the individual leader and not surprisingly we see kingship as a political concept wane in Greece. At the same time, it is counter-intuitive to see that process as a voluntary one from the standpoint of those who were privileged. Any mobilization of group cooperation presents a threat to the domination of established elites. Resistance is predictable.

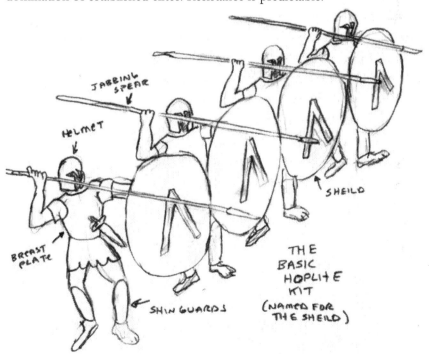

JABBING SPEAR

HELMET

BREAST PLATE

SHIELD

SHIN GUARDS

THE BASIC HOPLITE KIT (NAMED FOR THE SHELD)

And so an expanded warrior class overlapping the farmer class created inevitable challenges to the authority of the *eupatridae** whose preeminence, as we noted above, was based on control of the best land. It is in this context that we can interpret the appearance of what the Greeks called "tyrants." Over the period 700-500 we see insurgent elites taking power in many Greek cities and land re-distribution seems a common element of their appeal. This included Athens and naturally this is the city about which we know the most. In Athens, Peisistratus was the tyrant and his domination in the middle 500s BC was characterized by a number of what we might call populist measures. He was also responsible for the creation of the Panathenaia that we mentioned in the previous chapter. In most cases the tyranny was limited to a generation or two. Later Greeks defined tyrants negatively but it seems reasonable to think of them as intermediary figures in an organic transition from relatively oligarchic political forms prevalent before 700 to *more* democratic forms prevalent after 600.†

In ancient Greece, we can trace the development of social institutions in the parallel evolution of the language. For example, there are two words meaning approximately "law" in ancient Greek: *thesmos* and *nomos*. But *thesmos* is law handed down from above—as in perhaps from nobles or gods—whereas *nomos* is law rooted in custom or popular approval. This transition in linguistic usage parallels the very political transition we are here describing. Most of this evolution takes place before 500 BC and our evidence really only becomes consistently reliable after that date but sufficient bits and pieces survive for us to get a sense of what is going on. In the decades just before Peisistratus established his tyranny in Athens, that city was experiencing significant social upheaval. The controversy seems connected to major changes in an evolving economy that threatened middle and lower status landowners. Rather than face a revolution and lose everything, Athenian aristocrats commissioned one of their own, a man named Solon, to make some concessions.

---

* *Eupatridae*: literally, the well born

† It is necessary to emphasize *more* here because the temptation is to overstate the degree to which lower status Greeks benefitted by these changes.

In his program of reform, Solon paid a lot of attention to problems of debt bondage and standardization of weight and measures but his most important contribution was a re-allocation of political powers.* Every male citizen was classified according to his agricultural potential: how many measures of grain his land could produce. There were four such divisions; from highest to lowest 500, 300, 200 and less than 200 measures of grain. Access to political power was then indexed to these categories. Whereas before Solon's reforms the lowest grade of citizens (the *thetes*) had no power at all, afterward at least they were allowed to vote on matters of war and were eligible for jury service. The highest three classes composed those who could afford to equip themselves with hoplite gear and only these three classes were eligible to serve on the steering committee for the full assembly. The highest two classes were eligible for election to leadership positions and this included leading the army into battle. There is little data to provide proportion to these classes as percentages of the overall population, but on balance it seems likely that the *thetes* represented by far the largest class and to this class was arrogated the least importance. Most notably, the new system firmly rooted political power in the class capable of providing its own armor for battle, while the leadership was kept in the hands of the old elite. And so we see that the measures taken by Solon were only half measures because powerful aristocrats were still positioned to dominate the system as a whole. As a result, political instability continued in Athens for another 50 years or so. This is not yet the democracy we think of when we think of Athens, but it was a major step toward it.

Meanwhile, a parallel drama had already unfolded in the Greek city of Sparta and the result there was a much more stable version of what happened in Athens a few decades later. As it turns out, Sparta represents the best-documented and most stable example of a city that empowered the hoplite class. Sometime before 600 BC, Spartan hoplite forces conquered

---

* Debt was the most common pathway into slavery before 500 BC. In this case, farmers would use their body, or more technically the work their body could do, as collateral for loans. With coins suddenly coming into common use in the 500s, an alarming percentage of Athenian farmers found themselves hopelessly in debt, and therefore facing more or less permanent slavery. Solon banned this practice.

and enslaved their Greek neighbors. These unfortunates survived to become the so-called helots, a captive laboring class. Individual Spartan citizens were assigned these slaves and were debarred from alienating them. The existence of such a permanent slave class made it possible—and necessary it seems—for Spartan citizens to remain in arms *permanently* as well. From the time of this conquest, all full Spartan citizens were, therefore, full time hoplite soldiers and only they had full citizenship rights in Sparta. At the same time, the egalitarian nature of the hoplite phalanx tended to obscure any wealth distinctions that existed. The Spartans always claimed absolute equality among the citizens but there is plenty of evidence indicating wide disparities in land ownership.

In Sparta, there was also a small middle class of free craftsmen but these had no political rights. There were two kings whose responsibilities were limited to leading the army, presiding over the council of elders (*gerousia*), and supervising various ritual activities. The council of elders consisted of 28 men over the age of 60 as well as the two kings. Once elected, members sat for life. Every year, five men were elected as *ephors* (literally, overseers) whose collective power could overrule the kings. Their job was essentially to act as guardians of the laws and they undertook a number of administrative duties, including the inspection and enrollment of infant citizens. Each man was only allowed to serve a single term as *ephor* in his life. All full Spartan citizen males voted in the assembly to answer questions put by the council of elders. Technically then, all Spartan males had equal political power but realistically, the elders and the ephors effectively managed the political system. Voting was by acclamation and supervised by the ephors. The Spartan education system—called the *agoge*, in Greek—featured a long program of indoctrination to the will of the elders and the system guaranteed that their priorities were upheld. Since all important decisions were shaped by men over 60 years old, it is no surprise that, for the most part, Spartan foreign policy was extremely conservative.

As I said above, Sparta is the best example of a pure hoplite system. You could perhaps call it a *hoplite* democracy in that political power was evenly shared *within* the hoplite class. On the other hand, you could hardly call it a democracy without qualifying the term because the hoplite class was less than—and probably *much* less than—50% of the adult male population in Sparta. Nevertheless, it was a *pure* hoplite democracy in that its citizens engaged in no activity except military training. This makes it differ dramatically from all other Greek cities with hoplite forces. In all other cases of which we know anything, cities routinely trained young men of sufficient means as a hoplite army-in-reserve. This status made the hoplite class the most consistently important political class in all Greek cites-that is, in Greek cities without significant navies. This brings us back to Athens.

# Triremes and Democracy

Unlike Sparta, Athens *did* go through further stages of political development. After Solon and the instability represented in the tyranny of Peisistratus, the next most important political moment featured the reforms of Cleisthenes (shortly before 500 BC). In the ten years or so leading up to those reforms Athens had been torn apart in a bitter political feud between several powerful families. The figure head of one of these factions, and Cleisthenes' number one rival, Isagoras, was forced to flee the city after some especially underhanded tactics rendered him unpopular with the people. With the precipitous and unexpected departure of his main aristocratic rival, Cleisthenes had a window of opportunity of which he immediately took full advantage. He began by sponsoring sweeping political reforms designed to undermine Isagoras' power and political influence. The most important of these was a total re-organization of the Athenian voting districts. At least since Solon, Athens had been divided into four voting districts (*phyle* is the term in Greek; we use the term tribes to translate this). Each of these tribes was dominated by one aristocratic faction or another. This had the predictable effect of guaranteeing that all political contests ended up being contests between powerful families. By first increasing the number of tribes from four to ten and then assigning all of the 160 or so Athenian villages (called *demes*) to these tribes in equal measure from coastal, mountain, and flatland parts of Athenian territory, Cleisthenes made it impossible for any single family or any single economic constituency to dominate the voting process. The effect was immediate and dramatic in that *aristocratic feuding never again paralyzed Athens* and from this moment forward Athenian citizens celebrated their common Athenian political identity above all others. It was still not full democracy, but it was a *giant* step closer.

Cleisthenes was also associated with another political reform called ostracism. He came up with an extraordinary idea that allowed all citizens a vote to exile any one citizen from the city for a period of ten years. The theory behind this odd practice seems to be that the citizens could neutralize someone they thought was wielding too much power from behind the scenes. The individual would not lose his citizenship or his property; he just couldn't enter the city for ten years! The term ostracism comes from the Greek word *ostracon* for a broken piece of pottery, which must have lain everywhere in garbage heaps. It was the *de facto* memo pad of its time. Citizens scratched the name of the citizen they wanted to get rid of onto a pottery shard and dropped it into a vase. Afterward, the vase would be dumped out, votes counted and if the overall winner received a minimum of 6000 votes, he was forced to leave the city. The practice was eventually abandoned but its institution and use illustrates again the underlying intention of Cleisthenes' reforms: to frustrate the plans of overly ambitious aristocrats. Historians like to give Cleisthenes credit for creating the Athenian democracy but this is not entirely accurate. To think Cleisthenes was a pure humanitarian and altruist is to overlook his own ambitions (some historians think he was the first to be ostracized). Secondly, these reforms did little for the *thetes* who remained ineligible for elective office. Finally, it is clear that the real impetus toward democracy in Athens was the creation of a large navy and the patronage of two other important Athenians, first Themistocles in the 480s and then Pericles in the 440s.

So we can give Cleisthenes his due, but as it turns out the democracy for which Athens is famous has everything to do with war ships. Lots and lots of war ships. While not all Greeks took to the sea, many did, and Greeks from various cities over the centuries designed ships not only to carry trade items but also to protect that trade. The most successful of the warship designs was the trireme, the standard in widespread use after the year 500 BC. Although it was in the interests of every coastal city to maintain some ships to control piracy, they were extraordinarily expensive to build and maintain and so there was a practical limit to how many ships any one city could keep. In addition, each trireme required 170 rowers plus officers and marines, so a practical commitment to maintain even a modest a navy was a huge and costly affair. No single Greek city before 500 owned more than 60 or 70 triremes and most had substantially less. This all makes Athens' sudden acquisition of a 200-ship navy an extraordinary event. Around 483 BC, the city of Athens suddenly found itself with a huge surplus of cash. The city had been mining silver for decades on public land but when a huge new vein was discovered, the question then became: what to do with this windfall? Themistocles convinced the Athenians to build a fleet of 200 triremes.

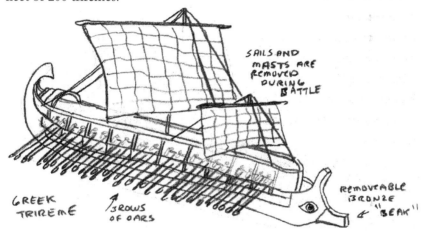

SAILS AND MASTS ARE REMOVED DURING BATTLE

GREEK TRIREME

3 ROWS OF OARS

REMOVABLE BRONZE "BEAK"

We really have no idea what arguments he used; perhaps it came from fears of the Persian empire or it might have been a power play to put Athens into a dominant position compared to other cities with significant navies (nearby Corinth and Aegina perhaps). In any case, the ships were built and the economic effects of this decision had to have been enormous; aside from the thousands of man hours required to build these ships,* harbor and storage facilities had to be created, tens of thousands of oars to be

---

* It took something on the order of one year for 20 man to build just one.

individually carved, not to mention 35-40,000 rowers, all *thetes*, needed to be recruited, trained, and paid. [As a side note, it is *not* true that the ancients routinely used slaves as rowers. In the few known emergencies when slaves were used, they were freed first.]

As it turned out, building this fleet elevated Athens to a position of dominance in the Greek world (we will cover some of the details of this story in the next chapter). The first step in this process was the naval battle of Salamis (in 480 BC) in which the combined Greek navy crippled a large Persian invasion fleet. The largest contingent in that navy was the contingent from Athens. We saw that with the earlier adoption of hoplite weapons and tactics across Greece, there was a corresponding shift of political power toward the class that could afford these weapons. The best example we have is Sparta, but to some extent this was true in most Greek cities. The implication of this shift prepares us for what happened in Athens with the navy. All of a sudden 40,000 or so *thetes* had a military importance to the city of Athens that they never had before. And a clever politician like Themistocles would certainly be in a position to use the popularity of the new fleet to reward and increase the political clout of the rowers. While the details are a little fuzzy, over the next 40 years we see a trend expanding democratic participation in all facets of the city government. The expression 'radical democracy' is often associated with this period. One example of the radical nature of the democracy is that by the time of Pericles' influence (470-430 BC), most elected officials and all jurors were paid for their service. And there were plenty of positions created over this period. By 430, there were over a thousand or so elective offices in Athens and about 90 percent were chosen by lottery, the ultimate form of democracy! In no other city that we know of did democracy expand to this extent. I am arguing here that the extraordinarily large navy Athens created was the engine for this change because it gave the lowest class of citizens—those without property—a military importance they never had before. The hoplites continues to exist as a class of course but their political importance was overshadowed by the *thetes* on the basis of sheer numbers.

In the next chapter, we will survey in more detail the rise and dominance of Athens over the course of the fifth century BC (the 400s). We have excellent detail for that period provided by two of the greatest ancient Greek historical writers, Herodotus and Thucydides. For now, we will skip to 404, when Athens was toppled from her position of dominance after Sparta made a grand bargain with the Persians for a fleet of ships. Thus began a much less glorious chapter in Greek history (c. 400 to c. 340) where a succession of Greek cities, fueled by Persian subsidies and stolen Delphian treasure, ripped each other to shreds. A political lesson emerged from this mess: no individual polis could sustain a position of dominance without some artificial support because of the limits of citizen manpower in any given city. Athens' position of dominance was originally predicated on a lucky silver strike. Sparta overcame the Athenian fleet by taking subsidies from the Persians. The Spartans in their turn were knocked down by Thebes in a devastating defeat in 371 but this happened only after Sparta had been weakened by an alliance of Greek cities that was also financed by the Persians. Thebes' power waned and collapsed first under the pressure of the tiny but surging Phokis, whose city war chest had been bolstered by the stolen treasure of Delphi, and then finally by the rise of Macedon under the leadership of Phillip II.

The details in this round robin of political and military failures do not interest us but the solution does. That solution was Philip II of Macedon and a new set of political and military policies that changed Greece forever. Macedon was a weak kingdom in the northeast of Greece. Its many small cities never went through the hoplite phase of political history—perhaps because of their relatively small size—and in some respects it resembled the old Dark Age model of kings and small entourages of hereditary elites monopolizing all political power. The Greeks of the southern cities were always ambivalent on the question of whether Macedonians were actually Greeks, even though they spoke a dialect of Greek. Southern Greeks pointed to, for example, the Macedonian habit of drinking their wine unmixed with water as a sure sign of a foreign and barbarous nature. But the central reason why the Greeks regarded their cousins from the north to be inferior is the fact that Macedonian cities lacked the political structures common in the southern cities. The *polis* was, for those Greeks that lived in one, self-evident in its superiority, and the only place in which a thinking person could imagine living. Hence the Greek expression made famous by Aristotle: "man is a political animal."

The kingship of the Macedonians was traditionally a weak position, that is, until Philip II took the throne in 359. Before he seized power, Philip had been a hostage in Thebes. While he was a young man there, he noted with interest the strengths and successes of Theban cavalry tactics and their modified infantry weapons. Later he adopted versions of these tactics and weapons when he ascended the throne in Macedon. He created a new unit of Macedonian cavalry composed of the elites of the various cities in Macedon. He called these his "Companions" and in so doing tied these elites much more closely to the person and fortunes of the king than had been the case in the past. He extended the lances that Theban infantry employed to an astounding 18 feet. The result was an infantry unit that was reminiscent of a hedgehog or a porcupine in appearance and just as daunting to approach. Traditionally in Greek hoplite combat, horses were used as taxis to arrive at the battlefield and to facilitate running down and slaughtering fleeing enemy soldiers. Now they were used as active elements in combat, a sort of hammer to punish those pinned against the infantry anvil. The integration of these two force structures became the standard foundation for the next generation of combat in the Greek world.

Philip also exhibited a keen interest in a new generation of weapons that was destined to change siege warfare forever, the catapult. And he was also not averse to multiple marriages to seal alliances (an un-Greek practice, but common in ancient kingships as a diplomatic tool). While the rest of Greece was tearing itself to pieces in pointless wars, Phillip was building alliances, and imagining a grand campaign against the fattest cow of them all, Persia. Although he did put plans in motion to achieve this objective, he was murdered before he could follow through and this grand adventure was left to his son Alexander to fulfill. Although Alexander proved himself equal to the task of leadership in the conquest of the Persian empire it was the structure Alexander inherited from his father that enabled him to succeed.

What remains for us in this chapter is to emphasize the political components of Philips's reforms and the ways these departed from the *polis* system dominant in Greece for the previous several centuries. Every Greek and every Greek city defined itself with respect to a single political center and its immediately surrounding land. The weakness of such a political definition of citizenship is that its potential membership is limited by how many souls the countryside surrounding the city could support. Philip fostered the creation of a wider political membership and, in so doing, he broke the political deadlock that had existed in Greece since the fall of Athens in 404 BC. By emphasizing an inclusive regional identity and by closely tying regional elites to the king, Philip fostered a new layer of political identity. To call oneself a Macedonian was to swear allegiance to an idea larger than that encompassed by a city wall. This does not mean that one abandons the identity associated with one's city of origin; one augments it with a *new* identity that has its own rewards. From a military standpoint, the advantage is obvious: one can obviously now think of a citizen army larger than one associated with a single city. Single cities can have allies, but alliances are always subject to breakdown along the lines of changing local interests. Meanwhile, all members of the Macedonian army are citizens of the same polity and their interest neither temporary nor *ad hoc*.

Reviewing briefly, we observe a threshold in Greek history around 700 BC. In the period before 700, political power was mostly oligarchic in form. Powerful families cooperated to control the land and maintained their supremacy with a monopoly on weapons. Conflict was low intensity and localized. After 700, new ideas about weapons and tactics, population growth, and economic change came into play and a period of political experimentation began. We have identified three political directions in which this experimental period developed; we associate Sparta, Athens, and Macedonia with these three models of development. In the case of Sparta we see a stable political system where political power is vested entirely in the hoplite class. As a general proposition, the hoplite class is that class of farmers with sufficient means to afford the hoplite equipment. If you are a Spartan citizen, you are a hoplite soldier and you don't bother with farming directly, although you do own farmland. Outside of Sparta, it was never this clear cut. In most Greek cities, political power was distributed, at least to some extent, over all the classes, but most tended to favor the hoplite class. We see this principle in Solon's reforms in Athens (c. 590). But when Athens system finally stabilized after 500 BC, we see a new and different political solution from the one we saw develop in Sparta. The difference is in the navy; Athenian political power shifted over the course of about 40 years (480-440BC) to the rowers of that fleet. Because rowers needed no equipment, and there was need of so many of them, the lowest property rating of citizens was necessary to fill the rolls. Political power followed. Once sheer numbers extended power to the lowest class, that class predominated in the political arena. It is also true that the rowers, once politically empowered, tended to advocate for war because, as the poorest class, they had the least to lose and the most to gain by war. Although Athens is our most clear cut example of these principles, it is also true generally that in all Greek cities with fleets of ships, there tended to be more political power vested in the lower tiers of citizens than in cities without fleets. Finally in the Macedon of Phillip II and Alexander the Great, we see something different. We see the logistical advantages inherent in creating a regional army with a single unified political identity. "Macedonian" became a political identity that subsumed and superseded local city identity. This integrated political identity enabled a quantitative increase in the scale of military endeavor and signaled the end of the *polis* era of Greek history.

# Chapter Four: The Difference between Classical and Hellenistic

*What were the dynamics driving Ancient Greek culture?*

This chapter is mostly about Greek ideals and aesthetics. The Greeks set intellectual and artistic benchmarks which will forever define core elements of western culture and these benchmarks provide an almost unavoidable idiom for any serious discussion of beauty, proportion, and even of justice. Unfortunately, many who are familiar with the idiom have little idea of the forces shaping its invention. And so the idea here is to put some of this into its proper context. When you read about ancient Greece or when you wander through a good museum, you always see tags referring to various periods of Greek art history: geometric, archaic, Minoan, Hellenistic, etc. To the casual observer or the beginner, there are two of these that really matter: Classic and Hellenistic, with Archaic perhaps bringing up a distant third. They matter because the periods they represent are the ones about which we know the most and, more importantly, they provide the context for much that is directly influential on our own culture in terms of, for example, aesthetic principles, the origins of western science and philosophy, theatre, and so forth. The goal of this chapter then is to explore what is essential about these periods; not so much to list and describe everything that happens but to see what defines them as periods both politically and culturally. In the process, we discover a consistent resonance between the political narrative and the evolution of Greek ideas of aesthetics and justice.

In the previous chapter, we outlined an evolution in Greek political models or, put another way, the relationships between Greek citizens. This chapter will provide a glimpse into relationships between Greek *cities*. The combination of these dynamics, one contained within city walls, and one standing astride them, are the prime dynamics informing the zeitgeist of any people. So since we are interested in the way the Greek mind developed it is logical to provide a sketch of the conflicts between Greek cities. This will not be a blow-by-blow description of Greek warfare; just enough detail will be provided to add substance to the assertions I make. First, a few words about the Archaic period.

Archaic is used as a tag corresponding to Greek art of the period 700-500 BC, more or less. As already noted in the previous chapter, this is a period of economic expansion, population growth and the rise of hoplite-based political systems. It is before the rise of democracy, which is key to the use of the word. The term *archaic* speaks volumes. It means old fashioned and out-of-date, obsolete even. The implication of the word is that what is deemed archaic can only be done so *in retrospect*. By definition, something has already been superseded by something better, or something more up to date. It is therefore not a term useful for understanding anything in and of itself. In this case, the term is deliberately deployed to foreshadow the thing that supersedes it (this will be Classic Greece, but more on that in a moment). In the Archaic period, cities all across the Greek world celebrated their expanded political membership and their community prosperity through temple construction, and gifts by powerful families to these sacred precincts were common. The aesthetic principles guiding the craftsmen doing this work seem formulaic and unoriginal. Obvious influences from Near Eastern and Egyptian principles and habits are abundant. Sculptural and architectural techniques gradually improved over the period, as one might expect, but the assumptions driving the proportions and styles remained moribund. Before 500, one sees better and better versions of the same old things. This aesthetic conservatism reflects the class paying for the art. All statuary and arguably most temples from this period were functions of aristocratic display, an inherently conservative constituency. Things changed however, with the rise of Athens.

Of all the hundreds of Greek cities, the one about which we know the most is Athens. There is no close second. What this means is that when we moderns talk about "what the Greeks did," chances are we are *really* talking about what the *Athenians* did. This is not always true but when we are

64

talking about "Classical Greece," it is almost entirely true. Classical Greece corresponds roughly with the period of Athenian democracy, that is, from about 500 BC to the death of Alexander the Great in 323. Within this period there is a smaller, even more focused period sometimes called the Golden Age of Athens. This corresponds with the first 100 years of the same period and corresponds with the time of Athenian dominance of the Aegean. Some like to get in even closer and talk about "Periclean Athens", the period when Pericles was the dominant figure in Athens, from about 450 to about 430. Carving history in this way allows those who worship the cultural beauty of Greece to exclude most of the nasty war that Athens brought upon itself in the last third of the so-called Golden Age. But however you slice it, Classical Greece really is a story of Athens.

Hellenistic Greece, on the other hand, is a much wider shot of the Greek world. As a referent to either art or politics, it refers to the period between the death of Alexander the Great and the Roman conquest of Egypt, 300 years later. Politically speaking, the emphasis is not on city level government as it was in Athens, but on the kingdoms torn by Alexander's generals from the shredded fabric of the empire Alexander stole from the Persians. The last surviving of these kingdoms (that bordered the Mediterranean) was in Egypt. The last Hellenistic ruler of Egypt was Cleopatra, nine generations removed from her ancestor Ptolemy I, who was a Macedonian general with Alexander throughout his conquests. In the Hellenistic period—and in the Roman period to follow—cities like Athens continued to exist and enjoyed some degree of self-rule, but they were never again independent political entities free to choose their own destiny, for better or for worse. In the Hellenistic period, we hear about Athens, but it is no longer the center of attention in the surviving evidence.

In order to use these words—Classical and Hellenistic—there are some subtle implications of which one should be aware. To say something is "classic" is to say that it sets a standard; it is an ideal against which all else should be compared. Ideals are inherently unreachable. And so nothing can be better than Classic. Hellenistic, on the other hand, has a not-so-subtle pejorative built right in. It's the *istic* bit. "Hellenic" just means Greek. *istic* is a qualifier implying, "not quite," or "sort of," or perhaps "like," as in *realistic*: something *like* real, but *not* real. By itself, the term Hellenistic makes a lot of sense because the kingdoms ruled by Alexander's former generals were not, for the most part, populated by Greek speakers. Greek speakers ruled, but the languages and cultures shared by nearly all the inhabitants of these kingdoms were decidedly not Greek. And so in most of the Hellenistic kingdoms, there was a Greek veneer because it was the language, culture, and idiom of power, but this veneer and the cultural idioms characterizing it possessed little relevance for most of the population.

It is when you put the two words together, whether explicitly or implicitly, that you convey another level of meaning. Juxtapose the words Classic and Hellenistic and you are automatically creating a comparison in which Hellenistic must suffer. It is built into the words and our use of these words says volumes about us. Here is a small example of something we discussed in the first chapter, namely, that History is as much about the present as it is about the past. In this instance our choice of language sets up a value judgment about which is the better idea: the democracy of Classic [ideal] Athens, or the monarchy of the Hellenistic [Greek-like] kingdoms. The judgment we make is predicated on our own value system, our own hierarchy of political goods. I do not take issue with the judgment; I merely point out that the words we use precondition our judgment.

However, when one surveys the actual democracy of Classic era Athens, one discovers a mixed bag and only with careful picking and choosing of the evidence can one come up with an unambiguous endorsement of Athens or of their version of democracy. Let us divide the period of Athenian democracy more or less into thirds and characterize each period separately. Then you judge for yourself.

# The Rise of Athens (500-430 BC)

In the year 500, Athens was a city of the second rank in the Greek world. Sparta was number one. Across the Aegean was the western border of a vast Persian empire stretching from Greek waters all the way to India and

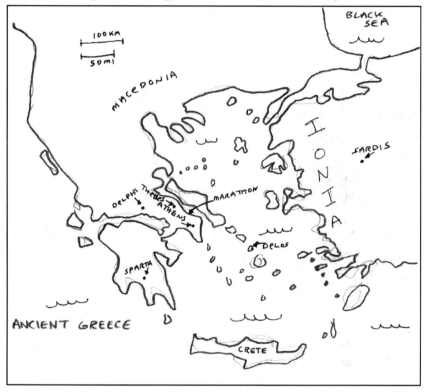

south to include Egypt as well. The western border of the Persian empire was the western coast of modern Turkey, known then and now as Ionia. Ionia was then entirely Greek. This means of course that the Persians had Greek cities under their control. But, as was their pattern, the Persians ruled with a light hand and the Greek cities of Ionia were free to run their own affairs (just don't be late with the taxes!). On balance, the Ionians had little to complain about. This makes it all the more surprising when the Greek leaders in some of these Ionian cities decided to revolt. In anticipation of the likely Persian response, Ionians visited various free cities in mainland

Greece seeking allies. Most cites wisely stayed out of the fight including Sparta. Inexplicably however, and perhaps because the Spartans chose not to, Athens went the other way and gleefully participated in a raid on the Persian provincial capital of Sardis. For the sake of illustration, let's make a modern imaginary comparison. Imagine that Puerto Rico decided to revolt from the United States and convinced Cuba to participate in burning down the city of Tallahassee, the capitol of Florida. In this imaginary scenario, Puerto Rico might be in for some trouble. But the Cubans? Watch out for some *serious* trouble!! And so this began the Persian Wars. Once Persia reeled in the Ionians, they turned their attention to Athens. In 490, they sent a punitive expedition island hopping across the Aegean and landed a large force of cavalry on a beach called Marathon in Athenian territory. Their likely mission was to destroy and burn as much of Athens' farmland and infrastructure as possible in a lightening raid. Only it didn't turn out the way the Persians imagined. The Athenians and a few neighbors sent hoplites to block the Persian force from leaving the beach area. After a few days of what had quickly become a tactical stalemate, the Persians attempted to reload their horses onto the transports with the intention of trying their luck elsewhere. The Athenians attacked the departing Persians, inflicting major casualties. There is good evidence to suggest that the Persians had a plan B, that they planned to land elsewhere in Athenian territory, but the losses their force suffered at Marathon caused them to withdraw from Greece altogether. Imagine the loss of face to the Persian King Darius and the likely scale of his intended response. However, as it turned out, the Athenians caught a break; actually, two breaks. Darius died before he could plan another attack a task effectively left to his successor, Xerxes. Meanwhile, the Athenians found a huge lode of silver and used the money to finance a huge fleet of ships. Athens was about to become a different kind of power.

Herodotus, our main source for this and what follows, gives us a blow-by-blow description of the massive invasion that came in 480. If you believe his every word, then several million Persians streamed into Greece drinking the rivers dry every time they stopped for a rest. While his numbers are obviously exaggerated, it was indeed an impressive and well-organized invasion. Faced with this existential threat, dozens of Greek cities put aside (most of) their petty grievances and agreed to cooperate for the first time ever. Sparta, regarded as the most respected city in Greece, claimed the leadership of the *ad hoc* alliance. But even united, the Greeks could not match the Persians in numbers. This called for a smart defense that emphasized geography and local knowledge. The main feature of the plan was to defend a series of narrow defiles where Persian numbers could not be used effectively. Meanwhile, ships from all the Greek cities would attempt to harry and harass the Persian fleet, as it waited for the stalled Persian army to advance. The thinking was that without their fleet to provide forward reconnaissance, communications, and supply, the enormous Persian army would be left blind and hungry.

| Persian Wars Timeline 499 - c.450 | |
| --- | --- |
| Cyrus the Great creates the Persian empire | 550-530 |
| Cambyses is Great King of Persia | 530-522 |
| Darius is Great King of Persia | 522-486 |
| Ionian Revolt | 499 |
| Ionia retaken | 494 |
| Marathon | 490 |
| The Athenians strike silver and build a huge fleet | 484/3 |
| Xerxes is great King of Persia | 486-465 |
| Battles of Thermopylae, Salamis | 480 |
| Battle of Plataea | 479 |
| Delian League formed | 478 |
| Battle of Eurymedon River | 468 |
| Athenian fleet stranded in Egypt | 456 |
| Peace of Callias (?) | 449 |

And it worked. And there was plenty of glory to go around. There were several key and dramatic battles about which we now quite a bit—a big thank you goes to Herodotus for this —and a few others about which we know very little. The long and short of it is that the Spartans lived up to their fearsome reputation on the battlefield and the Athenians gained a lot of stature in a key naval battle almost directly opposite the city of Athens. After the invasion was turned back, there was talk of revenge and the re-liberation of Ionia but the Spartans soon lost interest and they dropped out of the alliance along with most of their particular allies. In order to differentiate this new alliance from the one that included Sparta, we call it the Delian league after its treasury, originally located in the center of the Aegean on the island of Delos.

For Athens, this was a critical moment. By default, Athens was the most prestigious city in the new alliance. Moreover, the Athenians provided the largest single contingent of ships to the effort. Athens' fleet would become the key to dominating the league. Because of this, the rower class found themselves front and center in all discussions in Athens concerning the war. Unlike the hoplite class, the rowers were unambiguously pro-war because war meant jobs, the potential of war-booty, and a piece of the martial glory that had always defined Greek manhood. For the *thetes*, none of this could exist without the ships. And ships were expensive. Athens demanded that her allies without ships provide money instead. This system worked primarily to favor Athens, and Athenians rowers most of all, but few of the allies complained, at least at first. Hostilities against Persia continued on and off until the mid-450s BC by which time Ionia was mostly back in Greek hands. Some scholars believe a peace treaty was signed between Athens and Persian around 454 although the evidence is slim. What matters is that the ostensible reason the alliance was created was gone. There was no longer a war with Persia and, for the allies, no need to pay Athens.

But for the Athenians, the no-war thing was just a technicality. There was still a fleet, and there were still oars to carve and rowers to pay and the allies who tried to pull out were therefore punished for their impudence. The Delian League had become, for all practical purposes, an Athenian empire and, not surprisingly, the treasury of the league was moved to Athens. After 450 Pericles was the leading man in Athens and with his influence the democracy had evolved to its most radical version of itself. The number of committees and minor officials, all of whom were paid, exploded. The fleet grew in size rather than shrunk. Vast building programs were initiated, including the Parthenon. If you were a performer, if you were a teacher, if you were a craftsman, if you were a prostitute, there was good work to be had in Athens and the city swelled in consequence. If you were Athenian, it was a great time to live.

But not everybody in Greece was an Athenian, not by far; and the grumbling and the resentment about Athens' bullying grew louder and louder. Meanwhile the Spartans eyed Athens' growing power with concern. In the competition that was Greece, Sparta had been number one for a long time. This is no small thing. Spartans eyed Athenian bullying of lesser cities, especially those with ties to Sparta, as a challenge to their reputation and position as number one. The Spartan inclination to see things in this way made it inevitable that sooner or later the line of ambassadors at Spartan doors complaining about Athens would have an effect. The only question was which spark would light the fire of war. Historians looking at this moment cite several possible proximate causes for the war that inevitably came but it may be as simple as under-standing that Athens no longer agreed to be number two—that means not backing down—and Sparta was concerned to maintain a status quo wherein their preeminence was unambiguous. It all seems pretty silly when put in those terms, but the way the war progressed, tit for tat, start and stop, even until the very end, it seems to come down to a clash of symbols and pride rather than substantive strategic interests.

# 430-380 BC

And so Greece was divided into two sides: Athens and her allies, Sparta and hers. And all wars, especially long ones, become showcases for brutality and horror. Our main source for this period, Thucydides, pulls no punches in his heart-wrenching and matter-of-fact descriptions of systematic massacres. One cannot read his account without realizing how much Thucydides hated war and what it does to all that is good in us. But for all of that, the war dragged on and off until the Athenians made a blunder of colossal proportion. They decided to invade the island of Sicily and conquer its most prestigious city, a city at least as big as Athens itself: Syracuse. It did not turn out well and both the initial invasion force and the relieving forces sent to reinforce it were destroyed in a pointless loss of life. This did not end the war, but it certainly portended its end. In an ironic twist, one of Athens' leading citizens and most ardent warmonger, Alcibiades, went into exile in Sparta at the beginning of the Sicilian expedition (he was accused of impiety and was headed for a trial). On his advice, Sparta appealed to the Persians to subsidize a fleet of ships and this ultimately tipped the balance against Athens. The war ended with Athenian surrender in 404.

Surprisingly, the Spartans did not do to the Athenians what the Athenians had so often done to others. That is, they chose not to execute all the men, and not to enslave all the women. Instead they installed a puppet government. This was a surprisingly rationale decision in that the destruction of Athens would have left a power vacuum of which other cities would naturally take advantage. More to the point, the Spartans seized the Athenian outposts around the Aegean and installed garrisons of Spartan soldiers. Although there was not much Athens could say about the latter, it was in contravention of a) Spartan promises to the Persians (who paid for the Spartan fleet) and b) Spartan promises of liberation to Athenian subject/allies. Instead of liberating the Athenian empire, Sparta claimed control over it.

Unfortunately for Sparta, neither policy worked out in the long run. The puppet government set up by Sparta lasted only a year before Athenians re-established the democracy. Meanwhile, the former subjects of Athens chafed under Spartan domination (and their lack of humor). And we must not forget the Persians who, for their part, were not pleased to be denied that for which they had already paid. Their strategic response was to start giving money to various Greek cities (including Athens) to contest Sparta's new role. This opening gave Athenians cause to believe she could reclaim her former pre-eminence; in the ensuing decades there was a small scale revival of the Athenian league of cities but it was never again to be dominant in Greek affairs. The Athenian countryside never really recovered from the devastations of war and the now well-established Persian policy of paying the Greeks to kill each other kept matters in Greece in a state of confusion until the rise of Macedon changed everything.

# 380-330 BC

The last period of an independent Athenian democracy featured persistent fantasies of reclaiming a glorious past ultimately frustrated by the rise of Macedon. Although Macedon was busy shaping its destiny according to its own interests, it was easy for some Athenians to interpret Macedon's progress as intended to frustrate Athenian goals. In the short term, Athens used the growing resentment over Sparta to marshal support for a new Athenian alliance. The prospects for Athens seemed good when Thebes destroyed the Spartan army at the battle of Leuktra in 371. Although Sparta never really recovered from this crippling defeat, neither did Athens regain the kind of pre-eminence she enjoyed in the 400s. Throughout this period, it was the policy of Athens to seek strategic control over the entrance to the Black Sea, a perennial source of grain for the oversize city. In the longer term, Phillip of Macedon's reshaping of the Macedonian monarchy translated into a more assertive posture in the same region. This created An inevitable conflict of strategic interests; all of the Aegean ports of Macedon lay between Athens and the Black Sea. Athens and Macedon were actually in a proxy war between 357 and 346 with most of the fighting directed at each other's allies along the trade routes rather than with each other directly. A peace was made in 346 but it accomplished nothing except to highlight Athens' decreasing prominence in Greece.

Not all Athenians were ready to acknowledge their diminished role. Demosthenes was the greatest of these. A powerful orator, many of his surviving addresses to the Athenian assembly feature harangues directed against the integrity and intentions of Phillip II, the Macedonian king. One could argue that Demosthenes was personally responsible for the final blow to the Athenian democracy. In 338, he convinced the Thebans to join Athens against Phillip on the battlefield; the result was a decisive victory for Phillip. According to the Plutarch, an ancient Greek biographer, Demosthenes' performance on the field of battle was less than stellar: "in the fight, he did nothing honorable, nor were his actions equal to his words, for he fled, deserting his place in the line disgracefully." From this point until the appearance of Rome, the Macedonian monarchy would call the shots in Greece and our ancient sources no longer concerned themselves with the glory of Athens.

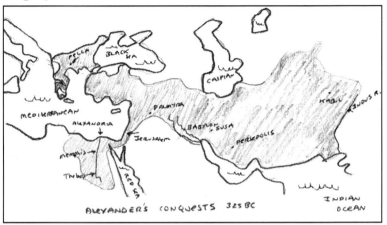

ALEXANDER'S CONQUESTS 325 BC

Over the whole period of the Classical democracy in Athens, one sees a clear narrative arc. Athens' democracy and the commoners whose votes empowered it arose in a flash of glory in a war against the hated Persian empire. After some decades, the cities that had once allied with Athens in a cooperative campaign against Persia began to see Athens as a bully, and it all slowly went bad. The leaders of Sparta, cajoled by abused Greek cities, and resentful of Athens preeminence, turned on Athens. Despite the disastrous defeat in Sicily, the Athenian democracy never blinked in its commitment to empire. Only a year after being beaten and admonished by Sparta, the Athenian democracy re-emerged and set about recovering her former glory, an effort nevertheless doomed to failure by the rise of Macedon.

The Athenians believed that their city, their form of government, had an inherent virtue that made it literally the greatest city in Greece. It is an alien thought process to most of us in this age, but the utter faith in the inherent virtue of the democracy empowered Athenians to believe themselves deserving of an empire because of that democracy. The intensely participatory nature of democracy in Athens—war policy was argued and decided by a direct vote of the enrolled citizens—and the thousand plus minor officials and committee slots made the democracy tangible to every citizen and imbued all citizens with a sort of persistent optimism. It is this sense of optimism that fired the spirit of the time, the age of the Classical Athenian democracy.

# Hellenistic Greece 323-30 BC

From a political standpoint, Hellenistic Greece could not be more different from Classical Greece; it was a world where kings were gods, or very nearly so. Obviously, monarchy was rare in the Classical era but it wasn't unheard of. In its Classical contexts, however, it was moderated and limited by interaction with other officials as, for example, in Sparta. The model of Greek monarchy in the Hellenistic era was more on the model of the eastern autocracy than it was on Greek precedent. For the eastern autocrat, justification for leadership was found in management of divine favor (remember chapter two). The king may not be god, but he is *honored* as if he were one. In any case, there was no room for critical citizen input in this sort of relationship and the palace cultures of the Hellenistic kings were bureaucracies centered on the king. It was of course much more efficient than having thousands of citizens rotate through endless committee spots but it also changed the citizens' perceptions of themselves with respect to the state. Moreover, the various Hellenistic kings spent an inordinate amount of time at war defending their territories from each other's incursions while the expense and scale of the battles was virtually unlimited thanks to the enormous quantities of Persian treasure taken by the Macedonians. These trends acted to emphasize the powerlessness of the individual in society.

The specific dynastic politics of Hellenistic Greece do not concern us much here. Suffice it to say that three major monarchies were created and a number of minor ones. One by one the Romans absorbed all of these. In 146, the Romans abolished the Antigonid dynasty controlling the Macedonian heartlands and Macedon annexed to Rome. In Syria, the

Seleucid dynasty faded away in the 60s BC, after being clients of the Romans for some time before that. The longest lasting of the a major Hellenistic kingdoms was in Egypt, the kingdom of the Ptolemies, which lasted until Cleopatra's suicide in 30 BC, after which Egypt was made a Roman province. To give you some idea of the political character of these times, let us choose one Hellenistic ruler to represent the period. Our token ruler is Demetrius Poliocertes.*

| Overall Greek Chronology | |
|---|---|
| Trojan war | c. 1200 BC |
| First Greek Olympics | 776 |
| Greek Alphabet invented | c.750 |
| Greek colonization period | 700-550 |
| Lycurgus in Sparta | 650 |
| Solon in Athens | 594 |
| Tyranny in Athens | 546 |
| Cleisthenes in Athens | 510 |
| Persian Wars | 499-c.450 |
| Pericles in Athens | 460-430 |
| Peloponnesian Wars | 450-404 |
| Spartan hegemony | 404-371 |
| Theban hegemony | 371-362 |
| Philip at Chaeronea | 338 |
| Alexander's Big adventure | 336-323 |
| Rome's Greek wars | 214-146 |
| Suicide of Cleopatra | 30 |

Demetrius was son of Antigonus the One-Eye, who was himself one of Alexander the Great's generals. The father put the son to work attacking his rivals, Seleucus and Ptolemy, also former generals of Alexander. In 312 Demetrius lost his first battle against his combined enemies and won his second. In 310 he lost of most of his father's kingdom in a battle in Babylon. In 307 he 'rescued' Athens from a tyrant and set up his own tyranny. In 306 he destroyed Ptolemy I's fleet in a major sea battle. In 305 he attempted to take the harbor city of Rhodes where he deployed some spectacular siege equipment but nonetheless failed. In 302, he "rescued" Greece from Ptolemy and demanded a ransom from Athens, which he reportedly handed over to his favorite courtesan. In 301 he lost a major battle with Ptolemy and returned to Athens, which he took yet again, and

---

* *Poliocertes*: from the Greek, meaning city-besieger. As I will mention in passing below, he developed a reputation for building giant elaborate devices and siege engines.

set up a tyranny there. Again, in 296, he conspired to kill the king of Macedon and established a new dynasty there that lasted until the Romans showed up. Unfortunately, he did not get much of a chance to enjoy this because he was driven from Greece in 288 and so he prepared to try his luck once again in Syria. After a famine decimated his troops, and the rest deserted, he was captured by Seleucus, who kept him a prisoner until he finally died three years later. Demetrius was just one colorful figure in a whole cast of opportunistic adventurers with ties to Alexander the Great. As fascinating a character as was Demetrius, one can see no enduring importance in his career nor in knowing anything in particular about him. The same can be said for virtually all Greek political developments in the Hellenistic period.

## The Connection of Politics to Culture

So what is the point of all of this? If there were no grand political principles at stake in the years following Alexander, perhaps it is also true of the period before. The carnage and mayhem that the Athenians inflicted on others and the astonishing waste of their own lives and fortunes provides much evidence for that assertion. But I would argue that the benefit to us in understanding these periods is not derived from any objective comparison of the quality of life of one period compared to the other, but in appreciating the degree to which the collective consciousness of the two times generated two completely different kinds of culture. In the Greek Classical period, in the moment of history that featured Athens' democracy, an exhilarating belief existed in the minds of citizens that they actually controlled their own destinies and it seemed self-evident to them that the reward of their self-determination was their empire. In the period that followed, that heady optimism, that elixir, disappeared. And when one examines and compares the transition in culture from one context to the other, one immediately grasps what is essential in both and more importantly, the importance of that transition in the mind of the Greeks.

Let us look, for example, at how Greek philosophy changed from one period to the next.

Philosophy as a term is rather vague. It is from the Greek and means, more or less, "wisdom that is loved." This covers a lot of territory but 'lovers of wisdom' have, over the long run, tended to ask increasingly difficult questions and nowadays the result to their popular reputation is that they care the most for things with no apparent purpose. This reputation also obtained in antiquity, but it came about only gradually. There was something about many ancient peoples that made them wonder about the universe, how it all worked, what mysterious patterns lay just out of sight, and how humanity fit into all of this. In Greece, as was also happening in China and India, the questions started out with an emphasis on the physical: "what is everything made of?" We might chuckle at the simplicity of the answers they came up with—earth, water, fire and air—but it's not an unreasonable conclusion given the limits of human senses. Any further progress in philosophy depended on some other path to knowledge and one actually existed: mathematics. The Greeks developed mathematical systems relatively early on that hinted at knowledge beyond the limits of human senses. Who has not heard of the Pythagorean theorem?* To discover that something is *always* true is a big enough revelation to suggest that perhaps everything can be explained with mathematics! Modern physicists certainly understand this enthusiasm but unfortunately the mathematical systems of the Greeks were too primitive to sustain this line of questioning for very long. Imagine doing advanced mathematics without either positional notation† or a symbol for zero.

Inevitably, the only solution is to move yet another step and argue from what is or can be known to what must be true. Logic, argument, discourse:

---

* $A^2 + B^2 = C^2$ Pythagoras (570-490) and Thales (625-550 BC) are the fathers of Greek mathematics. Both had traveled to Babylon and may have been inspired there by Babylonian methods. The abacus, a mechanical counting device, probably also appeared in Greece about this time, and this helped overcome the limits of Greek numerical notation

† *Positional Notation*: the practice of using position to assign value to a mathematical symbol. For example, each repeated use of the same Arabic numeral 1, in the whole number 111, carries a different value: one hundred, ten, and one.

these would lead philosophers--at least so they believed--to the next level of understanding. At the same time, the turn to logic carried with it certain intellectual risks. On what basis can we assume that a valid proposition about what is unknown can be drawn from what is known? Rules guiding logical discourse must be developed in order to avoid bogus conclusions. Does a line of reasoning generate a conclusion that ought to be true, but cannot be true? Unfortunately, the process of developing rules to avoid logical pitfalls influenced some observers to think of philosophers as engaging in meaningless mental gymnastics. For example, there is the consideration of paradoxes. A set of such problems is attributed to a man named Zeno, the most famous of which are his paradoxes of motion. The most well-known of these is this: if one travels half way to a given destination, and then half way again, and so on, does one ever reach one's destination? Since any space can be divided theoretically into an infinite series of intervals, the logical answer is no, but in practical terms this is impossible, at least so argued Zeno. Zeno used this paradox and variations of it, to argue that motion is impossible and, by extension, that what one perceives to be true is not true. Whatever one perceives, one knows nothing. Imagine taking notes at that lecture…

So how do men like Zeno pay for their wine and cheese? By teaching in general and teaching rhetoric especially.* To be able to argue effectively and convincingly is a useful skill for those who would make their living in public: public figures, legal advocates, for example. All important decisions were argued and passed in the public space and the arguments suffusing these processes provided a veritable spectator sport. One can see that the art of speech was integral to any serious Athenian education and a steady stream of such teachers came to Athens trolling for potential clients. One common method of advertising this service was to give impromptu

---

* *Rhetoric*: the art of speech was essentially invented in Classical Greece. The fundamental principle is this: in an argument, an effective rhetorician identifies a logical or ethical principle that both participants in the argument share and then goes on to prove, using that common principle, that an opposing argument is fallacious. Some rhetoricians go far beyond this however, and watching them argue was a spectator sport much admired in Athens.

demonstrations of oratory in public. This would be the first context in which an ordinary Athenian might see a philosopher/teacher that was new to town. Just as it is true now, many ordinary Athenians regarded these clever speakers with some suspicion that they were actually teaching the art of deception. This is how the common word for teacher in Greek, sophist, ends up with such an ambivalent meaning.*

We now introduce Socrates, the first of the three philosophers we associate with Classical Athens. Imagine him attending these impromptu demonstrations—as he apparently did—and engaging in kind of repartee with the sophists. What we gather from these conversations is that Socrates was primarily interested in justice and Socrates' persistent questions regarding justice reveal an abiding discomfort with relativistic argument. As far as Socrates was concerned, everything was *not* relative. Some things— truth, virtue, and justice—had enduring and absolute meanings. While Socrates never articulated what these meanings actually were, he was adamant that no one else had either and what we know about his dealings with public figures in Athens suggests he was not bashful in saying this. This hard line approach did not endear Socrates to authority figures in Athens and we should rightfully see this as contributing to his later legal troubles (Socrates was eventually put on trial for corrupting the youth and for impiety).

Plato was 30 years old when Socrates was put on trial and he was himself present for the arguments. Later, he wrote a series of dialogues that dramatized the events surrounding the trial and what he believed to be essential in Socrates' system of ideas. Plato went on to found a school called the Academy that he headed for the next 40 years. Aristotle studied with Plato at the Academy, and later he founded his own school, the Lyceum. And so the three of these men have a connection; they are a series. Socrates asked the essential questions; Plato and Aristotle attempted to answer them. As it turns out, Plato's and Aristotle's answers featured fundamental differences concerning the nature of truth and one's proper

---

* In modern English, the term sophist is *definitely* a pejorative. It means someone who twists or undermines the truth with clever speech. The *art* of twisting the truth with clever speech is *sophistry*.

approach to finding it.   These need not distract us here because straightaway one sees a commonality in the ideas of all three men that obliterates the importance of what separates them, at least for our purposes; that commonality is in what one *does* with knowledge once one has it. This is the essence of Classical philosophy.

What binds these men together as a group and what binds them to their period is their assumption that knowledge should be applied to benefit society in a practical sense. *It is all about justice and the principles informing civil society.* Everything we know about Socrates makes it clear he believed his *most important mission as a thinker was to pursue and advance the cause of justice in the public space.* In one of his most famous dialogues, *Crito*, Socrates argued that even though his fellow citizens might resent him and wish him ill for his efforts, he was duty bound not only to continue his mission, but to submit to execution were it the judgment of the law, however flawed be that judgment. He was quite fond of saying that he was the midwife to the virtue of Athenians. Plato, Socrates' most accomplished student, wrote a great deal but his most famous surviving work is his *Republic*, a description of what Plato regarded to be the perfect state. Neither Socrates nor Plato would have sustained such an interest in a proper society had they believed it was a waste of time. Both regarded public justice as the ultimate good. Later in his life, Plato tried to advise the rulers of Syracuse how to be better rulers; that didn't go so well for Plato,* but it still underscores that he envisioned that the practical application of his ideas was possible. Aristotle was a student of Plato and he fits the same pattern etched by Socrates and Plato. For all of Aristotle's interests—he had many—his most important work centered on ethics and politics and he wrote scores of books describing the political systems of various Greek cities. His most famous

---

* He was briefly enslaved by one such ruler (Dionysius II of Syracuse) and only rescued by the intervention of one of his richer students from Athens. None of this should be taken to mean that Plato, or any of these philosophers for that matter, liked democracy, *per se*. Plato actually hated democracy; if you read his *Republic*, his ideas about the perfect government have more in common with modern China than any modern liberal democracy. Given that the Athenian democracy had, in effect, killed his mentor and friend Socrates, Plato might be forgiven for this.

student was Alexander the Great. What greater opportunity for a teacher who cared about politics than to influence the son of the most powerful ruler in Greece? The point of all of this is that Athens' democracy engendered thinking about the good of the community as opposed to the good of the individual. It was never about democracy *per se*, but the self-actuating atmosphere in a city like Athens encouraged thinkers in their belief that *endeavoring to improve society* was not only a good idea, but *was the whole point of higher learning.*

So what happened to philosophy in the Hellenistic period? Right off the top, let us be clear: it was never about justice, or the community. And why should it be? What kind of sense does it make to prattle on about truth and justice in a political system where the king can kill you just because he wants to? Philosophy went off in a different direction and some of this might seem familiar, at least in outline. The Epicureans and Stoics were the most enduring and familiar of these but other less well known variations also existed. Epicureans believed in the idea of atoms, that everything is made of collections of identical particles, and so differences that are apparent to us, even social differences, are not essential, but merely the result of cosmic randomness. Stoics believed that the universe is the result of an interaction of matter and fate and that emotional reactions to the machinations of fate impede one's ability to live in accordance with fundamental laws of nature.

Both of these systems of ideas are predicated on the notion that individuals have no real power in this world and the key to a balanced relationship with the universe is to come to terms with the essential powerlessness of humanity. The practical thread that ties these together is that each emphasized ways to approach life, to avoid conflict and pain, and to find peace of mind in a universe that had no room for individual initiative. *It was all about the individual, not the community.* Another philosophy commonly grouped with these is Cynicism. However, Cynicism is best understood as a bridge between Classic and Hellenistic philosophy especially because the lifetime of its most famous advocate, Diogenes the Cynic, spanned the dysfunctional fourth century BC during which all the cities of Greece beat each other to a pulp. If you were a witness to this, you would be a cynic, too. Diogenes' long life during the most dysfunctional period of Greek history gave him every reason to conclude that the customs and laws of civilized society were foolish in their conception and contrary to both nature and reason. So much for the heady idealism of the Classical philosophers.

The premise of my argument in this chapter has been that the cultural transition from Classic to Hellenistic was actually driven by the political transition it paralleled. We have now seen this at work in Greek philosophy and it also is evident in Greek sculpture. At the top of this chapter I briefly introduced the term "Archaic" as it referred to the period before Classical Greece. I mentioned that Archaic sculpture as a form should be associated with noble initiatives and interests and was intended to display noble wealth and preeminence in a world in political flux. Archaic sculptors gradually improved in skill levels, but the principles they applied to their work remained conservative because their patrons were deeply conservative in outlook. But a wider political constituency newly energized by democratized political ideals drove the aesthetic principles evident in the new Classical-era sculpture. The art form naturally followed the same trajectory as Classical philosophy which itself was a product of the same democratized ideals. While it is true that aristocrats in fact paid for much classical sculpture it was done so in solidarity with the ideals the new form represented. Whether they be city authorities, or nobles intent on remaining relevant, patrons of Classical sculpture urged their sculptor craftsmen to capture perfection. The results were expressed in two fairly predictable elements: realistic depiction of the human in ideal proportions, and the triumph of reason over passion. There are no potbellies or warts in Classical sculpture.

CLASSIC
SCULPTURE
EMPHASIZES
IDEALS

440 BC

450 BC

450 BC

150 BC
(LATE EXAMPLE)

460 BC

But when the Classical world melted down in the 300s, patrons of sculpture abandoned these principles just as Diogenes the Cynic ran away from the principles and interests of the Classical philosophers. While Stoics and Epicureans introduced new systems of thought representing an accommodation with the world as it was, Hellenistic sculptors started adding the warts of human existence. One sees pain, one sees despair, and one sees pleasure. It is an aesthetic that captures the world as it was actually experienced by individuals rather than one imagined by idealists. And the why of it is clear. The public space had ceased to be a practical forum for the pursuit of justice; citizens' role in government was by practical necessity a passive one because the Greek world was subsumed by the ambitions of powerful dynasts. And while the emerging form of sculpture still cared deeply for realistic depiction of the human form, it de-emphasized idealism altogether. In consequence, public tastes and preferences in sculpture shifted to the private experience of individuals, just as it did with philosophy.

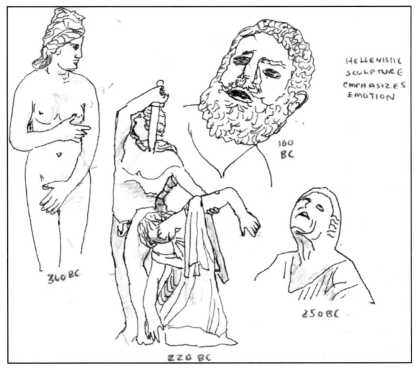

The nature of the transition from Classical to Hellenistic, in all its facets, is now quite clear. In the Classical period, the political experimentation that created the Athenian democracy inspired intellectuals with the premise that knowledge of justice and virtue was a proper prerequisite to an ideal society. Patrons of art chose to emphasize ideals in their work because Greek society, on the whole, worshipped this same principle. In the Hellenistic period, intellectual interest in political experimentation was set aside in favor of an accommodation with a disturbing reality; powerful men would rule society, not principles of justice. For everyone else, there remained no sensible place for the practical application of virtue beyond the bounds of one's private space. It is no surprise then that intellectuals and artists turned their focus inward. While this is, on a superficial level, a function of a transition from democracy to monarchy, it is more essentially about the transition from a society that encourages a belief in the possibility of perfection to one that does not. And that is the difference between Classical and Hellenistic.

# Chapter Five: the Secrets of Roman Success

*How did the Romans translate military success into a stable empire?*

We turn now to Rome. We will devote three chapters to Rome and this will hardly suffice to scratch the surface. Rome existed for more than a thousand years and during that period it evolved from a monarchy to a republic and then back to monarchy again. The period of the Roman Republic (c. 500-30 BC) is of special interest to us because the political system the Romans used during that period provided an important model in which the framers of the US constitution were keenly interested. In the meantime, the Romans created an empire that connected the entire Mediterranean world under one political system. This had never happened before and it is unlikely to ever happen again. The civil wars surrounding the life of Julius Caesar marked the end of the Roman Republic but the empire the Romans had accumulated continued to grow and prosper. We call the period after the Roman Republic by various names: "Imperial Rome," the "Principate," or sometimes just the "Roman Empire." The key thing to remember is that after Julius Caesar, Emperors ruled Rome; before Julius Caesar, laws and institutions ruled Rome.

To complicate things somewhat, the empire was split into two loosely connected halves, East and West, about the year AD 400. The Western Roman Empire disintegrated during the 400s within a few decades but meanwhile the Eastern Roman Empire continued to exist for another thousand years. Historians like to call the eastern half of the Roman Empire the "Byzantine Empire" in order to differentiate the two halves but as far as the Byzantines were concerned, they *were* the Roman Empire, even if the city of Rome was no longer part of it.

Each of the three chapters on Rome will present a different topical approach to the same overall material. Chapter five, this chapter, will highlight the customs and policies that the Romans employed to create and sustain the empire they accumulated and take a brief look at why it all came apart when it finally did. In essence, *chapter five is about the relationship between Romans and the people they conquered.* We ask two questions: why did it work so well, and why did it fall apart when it did? In the next chapter, chapter six, we will return to the Republican phase of Roman History and analyze the institutional breakdown that brought the Republican system to an end. Whereas chapter five looks outward from Rome, *chapter six looks inward and only considers the Republican period* (before Julius Caesar). We will ask the same question that the US founders asked when they considered the Roman political system as a possible model for our own: what went wrong with it? In chapter seven, we will look at two related phenomena having to do with early Christianity. On the political side of the equation, we will chart the changing relationship of Christianity with the Roman state. On the social side, we will examine the role that the heroes of the early church—the Saints—played in the growth of the religion as a social movement. These two subjects are of course closely related. The primary question we will attempt to answer in chapter seven is how and why did Christianity evolve from a strange and misunderstood cult into an official state religion.

# The Roman Culture of War

To understand the culture of Rome you must begin by considering war as a permanent and beneficial reality. Romans embraced war. And the more closely one examines the rhythms of Roman society it is easy to see why. During Rome's long march to the domination of their world, every constituency in Rome derived a significant benefit from war, either directly or indirectly. We are certainly not surprised to see that Roman elites benefitted from war but the greatest benefit for the elites was that derived from their distribution of favors to lesser and non-elites. This is a form of patronage that can be defined, more or less, as the giving of favors in return for political loyalty. Patronage, unlike money, cannot be stored and put away, it must be distributed for it to have any value. The Romans went to war because it created numerous opportunities to distribute patronage. In Rome, patronage was power.

In the Roman period before Julius Caesar—we call this the Republican period—the most eagerly sought political office was that of Roman consul.* Consuls were the highest-ranking military position in the Roman system and military positions were the gateway to enormous patronage possibilities. Every year the Romans elected two consuls and each of these was given unlimited power to wage war within a defined area and an army with which to fight it. The Roman Senate, a deliberative body composed of various elected officials and priests (remember chapter two), decided where to send the consuls and whether to extend the commands of previous years' consuls (the Romans called consuls with extended commands *pro*consuls). This means that in any given year, the Romans would have two or more armies fighting in parallel conflicts along with any number of smaller military operations conducted by lower level officials called praetors and *pro*praetors. Each commander recruited his own staff of senior officers from his friends and clients, all of whom served without pay. Despite lack of pay, there was never a shortage of candidates as this was how young nobles gained practical experience leading men in battle. Only rank and file soldiers were paid; officers' rewards came indirectly from the distribution of the fruits of war, each with its own potential for patronage: portable booty, land, slaves, and coopted local elites.

A returning consul (or *pro*-consul) would, after returning from a successful campaign, petition the senate for a victory celebration; the Romans called this a triumph. Were the request granted, the commander would then enter the city with his army, something otherwise prohibited. He would paint his face purple (a color reserved for the gods) and lead his army in formal procession through the city. The senior surviving leaders of the defeated foe might be chained to the *triumphator*'s chariot.

---

* *Roman consul*: a common mistake is to confuse the term consul with council. They sound alike but are two vastly different things. Roman consuls are individuals given the right to command an army for a fixed period of time. A council is a generic term meaning a group of individuals who meet to consider something

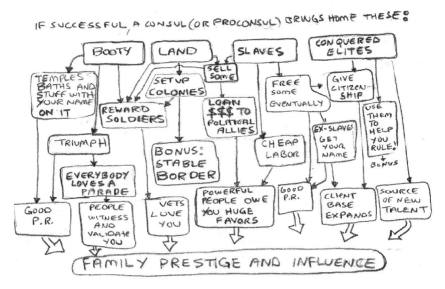

IF SUCCESSFUL, A CONSUL (OR PROCONSUL) BRINGS HOME THESE:

Along with the army came wagons full of booty while soldiers carrying storyboards illustrating the progress of the war walked alongside. It was apparently customary for the soldiers to sing ribald songs and the Romans loved brass and drums. Of course, the grandeur of the triumph could vary quite a bit, and a toned down version of the triumph, the ovation, was also possible for what the senate deemed lesser victories. One can see the obvious and immense possibilities for self-promotion that a triumph provided. A well-organized triumph might feature distributions of food and wine and perhaps coins and baubles tossed into the crowd by the passing procession. Just being in the procession was a reward for the soldiers and the successful commander would have a chance to display his glory under the watchful eyes of his peers. In one sense, the triumph represented a social signal that the benefits of war were about to be distributed.

First, you have to take care of the soldiers. Distributions were allocated by rank after campaigns were finished. Sometimes these gifts were in the form of land. Early on, when armies marched on relatively short campaigns within Italy and the army was dismissed at the end of the year, some of this land was divided and distributed directly to individual soldiers. Over time, individual distributions of land evolved to mass distributions in the form of organized colonies and then, as service in the army became a professional career, finally to periodic cash donations. Ex-consuls were usually involved in the process of enrolling colonists, an obvious form of patronage.

Ordinary Roman soldier 100 BC

Upon their return, all commanders were obligated to account for what they spent on campaign and the plunder they won but the evidence suggests most commanders had wide discretion. In some cases huge piles of loot were turned over to the city treasury. These funds financed all sorts of infrastructure in the city including the first basilicas that were, in their original intention, a kind of shopping mall. Commanders could, in fulfillment of personal vows, dedicate temples to the gods they deemed responsible for their victories and they endowed these temples with the resources to remember the victory for years to come. This provided a continual reminder of the prowess of the commander in the form of an annual barbeque of sorts.

Commanders would accumulate villas in captured territory, they certainly kept some cash for themselves and frequently they 'loaned' huge piles of cash to members of the aristocracy who have, for whatever reason, fallen onto harder times. Early in his career, Julius Caesar was in this category. Although his family had been successful in Roman politics, his branch of the family was relatively broke. He grew up in an

Interior view of the Pantheon in Rome

apartment house owned by his mother in a slum of Rome called the Subura. As he was climbing the political and military ladder* of Roman prestige, he was helped substantially by Marcus L. Crassus, one of the richest men in Rome. Eventually, Caesar became worth many times what Crassus was worth. In the meantime, Caesar was very useful to Crassus by helping to protect Crassus' political and economic interests.

So far we have talked about portable booty and land but what of slaves? When war was conducted on a small scale and relatively close to Rome, it is likely that a personal relationship existed between a captured soldier and the man who took him in battle. The details in the evidence are fuzzy but early on at least some captured soldiers could redeem themselves either by ransom or by working themselves free after some interval. In early Roman history, there was no large-scale labor requirement and so there really was not much else to do with adult male captives. Women and children were much more manageable acquisitions for domestic or sexual service. But several factors conspired to change some of this dynamic. First, the Romans began keeping soldiers in uniform for longer periods of time meaning that, for all practical purposes, their labor was permanently removed from the economy. At the same time, large-scale state contracts for logistical support of this mostly permanent army created a concentrated demand for labor that had not previously existed. Finally, with military campaigns becoming longer and taking place farther away, there was an inevitable transition to a system where slave dealers would follow an army and buy captives wholesale. Captives were by this process converted into another form of portable booty. Something similar happened in ancient Athens because their large permanent fleet of oared warships took tens of thousands of free men out of the labor market.

We can see that when Rome institutionalized warfare, it forced an existential shift in the nature of slavery. In all societies bordering the Mediterranean, some form of bondage had always existed and in some

---

* The Romans called this military and political ladder, the *cursus honorum*. It is Latin and means essentially, the "schedule of offices" that ambitious men ordinarily sought as they worked their way up. The term is occasionally used in modern political discourse to mean the same thing.

cases, multiple forms existed in parallel. While there were certainly varieties of slavery that were considered permanent, this was *not* the most common type. Outside of Athens and Rome, the most common path into bondage was debt from which one would ordinarily expect release after a set period of time. As Rome's empire stretched farther and farther from the city, the default for slaves evolved to a system where they had no expectation of freedom, unless the owner released them. This sounds pretty dreadful in theory and probably for most slaves it was truly a harsh and dreadful life. On the other hand, if Roman slaves were freed, and quite a few were, the Romans had regular and formal provisions for slaves to re-enter civil society as partial citizens. The children of freed slaves were full citizens. This was something unique to Rome, and part of the reason for its stability.

How did all this work in practice? First, the owner had to free the slave; the most likely moment for this was in the owner's will. At this point, the slave became a citizen, but his status was similar to that of a minor child; he or she had to get the former owner, or the son of the former owner, to sign off on certain kinds of contracts that the freed slave might enter. Marriages, wills, and land sales were all in this category. So the legal connection of the owner to his former slave did not cease after manumission,* it changes to something else. So long as the former slave lived, he or she was a legal dependent of the former owner, more or less in the way that children were legal dependents of their father. If the former owner should die, the dependency of the freed person passed to the heir of the former owner. At first glance, it seems utterly depressing for a slave to consider that even when free, he would have to kowtow to the wishes of his or her former owner. But there is an upside. If the family that freed a slave were financially stable enough to have freed the slave in the first place, then a continuing association with that family was likely to be beneficial to the ex-slave. In a world where one's existence depended so much on who you knew, this was not a benefit to be undervalued. One can easily see that to be the ex-slave of someone powerful would likely mean a better life than that of a free but unconnected commoner.

---

* *Manumission*: the act of releasing someone from slavery or other custodial status. From the Latin, it means literally the process of "releasing from the hand."

Now we turn to the last of the four categories of benefits derived from successful campaigns, coopted local elites. The Romans never had an elaborate bureaucracy for ruling conquered areas. They preferred, when possible, to rule through the existing elites. This means, for a start, that the conquest of an area should not be accompanied by the total destruction of local elites. This is a principle occasionally forgotten in the modern era, (as in the US invasion of Iraq). The most important question is whether one can convince the surviving local elites to cooperate. This they will do if they perceive that their long-term interests are best served by cooperation. The first step in this process was often a grant of Roman citizenship. We see one well-known example in Paul the Apostle. A glance at Paul's career shows him trumpeting his Roman citizenship whenever he got into trouble. Paul had this benefit because he was a Pharisee in Roman Judea.* Although Paul became an irritant to the Romans (see chapter seven), the practice of extending citizenship to provincial elites usually encouraged them to cooperate with Roman authorities.

Once someone had Roman citizenship, this meant they were theoretically eligible to run for Roman political office. The granting of citizenship provided ambitious elites with clear opportunities for upward mobility and, by drawing talent to Rome; it cemented a relationship between imperial center and provincial periphery, an absolute must for a stable empire. Scholars have charted a consistent pattern of lateral movement of elites to Rome and then, after a generation or two, vertically up the hierarchy of offices. All successful management structures provide conduits for recruitment of outside talent. Meanwhile, the gateway to the political and economic opportunities Roman citizenship afforded was guarded by older Roman elites, whose management of newcomer elites was an important example of patronage and a cornerstone of Roman power.

---

* *Pharisees*: one of the two established priesthoods in Judaism as it was practiced in the time of Jesus (the other was the Sadducees). The Pharisees were responsible for interpreting the laws of Moses by resort to an oral tradition (the Talmud) developed in the previous centuries. The doctrines of an afterlife with consequence for earthly deeds and of a messiah both had their roots in their influence. Because of their political importance in maintaining social order in Herod's Judea, the Romans extended Roman citizenship to them.

# Inclusive Citizenship

Like the Greek cities we looked at in chapter three, Rome's political evolution had much to do with empowering the classes most relevant to the conduct of war. But there are some important distinctions. In Greece, we saw that local elites tended to emerge with localized urban identities but the physical focal points for these identities, the cities, were already in existence and mostly had been since the distant Mycenaean past. The convergence of villages that we saw celebrated in the Panathenaia (chapter two) did not mark the convergence of elites nor did it celebrate a physical move from country into city. It marked the extension of unified political identity outward to include all the villages. *In Archaic Italy, the situation was fundamentally different.* Central Italy before the rise of Rome featured regional elites in control of a countryside that was studded with small settlements at convenient market locations and river crossings. In the 700s and 600s BC the nobles shifted the focus of their power toward these nascent urban centers, which we see represented in a new habit of noble display; the wealth that used to decorate noble tombs began in that Archaic period to organize and decorate the cities.*

We can only talk about Rome as a city after the forum area was drained in the 600s, even though the area had been inhabited for centuries. The new forum provided a focal point and a ritual center to celebrate the new political identity being imposed by what was formerly a rural elite with no connections to the city. This history, quite different from that of Greece, resulted in a two-tier identity with political institutions corresponding to both city and country. We note, for example, that one citizen assembly met outside the gates of the city (the Assembly of Centuries) to decide matters of war and to elect military officials while a second citizen assembly (the Tribal Assembly) met inside the city to decide on laws and other matters of domestic concern. The same citizens voted in both, but they were organized differently.

---

* After about 650 BC or so, nobles stopped burying their wealth and started investing in city infrastructure.

All scholars agree that by the time Rome emerged from the mists of legend she was a member of a league of cities conventionally called the Latin League. In the Latin, the term for the league is *Latinum Nomen*. For the moment, I prefer to suggest a slightly different translation of the Latin phrase, 'those of Latin status.' Even if this is more awkward, it tends to emphasize that the political identity connoted by the phrase is not tied to a place but rather to inclusion in a political category. Every year representatives from all the cities in the league met on a mountain outside of Rome and celebrated their regional ties. At least until the year 338 BC, residents within any of the thirty or so member cities could move from one city to another and in so doing, they effectively traded one local citizenship for another. This is unheard of in any Greek city. Having Latin status had other benefits emphasizing reciprocity of marriage and contracts, but *what truly sets the Latin League apart from any other political status was this portability of political identity*. It seems also to be true that individual cities within the Latin League retained their sovereignty. We know this because individual cities could conduct war individually as well as together, but wars fought cooperatively led to the establishment of new Latin-status cities populated with citizens from all the member states of Latin status.

As the largest single member of the Latin League, Rome was, practically speaking, the hegemon* of the league before 338 BC and *officially* hegemon afterwards. The war (the Latin War: 340-338 BC) that resulted in this change exists at the very edge of reliable evidence and so scholars disagree vehemently about the degree to which Rome managed the League before 338. That we might avoid tangling ourselves in this and other arcane controversies, we will restrict our discussions to the period afterward. From 338 until nearly 200 BC, Roman citizenship was available (by virtue of this overlap in citizenship status) to any resident in any city with Latin status. As the primacy of Rome became ever more clear with each succeeding decade, the real prize became Roman citizenship and Romans increasingly extended Roman citizenship directly to cities without a previous Latin connection. In one sense, this was just a continuation of the Latin citizenship policy in

---

* *Hegemon:* an indirect ruler over other political entities.

place before 338. By either path, and by whatever timetable you should choose to emphasize, the fact is that there were routine paths to Roman citizenship from the earliest moment for which we have any reliable evidence. *This set them apart from any of their rivals and certainly from the Greeks.*

So far we have mentioned a horizontal path to Roman citizenship. That is, the social status one had in one's former city of residence would presumably pass unchanged as one became Roman or exercised some other privilege of being Roman. But there was also a vertical path from no citizenship at all to Roman citizenship, something else that set the Romans apart. We have already mentioned that the Romans routinely admitted freed slaves to Roman citizenship. So Rome is unique in the ancient world in providing two regular paths to becoming Roman, one horizontal and one vertical. In practical terms most of those who called themselves Romans were actually products of a process where they or their ancestors had become Roman. It was not merely a question of being or not being Roman as one would ordinarily imagine ethnicity. In ancient Rome, technically, you could be both Greek and Roman at the same time because they meant two different things. This has important ramifications for understanding Roman culture. The *culture* of Rome was obviously a composite of the cultures that it absorbed. Of those absorbed cultures, the most dynamic and obvious contribution was from the Greeks. This leads to a knee jerk criticism that the Romans were unoriginal; they were a bunch of copycats. But this misses what is truly connoted by being Roman. "Roman" was a *political* construct that was accretive of culture, but was independent of and preceded culture.

# A Matrix of Treaties

We know Rome was successful in creating their empire and it is all too easy to assume that they were always successful in battle, but close examination of the evidence shows that the Romans lost *a lot* of battles. Some of these were genuine disasters that really should have buried them. But they weren't buried. They bounced back, again and again, and always managed to outlast their opponents. This was not luck. The factors we have already mentioned are obviously part of the explanation, but the Romans had a significant advantage over the rivals in the way they organized for war. It was a system of treaties that distributed the cost of war, both in manpower and material, over a wide base. The most important of these was the Latin League, at least until the end of the Republican period. We have already mentioned the practical benefits the league offered to its members and its role in promoting a common identity. As always when you are talking about early Rome there is much we do not really know, but the evidence suggests that somewhere before 500 BC the members of this Latin League began to use the framework of the league to organize a common army. The members of the league paid and equipped their own men. Once the Romans took over the league in 338 BC a second category of ally was added to the mix. The Romans called this category "Italian" which for them was a sort of catchall category for allies who did not have Latin rights. In any given year after 338 BC, a Roman army would have three political categories of soldier: Roman, Latin, and Italian. There was no set proportion but normally the army would have many more allied soldiers than Roman ones. Some allies provided material instead of men. Naples, for example, supplied one or two warships to the Romans every year and there is evidence to suggest other cities did as well. All these categories of ally were useful to the Romans of course, but the Latin league was the backbone of the alliance system.

There are several really good early examples of how this system of treaties gave Rome a significant edge over rivals. The first of these is the war with Pyrrhus (282-275BC). We already mentioned the beginnings of this episode in passing (in chapter two) where we discussed the Roman

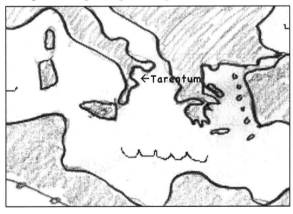

*fetiales*, the priests of war. When Rome declared war on the southern Italian city of Tarentum, Tarentum invited King Pyrrhus of Epirus to fight Rome on their behalf.

Pyrrhus fought Rome in three battles and in at least two of those battles Pyrrhus won *if you emphasize casualties*. At the battle of Heraclea in 280 the Roman army and Pyrrhus' army were evenly marched in numbers (probably around 30,000 each) and Pyrrhus's army inflicted twice as many casualties as it received (there were around 7000 Roman casualties to 3000 or so of Pyrrhus' men). But because of the treaty system, the Romans could easily replace these casualties. In the next year Rome fought Pyrrhus again at Asculum and the same thing happened: Rome suffered twice as many casualties as did Pyrrhus. But Pyrrhus was running out of men and Rome was not. Pyrrhus is reputed to have said after Asculum that if he won one more battle with the Romans, he would be beaten (hence the expression, a Pyrrhic victory). Ambivalent about his chances with Rome, Pyrrhus left Italy for a few years before returning and having one more battle with Rome (Battle of Beneventum in 275). We don't have any details from this battle, but we know that Pyrrhus gave up and left Italy shortly afterwards. The major lesson of this contest was that Rome could survive much heavier casualties on the battlefield than could her opponents.

Other set of examples comes from the three wars between Carthage and Rome (264-241; 218-202; 149-146 BC). Carthage, a Phoenician colony dating back to the 700s, was located on the North African coast and boasted a great harbor and many ships. Her wealth and power were built, first and foremost, on control of nearby trade routes. After the defeat of Pyrrhus in southern Italy, Rome and Carthage faced each other across the island of Sicily and conflict between these two growing powers was inevitable. The first of the three wars was fought mostly at sea and involved colossal losses of ships and men to both storm and battle. We know that at the end of this war Carthage was practically broke because her mercenaries refused to fight for not having been paid and her coinage had been debased. Clearly, the cost of replacing war losses had staggered the Carthaginian economy. Meanwhile, Rome's system of treaties made it possible for her to replace loses much more easily and win the war even though Rome never defeated the Carthaginians decisively on the battlefield.

An even more dramatic example comes from the second war with Carthage. Hannibal was the supreme commander in this war and most scholars credit him for being a military genius. In the first four years of the conflict, Hannibal faced Roman armies that were larger in size and beat them every time. The Roman eventually learned from their mistakes but in the short term they suffered what should have been catastrophic defeats. The greatest of these was at Cannae in 216. On August 2 of that year, an army of 90,000 Romans and allies faced Hannibal's army of half that size. At the end of the battle, three quarters of the Roman army was destroyed, one of the two consuls was dead, and nearly a third of the Roman senate had been wiped out. And all in a single day. Yet the Romans never recalled the army they had in Spain and they fielded another army in Italy the following year, and sent yet another to Sicily in 214. Despite Hannibal's brilliance on the battlefield, he could not defeat the Romans so long as Rome's allies stayed loyal. And mostly they did. This was the basis for Roman success.

# The Fall of the Western Roman Empire

So, the Romans were at war almost continuously for two important reasons. All levels of society benefitted by war, and war provided a dependable source of prestige for the nobility. The Romans were successful in war because they developed a huge network of allies who shared its cost. They kept the empire together by extending their citizenship and by convincing conquered elites that they could benefit from being a part of the Roman system. There were many wars that followed those with Carthage but there was little question that Rome could win any war that she chose to pursue and, for the next 400 years, Roman power dictated the political realities of the Mediterranean world. In the center of that 400-year period the Romans turned on themselves in a bitter civil war (more on this in the next chapter) but that political contention within the ruling oligarchy of Rome tended not to affect the overall stability of the empire. This is a testament both to the strengths of the policies Romans used to gain their empire and to the unanimity of interests all the Romans understood in keeping their empire.

Meanwhile, bit-by-bit, the respect Romans had historically shown their partners eroded. Around the year 90 BC Rome's allies in Italy revolted after a failed effort to extend them Roman citizenship. Tired of what was becoming clearly a second-class status, the allies plunged Italy into one of the most destructive wars in Italian history. Rome won that war only after relenting on the question of citizenship, at least to some of the rebels. This could have been a learning moment for the Romans but since there was no credible external threat to the awesome power of Rome at this point, Rome did not need to learn a lesson.

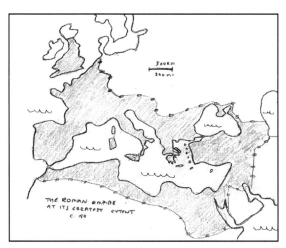

THE ROMAN EMPIRE AT ITS GREATEST EXTENT c. 150

The Roman empire did fall apart eventually. The period from AD 235-284 saw the Roman empire plunged into civil war, beset by invasion, and victimized by disease and inflation. After some stability was restored in the 300s, the wheels came off completely in the 400s. Scholars have spilled much ink on this topic and each has their own pet theory about the critical dynamic that made it fall apart. It is easiest to point to the barbarian invasions and say "Aha! That's it!" But Rome had dealt with similar patterns of migration and invasion many times. So the reason for the collapse of the empire is not simply outside pressure; there was something rotten *inside* Rome. This volume has already set forth some principles that bear on the question. In this chapter I have already noted how conquered elites were coopted and encouraged to, in essence, *become* Roman. We have also noted the extension of citizenship and the advantages of that status. In chapter two, in our discussion of religion and community identity, I argued that individuals have always defined themselves according to categories that they find practical and useful. In that same chapter, I stressed the importance rulers put on aligning themselves, in the minds of the people, with justice. The argument was that rulers could expect their citizens to be satisfied with their performance so long as citizens believed their rulers to be ruling justly. If we take the sum of those observations and apply them to the period of Roman decline and fall, we see the Romans violating both principles.

First, by the time we get to the later Roman empire, we are talking not of conquered elites but of provincial elites. The premise, however, is the same: for the Roman empire to be stable and resilient enough to survive, the provincial elites must continue to view their alignment with Rome as being advantageous to their class. Over time, we can see this is less and less the case. By the time you get into the AD 400s, Roman emperors were issuing edicts *requiring* local elites to maintain physical provincial infrastructure—something they used to do voluntarily—while at the same time routinely offering senatorial privileges to those at the very top. Senatorial privileges included getting a pass from those requirements and moving to Constantinople, the capital of the Roman empire from the time of Constantine. Previously, local elites maintained provincial infrastructure even after they had moved to the capital because that was one of the most important ways in which their own lines of patronage—and therefore political power—were defined. The new policies essentially turned ambitious elites *against* the local power structures from which they had emerged. Furthermore, this new system deprived local economies of the cash flow necessary to sustain an urban center with all the iconic accouterments of a Roman style city (baths, amphitheaters, etc.). The net effect was to abandon a system that glued the provinces to the center and replaced it with one that drove a wedge between center and province.

Meanwhile, on the local level, Roman citizenship meant a lot less after AD 212 than it did before. To some extent this is an inevitable consequence of the long term policy of extending citizenship to more and more people. Citizenship only has value if it confers an advantage. If everyone has the same privilege, it has no exceptional value. In the year 212, the emperor Caracalla extended citizenship to all free persons inside the Roman empire. He did this to increase the tax base because the Roman taxation system had loopholes that in some cases favored non-citizens. For example, only Roman citizens were eligible for an estate tax. So the net effect of extending citizenship was to make *everyone* subject to an estate tax. Two hundred years earlier there were any number of advantages to being a Roman citizen that would offset this apparent disadvantage. For example, no Roman citizens in the time of Julius Caesar could be summarily beaten or executed. Every accused citizen was entitled to have this case heard in an official judicial setting. We see the practical effect of this difference in the respective treatments of Jesus and Paul the Apostle. The non-citizen Jesus was beaten and summarily executed on the orders of the Roman governor of Pontius Pilate, while the apostle Paul, a Roman citizen, was shipped back to Rome for trial. But by the time of Caracalla's edict, Roman citizenship had been divided into subcategories such that punishments and procedures previously reserved for foreigners now applied to Roman citizens below a certain wealth/status rating. There was therefore no longer any increase in social status associated with Roman citizenship. It is no coincidence that Romans stopped noting their citizenship on funeral inscription in this context.

Finally, we can see real signs of local withdrawal from active engagement with community and Imperial identity. It starts slowly and builds. The physical remains of the buried Roman city of Pompeii provide an early example. Most of us are familiar with the eruption of AD 79 in which Pompeii, Herculaneum, and hundreds of Roman villas were buried. But few of us are aware that there had been an earthquake seventeen years earlier, in 62. When the volcano erupted in 79, the debris from the earlier earthquake had been cleared away, but none of the public buildings lining the forum had yet been reconstructed. This included the most recently built temple to Augustus, located in the very center of the forum. The only temple that was fully repaired was the temple to Isis, a recent import religion. Traditionally, the richest citizens in any city maintained big households in the center of the city. But in Pompeii, most of the larger houses in the neighborhoods closest to the forum had long since been subdivided into apartments, and their former occupants moved out to the suburbs. The center of Pompeii had lost its attraction as a focal point of community identity.

Since the Republic had been turned into a monarchy, public religion had shifted its focus from the safety and well being of the community to that of the emperor. Imagine the fourth of July evolving into a celebration for the health of the president! Most major cities of the empire featured a temple to Augustus, which had become the unifying ritual focus for all Romans, all across the empire. Augustus was enormously popular as an emperor and this explains the early success of the cult, but the same cannot be said for many of the emperors who followed him. The failure of Pompeian officials to rebuild this most important civic temple indicates a lack of interest in the temple, the rituals associated with it, and by extension, the whole idea of a unifying Roman identity. For local elites, there was less prestige available in supervising these rituals and they fell into neglect. This growing disconnect puts the increasing popularity of various eastern cults into a meaningful context. As we have already mentioned, we note that the temple to Isis was the only public building completely rebuilt in Pompeii after the earthquake. Constituent communities around the Roman empire were not actively owning their citizenship anymore, nor were they celebrating it.

Fast forward to AD 400; by this time Christianity had become the official religion of the Roman Empire and there had not been any persecution of Christians for nearly 100 years. In fact, the shoe was on the other foot; the Christians were now going after the pagans.* Under the influence of the radical Bishop Ambrose of Milan, the Emperor Theodosius I (378-395) ushered in a period of radical anti-paganism and anti-Judaism in the Roman Empire that resulted over the course of a few decades in hundreds of temples and synagogues being thrown to the ground and public pagan rituals being banned. Neutral bystanders watched in amazement as gangs of zealots engaged in wanton acts of destruction and assault while Roman officials stood by and watched. In 415, the pagan astronomer, philosopher, and teacher, Hypatia of Alexandria, was publicly torn limb from limb by a private gang loyal to the fiery bishop Cyril of

---

* *Pagan*: the word is slippery and inexact. The original connotation of the word was rustic, or unsophisticated, and so carries with it a pejorative sense, as does the modern American word hillbilly. Nowadays we use it to refer collectively to religious practices that are folk-ish in nature. In the period we are now treating, it referred to all who were *not* either Jew or Christian. So it is more *what something was not, than what it was.*

Alexandria. Her only crime was the belief that Christians should be subject to the law.

There are many things people might consider in asking how connected they feel to their political identity. I think it likely that a people will put up with a lot of grief before they get to a point of rejecting their own government, whatever its form. When the big moment comes, let's say an invasion of outsiders, you are faced with a decision: does one resist and pay the cost of resisting or does one join the invaders? "Is being Roman something I really want to hang onto?" In Italy, this became the important question in the 500s. The Roman empire had already been split, practically speaking, since the death of Theodosius in 395. Theodosius' sons and grandsons proceeded to rule the two halves of the empire as they drifted in two different directions. The east with its capitol in Constantinople had a bigger tax base and the city was in a strategically safer position. It survived for another 1000 years. Because the west had a weaker tax base and was more difficult to defend, the emperors in Constantinople lost interest in maintaining direct control. It was too expensive and the city of Rome no longer had the symbolic importance that it used to have.

By 476, Italy was only nominally part of the Roman empire and was ruled by the German king Odoacer. But Odoacer proved difficult to control and in 488 the emperor in Constantinople sent another barbarian king, Theodoric of the Ostrogoths, to kill him. Theodoric did so, and ruled Italy until his own death in 526, after which the emperors in the east tried to rejoin Italy to the Roman empire. The general that was sent to do the job, Belisarius, is often hailed as "the last Roman" at least partly because he was the last Roman general to hold the title of Consul and the only consul from the Eastern Empire to have a Roman triumph. Ironically his campaigns were responsible for the worst destruction in Italy since the war of the allies in 90 BC and, in a sense, they mark the practical end of Classical history in Italy. Campaigns by Belisarius in Italy between 537 and 547 destroyed the infrastructure of all the major Italian cities, turning them into shells of their former selves. In any case, never again would Italy be part of the Roman Empire.

## Overall Roman Timeline

| | |
|---|---|
| Legendary Aeneas flees to Italy | 1200 BC |
| Archaic monarchy | 753-500 |
| Roman forum area drained | c. 650 |
| Temple of Jupiter in Rome | 509 |
| Roman Republic | 500-48 |
| Latin War | 340 |
| Pyrrhus in Italy | 285-75 |
| First Punic War | 264-241 |
| Second Punic War (Hannibal) | 218-202 |
| Greek Wars | 214-146 |
| Destruction of Carthage | 146 |
| War of the Allies | 91-0 |
| Roman Civil Wars | 48-30 |
| Egypt annexed | 30 |
| Imperial Monarchy begins | 30 BC |
| Britain conquered | AD 43-84 |
| Dacia conquered | 101-6 |
| Mesopotamia conquered | 117 |
| Fifty years of chaos | 235-284 |
| Diocletian/Constantine | 284-337 |
| Western Imperial Rome collapses | 395-476 |
| Eastern Imperial Rome continues | 395-1453 |

# Chapter Six: Why did the Roman Republic fall apart?

*Why did Americans like Jefferson, Madison, and Adams ask this question?*

Now that we have surveyed the Roman strengths and weaknesses as an imperial power over the whole course of about 1000 years, let us go back to the first half of that period, the period of the Roman Republic (the period before Julius Caesar). The political system in effect during the Republic has fascinated modern thinkers for hundreds of years. Where Athens represents in our mind an early version of democracy—one man one vote—the Roman Republic represents a system much more like ours, a representative democracy. This is no accident. As the American founders argued and debated the shape of the America-to-be, they evaluated the merits of both Athens and Rome as political systems and ended up choosing and inscribing much of what was Rome into the US Constitution. The founders, John Adams in particular, concluded that the democracy in Athens was too prone to the passions and whims of a hotheaded and irrational mob. He preferred the Roman Republic as a system where a sober aristocracy in the form of a senate kept the excesses of the democracy firmly in check. There was only one small problem: the Roman Republic collapsed in the time of Julius Caesar and was replaced with a monarchy. So Adams and the other founders were keenly interested in what went wrong on the premise that, if they could figure it out, they could design a system that incorporated the best of Rome while avoiding its weaknesses. In a sense then, the American system was and is a political experiment, the long-term success of which remains to be proved.

This means that in even in our own time, the fate of the Roman Republic remains relevant. The question comes down to this: can we blame the collapse of the Roman system on the acts of a few men? Or was the collapse of the system the inevitable result of something systemic? Or a combination of both? I will take the position that there are several systemic problems that made it unlikely that the system could survive. Individual actors did matter, but their decisions were constrained and shaped by forces beyond their control. I will divide these forces into categories and treat them one by one. This will cause us to treat the same time period multiple times, but each time with a different focus.

# Dangerous Political Precedents

The Romans did not have a constitution. This means that a law could be passed at any time changing the way things were done. This sounds like it might be a good thing but a problem arises when an important principle is swept aside under the pressure of short term convenience. Once it is gone, it is gone forever. Having no constitution also means that the rules of what it takes to pass a law can also change and who is to say, "well, you can't do it that way?" Once it is done and no one has spoken up to say, "wait, that's not right!" it is done differently now, for better or for worse. When one looks at the collapse of the Roman Republic one sees many such moments. There was never one thing, no one key moment that were it undone, it all would have turned out differently. Perhaps this is why the Romans never saw the end coming until it was too late and, moreover, it helps to explain why the American founders were so keen to have a written constitution.

Perhaps ironically, the first dangerous precedent is buried within a shining moment in Roman history. In chapter five we mentioned the second of the three wars between Rome and Carthage as an example that proved Rome's structural resiliency. Although Hannibal beat the Romans repeatedly on the battlefield he could not hope to win the war so long as Rome's allies stayed true. They did and Rome prevailed. Of course, it did not hurt that Hannibal taught the Romans some important lessons on battlefield management, but the benefits of those lessons were slow in coming. After the disaster at Cannae in 216 BC, Hannibal's army had been pushed into the south of Italy and any immediate danger to the city of

Rome had subsided. Rome had armies and navies deployed all over the Mediterranean and her resources were stretched to the limit. One of those armies was stationed in Spain and was fighting to wrest control of the Spanish gold mines from Carthage. The campaign was not going really well. The Carthaginians were keen to hold Spain as it was financing their war and they had three separate army groups stationed there including one commanded by Hannibal's brother, Hasdrubal. In 211 two brothers, Publius and Gnaeus Cornelius Scipio, commanded the Roman army in Spain. Theirs was an illustrious and successful family and both had served as proconsuls in the Spanish campaign since the war began. The brothers gambled and split their force with disastrous consequences; their army was destroyed and both were killed. When news of the disaster made its way back to Rome, the son of the younger brother, Publius Cornelius Scipio, lobbied to avenge their deaths. The problem was that he was only 25 and, although he had served with distinction as a staff member in at least two battles, he was too young by five years to be elected consul. In fact, young Scipio had never been elected to any military position. However, the perfect combination of the family's popularity and the emergency convinced the senate to confer consular imperium, breaking all these important precedents. This was the first time a private citizen was made commander of a Roman army without having been elected to either praetor or consul.

As it turned out, young Scipio did not abuse his huge popularity or his sudden rise to the very top; in fact he went on to defeat Hannibal in the final battle of the war. The Romans thus paid no *immediate* penalty for their abuse of procedure. This is good news and bad news. The senate bent the rules and everything turned out well. That is the good news. The bad news is that the senate was now free to ignore the normal procedures for assigning the most powerful positions in government. In addition, the incident also hints at how the crowd in Rome had become a constituency of real importance. The senate had folded under public pressure. For them, because Scipio had the right family, it was not such a big problem. Both the precedent established in the case of Scipio and the role of the crowd in Rome would be revisited in the person of Gnaeus Pompeius Magnus (or just Pompey), someone far less concerned with the rules of government.

Like young Scipio, Pompey was the scion of a successful family and, also like young Scipio, Pompey was thrust prematurely into the political spotlight. At the age of 24, he found himself a major player in an expanding crisis in Italy. In the 90s BC, many of Rome's allies in Italy turned against Rome—a topic mentioned in chapter five and to which we will return later—and this evolved into a brief civil war between two major factions in Rome, the friends and allies of two men, Sulla and Marius. In support of Sulla, Pompey raised several legions of soldiers and financed them from his own pocket. Afterwards, with Sulla winning, Pompey demanded and received a triumph for his services despite the fact that his forces were technically mercenaries, and his command was technically illegal.

After Sulla died, Pompey demanded that the senate appoint him proconsul for a war in Spain he wished to pursue against one of the holdout supporters of the defeated Marius. On his return from Spain in 71, Pompey stumbled into remnants of the slave army of Spartacus. Despite the fact that Marcus Licinius Crassus (or just Crassus) had already defeated this renegade army, Pompey ended up getting all the credit. This made the two men bitter enemies and political rivals. But Pompey was riding a wave of popularity and the senate reluctantly granted him a *second* illegal triumph. So far, Pompey had been commanding armies for nearly ten years without having run for a single election. In 70 BC, Pompey ran for and won the consulship, despite never having held any lower offices. Crassus also won that year. Crassus, still smarting from the insult inflicted on him by Pompey, tried to offset Pompey's popularity with the people in Rome by paying for a three-month grain distribution in Rome and hosting a public banquet for 10,000. The incredible wealth of these two men and their willingness to bribe the mob was changing the political dynamics of Rome in a dramatic way.

In 67 BC, Pompey won another chance to boost his popularity. By this time the population of the city of Rome was approaching a million souls. The grain to support this huge population was imported from Sicily and Egypt and this traffic had become increasingly vulnerable to pirates. Attacks on the shipping lanes of the Mediterranean threatened to drive the price of grain off the charts and the situation was made even worse by price speculation and hoarding by grain dealers. The word in the street was that Pompey was the only answer. The senate, already fearful of Pompey's enormous power, was reluctant to authorize any more special commands for Pompey but it was too late to stop him. Using the same procedure that granted young Scipio special authority in Spain, the people passed a special law giving Pompey five years of what they called *maius imperium.*\* This startling precedent meant that Pompey's command would automatically overrule anybody else's if he found himself crossing any boundaries in hot pursuit of pirates. Now this sounds like a logical idea, but until this point, commanders' authority over their troops was always limited by some geographic boundary. Pompey now possessed more power than any person or institution had ever possessed in Rome. This super-command absolutely begged for abuse.

So confident were the people in Rome that Pompey would handle the pirate problem that the price of grain dropped when word of Pompey's appointment went out. As it turned out, Pompey finished the job in a matter of months. Before returning to Rome, he spent time in the East re-arranging affairs with various allies and friends of Rome. Back in the city of Rome, his popularity soared and the people clamored to appoint him for another five-year command against the eastern King Mithradates who had been raiding Roman possessions in the east. This campaign lasted from 65-62 BC and resulted in several new provinces added to the Roman Empire, a river of loot and tribute unmatched in Roman history, and a popularity that was virtually unstoppable. In 61 BC Pompey celebrated the greatest and most elaborate triumph up to that point in Roman history. It lasted two days and one can imagine the looks the other senators gave each other as they considered how powerful Pompey had become. Pompey's rise to

---

\* *Maius Imperium:* Latin for "higher command." The pirate problem presented a special situation. At any one time, there were consuls and proconsuls assigned to areas all over the empire. Normally, the authority of Roman commanders was restricted to geographic boundaries, this side of the river, that side of the mountain, etc. But the pirates were presumably at sea and had bases all over. Who is to say which Roman commander was in charge in which location? But the creation of this new overarching category of authority was yet a new precedent for expanded military power.

Why did the Republic fall apart? 111

power was characterized by two very dangerous factors: blatant disregard for political precedent and an obvious manipulation of mob passions. Meanwhile other troubling signs of dysfunction were accumulating.

## Political Paralysis in the Legislature

With Pompey's conquests in the east, most of the pieces that comprised the Roman empire were already in hand. Nevertheless, it was still, for better or worse, a Republic: a system of laws, rules, procedures by which a people governs itself through elected representatives. Unfortunately, these laws, rules, and procedures were invented when Rome was a city with no significant power or possessions. Commands were short, the booty taken in conflict was modest, and the crowds were not dangerous. In those earlier years, it was easy for the senatorial aristocracy to hold the ambitions of its members in a kind of balance. But by the time of Pompey, everything was different. One sees not only how easily rules might be bent, but what rewards lay in store for those prepared to bend them. One might argue that it was the attraction of these rewards that ultimately warped and undermined the laws, rules, and procedures that defined the Roman Republic.

We also noted how those rewards were distributed thorough lines of patronage. These lines of patronage and patterns of cooperation within the senate might vary from generation to generation but the accumulated prestige of previous generations had always pre-positioned certain families for dominance. But once the Roman empire had developed into a colossus, the possibility for a dramatic advancement became much more tangible because a single campaign could yield profits so immense as to dwarf all that came before. The predictable reaction by the senate was to contest the elections of any whose ambitions might seem to threaten established lines of influence and dominance. The normal rules whereby consuls were elected tended to help in this regard. Elections to that position took place in the Assembly of Centuries where the voters were divided by wealth and factions of aristocrats organizing their clients to vote in blocks largely controlled elections. In part, this explains why the aristocracy resisted these special commands given to Pompey—because they originated not in the Assembly of Centuries but in the Assembly of Tribes, where voters were divided by residence and not by wealth. Votes in the Tribes were much more difficult to control and successful families in the aristocracy regarded any shift of power or initiative to the Tribes as a dangerous bypass of their power. It is in this way that we can understand the important events of 133 BC.

In that year, an ambitious young noble named Tiberius Sempronius Gracchus was elected to the tribunate.* Tiberius' family (the Sempronii) had already taken their place at the top Rome's power structure and there is every reason to think that Tiberius was destined to be a significant leader in Rome. His father and grandfather had both been Consul and young Tiberius had married the daughter of the *princeps*.† He had already been to Spain as a lower level official and was now ready to take his next political step. He ran for and won a position as Tribune for 133 BC. From the beginning, Tiberius's tribunate was marked by controversy. He proposed a bill that some Roman public lands be distributed to Roman citizens so that they could repopulate deserted sections of Italy and, as landowners, be then subject to the military draft. There's nothing really controversial about the idea except perhaps that there had been no such distributions for 50 years or so and the land intended for distribution in Tiberius' bill was not located near the frontier, as was usually the case, but in central Italy. The proposal sparked a great deal of controversy and led indirectly to his assassination a year later. That seems an extreme response to a proposal to do something the Romans seem to have done many times before. So why all the fuss?

At first, some senators complained that the land wasn't really vacant, that it is was being leased out to Roman ranchers. So Tiberius allowed for Romans currently using the land to keep it, up to certain limits. Then

---

* *Tribune*: one of ten men elected for a single year. Their job was to convene and preside over the Assembly of Tribes, in which the people decided matters of domestic concern. Tribunes are usually younger men near the beginning of their careers.

† *Princeps*: literally the "first citizen." Members of the senate acclaimed one of their members the most prestigious and granted him the right to speak first on any issue.

senators complained that Tiberius intended to pass out land to his supporters as a way of making himself some kind of tyrant. All of this whining and complaining from the senate convinced Tiberius he would not get their approval and he decided to bypass it altogether. According to Roman precedent and custom, proposed laws were usually given rubber stamps by the senate before the people were allowed to vote but this approval was never technically necessary, except for a brief period in the 70s, fifty years after these events. And so Tiberius went right to the people because he expected an easy passage. Meanwhile, the opposition in the senate went wild, accusing him of every sort of criminal ambition. There were a number of good ways of explaining this controversy but ultimately the best one is that Tiberius had stumbled into a way to bypass the usual rules governing access to patronage. Remember, the fruits of war feed patronage networks, and patronage was power in Rome.

When the bill came up for a vote in the Assembly, one of the other Tribunes (Marcus Octavius) promptly vetoed it.* Tiberius, enraged by this obvious political ploy, called for a vote to expel Octavius for working against the interests of the people. On the verge of that vote passing unanimously, Tiberius pleaded with Octavius to desist; but Octavius, even knowing he was about to be expelled, refused to back down. The vote continued, Octavius was dismissed, and the land bill was passed. The people rejoiced but the senate was even angrier. Although they couldn't undo the law that was passed, they tried to starve the new land commission by withholding a budget, because they normally controlled the finances in Rome. But Tiberius outsmarted his foes yet again by passing another law in the Assembly diverting money from a large inheritance that had just been given to Rome by the deceased King of Pergamum. Confounded in their opposition, Tiberius' enemies in the senate counted the days until Tiberius would be a private citizen again so they could make his life miserable by dragging him into court on some pretense or other. But so long as Tiberius was in office, he was legally immune from prosecution. So Tiberius decided to run for re-election. It was not common for Tribunes to run in successive

---

* *Veto*: Any of the ten tribunes could call a halt to the proceedings, effectively preventing a vote for the day.

years, but it was not unknown either. When Tiberius announced his intention to seek another term as tribune, Tiberius' opponents began to froth at the mouth and they trotted out every accusation they could think of to paint Tiberius as a threat to the state. In the climax of the drama, the *Pontifex Maximus,** the highest-ranking priest in Rome, whipped up a crowd of his supporters to confront Tiberius. Tiberius was then beaten to death along with 300 of his own supporters.

That seems a bit extreme! Tiberius was accused of breaking rules and insulting the dignity of the senate by bypassing it, etc., etc., but there was a precedent for everything he did with the single exception of dismissing Octavius. The real issue was the politics of the situation. The Romans, like us, liked to paint their political struggles as dichotomies: one thing versus another. But politics are always more complicated than this. In this case, it looks like Tiberius was setting himself up as a champion of the people and the entire senate stood in the way; the people versus the big-wigs. The truth is more complex as this depiction ignores the powerful players who very clearly supported Tiberius. The composition of the land commission illustrates this clearly. Tiberius' father-in-law, who, as Princeps, was the most powerful individual in the senate, headed the three-man commission. When Tiberius was killed, Crassus Mucianus, the man who ended up replacing Nasica as *Pontifex Maximus* took his seat. It is bizarre to argue that the land commission was hated by the leaders of Rome and loved only by the people. Here we have the *princeps* and the *Pontifex Maximus*, the two most powerful men in the senate, controlling the very same land commission that was supposedly opposed by the senate! Obviously, there is something else at stake here.

That "something else" was the political benefit the commission might confer on its members. Think of the patronage possibilities: each land recipient would credit his good fortune to Tiberius and the powerful aristocrats associated with him and many could be counted upon for political support in the future. In the traditional course of events, new lands were added to the Roman empire in the course of military campaigns

---

* *Publius Cornelius Scipio Nasica:* a powerful rival of the Sempronii and actually a cousin to Tiberius.

conducted by Roman consuls, and proconsuls. The rights to distribute those lands were one of the perks consuls and ex-consuls considered as belonging to them. Tiberius' bill represented a departure from that model because it dramatically expanded the patronage possibilities of the tribune, a lower level official and, in a sense, reduced the patronage possibilities belonging to the consuls. And so Tiberius became the focus of the controversy because he changed the political game and *not* because he was suddenly a champion of the people. This episode represents *a flashpoint within the aristocracy not between the aristocracy and the people.*

From this point on, all votes in the Assembly of Tribes that had ramifications for patronage became controversial. Ten years later (123 BC), Tiberius' younger brother Gaius ran for and won a seat as a tribune and proposed a number of sensible solutions to a host of very real problems. He changed the court system, he sponsored colonies, he raised pay for the army, and proposed that citizenship be extended in everyone in Italy. Some of these passed and it became clear that Gaius' ambitious ideas were too powerful in terms of creating a political base and like his brother before him he paid for it with his life. His mutilated body, along with those of 3000 of his murdered supporters, was thrown into the Tiber River. Twenty years later, another Tribune, Marcus Livius Drusus, was assassinated for sponsoring controversial proposals including, once again, citizenship for all Italians. His death and the consequent demise of his citizenship proposal sparked a major war between Rome and her Italian allies. Rome recovered from that war, but the political paralysis went on.

In summary, we can see that a number of Romans who were willing to tackle real problems with legislation were met with vehement opposition, even to the point of assassination. The criticisms thrown at these would-be reformers is that they were all *populares* that is, they appealed to the undisciplined people instead of to the sober and tradition-minded aristocracy, and they sought to overthrow the Republic and make a tyranny for themselves. This kind of political tactic should look familiar to us: if you can't attack the program, attack the motives of the one proposing it. But the real issue is that all of these reforms had huge political ramifications and whoever managed to solve the problems would reap a massive benefit in patronage. It was therefore better to have problems go unsolved than to have somebody else get credit for them.

# Alienation of Soldiers

Before 100 BC, soldiers were not drafted directly; a patron who was responsible for providing manpower from his clients referred them. The wealthier you were, the more bodies you provided. If you had no property, you received no draft notice. Does this mean that poor people did not serve? Hardly. It means that those who were responsible for providing bodies chose men from among their clients, gave them weapons and uniforms, and sent them off to report. New soldiers were not put off by this as service in the army might result in plunder, it was a paid position and, after all, this was a culture that honored warfare; to be a soldier is to seek honor.

The patronage system is the key to understanding how this all worked. A patron provides a man with the opportunity to serve, and if the campaign is successful, to enrich himself. That man remains connected to his patron partly because of this favor done for him. That man, now a soldier, will also develop a relationship with the commander to whom he is assigned. After each campaign, the soldiers were released because there was no permanent professional army until after 100 BC. Before that date, one can see that over the course of three or four campaigns, a man might have three or four commanders and develop at least some relationship to each of them but he will always have the original patron who sponsored his enrollment. Since all men will actually have several patrons in a sense, it is less likely that any one man, however successful, will be able to manipulate the loyalties of soldiers and ex-soldiers enough to threaten the state. But this all changed around 100 BC.

The decade preceding 100 BC saw the rise of a new and powerful man in Rome: Gaius Marius. A second generation Roman, he is a poster-example of how the Romans coopted local elites and introduced new talent to the middle echelons of Roman politics. Before he was twenty, Marius moved to Rome as a client of the most powerful family in Rome (at that time the Caecilius Metellus family) and with their assistance won several important lower level positions. Marius was a very ambitious man, and when he reached the age where he was eligible for the consulship, he made his move. In 108 BC, while on campaign as a staff officer with the *princeps*, C. Metellus Numidicus, Marius asked Numidicus to support him for the consulship. Normally a family as new to Roman politics as was Marius' might take several generations to work their way to the top rung and Numidicus was neither pleased nor amused by Marius' impatience. But Marius was not deterred. He returned to Rome and ran for the consulship anyway and, thanks to massive bribery, managed to win the consulship for 107. Stupidly pushing the insult to Numidicus, Marius sought the command in Africa that Numidicus had not yet finished. The Senate, stubbornly loyal to the *princeps*, refused to award it so Marius then convinced the Assembly of Tribes to give it to him as a special command. Numidicus must have been livid! As it turned out, Marius actually was a capable commander and soon won the victory in Africa that had escaped Numidicus, thus guaranteeing the permanent hatred of the Metellus faction.

Marius would pay the price for this disrespect, but not right away. As it turned out, shortly before and during the campaign in Africa, there had been a series of military disasters along the northern frontiers of Rome. To those in Rome, it seemed that the only competent commander the Romans had was Marius and he was elected to his second consulship (in 105) before he even returned from his African campaign. Indeed, he won his second through sixth individual consulships in consecutive years (105-100 BC), during which period he successfully defeated the northern barbarians and returned to Rome a hero.* But before he could leave to do that job, he had a major problem on his hands, a depleted army, and his solution to that problem would unintentionally make the crisis brewing in the Republic even worse...much, much worse. There are a number of possible reasons

---

* Our sources for this period are very problematic but this is a very odd situation that demands attention. Normally, consuls would have their commands extended in order to finish the job they had been elected to accomplish. That Marius's command was not extended in the usual manner, but extended by repeated and potentially illegal elections, suggests that the senate was reluctant to support him, despite the enthusiasm of the people.

for Roman difficulty filling the draft quota, but what matters for our discussion here is that Marius was forced to resort to an emergency measure the Romans had used before, that is, ignoring both the property requirement and the patronage structure and enlisting men directly into the legions. Marius was not the first to do this, but from Marius on this became the rule instead of the exception. Entire armies could be and were created from landless men with no history of loyalty to any of the traditional power brokers in Rome.

Once Marius had won in the north and the danger to Italy was abated, the old patterns of politics returned in the Roman Senate. The Metellus faction was still the most powerful and Marius was still an overly ambitious outsider trying to be accepted into the inner circle. Marius' enemies in the senate had not been able to stop Marius from having his victories in battle, but now they saw an opportunity to hurt him by denying his soldiers their reward. When proposals were brought forth in 100 BC to give his veterans land, Marius' enemies contrived to block these measures. All of a sudden, the soldiers, fiercely loyal to Marius, had become pawns in a high-stakes political game. Their reaction was violent and immediate; they took to the streets and rioted. Now we have one of those "what if" moments. Had Marius decided on backing his soldiers, he could have seized power in Rome because he had an army personally loyal to him. But as far as Marius was concerned, his most important ambition was to be among the traditional power brokers in the Roman senate and he turned away from his soldiers by arresting some of their leaders, and having others murdered. And so Marius did not choose civil war, at least not yet. For our purposes, the episode illustrates systemic pressures and responses that contributed to killing the Roman Republic. The most dangerous of these was how Marius' soldiers were treated. Sooner or later, they would turn against the state.

# The Romans Abuse their Allies

One of the strengths of the Roman system we already noted in the previous chapter was the Roman system of treaties. Those treaties spread the cost of war such that the Romans and their allies could outlast any opponent and opened paths to Roman citizenship. The treaties left allied cities to run their own internal affairs and for allies in the Latin category, there was little practical difference between their own citizen status and being Roman. The Italian allies were in a slightly different position however. Unlike those with Latin rights, each Italian treaty was unique and, so far as we know, they only recognized a path to Roman citizenship for their political leaders. But this was not really a problem until Rome started abusing her allies.

Our first obvious example of this takes place in 186 BC. In that year, rumors of a strange new cult that appealed to women and slaves started to appear in Rome. A combination of Greek and Roman wine festival, the cult seemed to celebrate drunkenness and lascivious behavior and this shocked Roman officials. We moderns like to think of the Romans as engaging in non-stop drunken orgies but in fact the Romans were much more prudish than we are accustomed to think. By way of example, Roman married couples tended to have sex only with clothes on and in the dark. Disturbed by what they perceived as a dangerous cult attacking the virtues of Rome, the Romans issued an all-Italy decree outlawing the cult. This was the first time that the Romans had ever interfered in the internal life of Italian cities outside of Rome itself. The Romans had simply not concerned themselves with what happened in other communities so long as they respected their treaty obligations for manpower and such. Now Romans were interfering in the internal affairs of their allies for the first time.

The Gracchan land bills of 133 and 123 BC also created problems for Italian allies. We mentioned above that Roman squatters on public lands scheduled for distribution were allowed to keep their land, but we note here that non-Romans were kicked off. This is probably the most important single explanation for attempts by tribunes like Gaius Gracchus and Marcus Livius Drusus to extend citizenship to Italian allies. If all Italians were Roman citizens, they would be treated the same as Romans with respect to

Roman public lands. In 91 BC, the Italians exploded in revolt after the latest plan to give them citizenship failed. So why was there resistance to awarding citizenship to Italian allies? It is simple: whoever would get credit for enrolling thousands of new Romans would gain thousands of new clients. No powerful Roman wanted anybody else to benefit from new voters and the idea was shot down every time it came up. So in 91 BC, the enraged Italians finally rose in revolt; they were quite serious: they even issued a joint coinage for the first time and established a capitol that they named Italica.

It was a brutal war as the Italians were long-time allies and veterans of Roman wars and understood very well how the Romans fought. They were able to put as many soldiers on the battlefield as the Romans and it only ended when citizenship was reluctantly extended to enough of the Italians to turn the tide. It took decades for Rome to bring all of Italy under control again. Afterwards, citizenship extensions became a regularly controversial proposition. We see this demonstrated later in the career of Julius Caesar. Caesar carried the Roman policy of extending citizenship to leading figures in new allied communities to new heights, extending the rights to entire communities. His rivals in the senate, rightly understanding the political benefits this gave to Caesar, did all they could to attack these gifts. The predictable effect of course was to drive these new citizens even closer to Caesar as their political futures were then tied directly to his. And Caesar cashed in these chips when his own civil war began in 48 BC.

# The Ides of March

Julius Caesar won that civil war but was murdered on March 15th, 44 BC, only a few days before he was due to leave on a major campaign to conquer Mesopotamia. Meanwhile Caesar had "forgiven" his enemies and showed considerable magnanimity in assigning many of them key positions in his government. But these acts only served to further insult those who imagined themselves Caesar's equal or better and their hatred of him inspired the most famous assassination in western History. Given that he was likely to be in Mesopotamia for the next five years, it makes you wonder why they bothered to kill Caesar. Perhaps they felt insulted for being "forgiven." In any case, Caesar's life and death make for a great story but the question that we have set out to answer is already answered. Even if Caesar hadn't been Caesar, someone else would have been, probably Pompey. Caesar's dramatic assassination certainly did not result in the restoration of senatorial dominance. That it did not is further evidence for the inevitably of the Republican collapse. The civil war resumed under new management and only ended in 30 BC when the nephew of Julius Caesar— Octavian, later to be called Augustus—emerged as true master of the Roman world. Exhausted by several generation of civil war, most Romans were grateful for the respite. It's pretty obvious Augustus became a king of sorts but he was clever enough to avoid the word. He preferred traditional Roman titles like *princeps* or *imperator*.

So did Julius Caesar want to be a king? It's not clear. Except for during a relatively short period at the end of 48BC, his acts can all be interpreted within the context of established precedent. It *is* clear that Caesar's rivals in the senate saw Caesar's success as putting a limit on their prestige and they certainly resented having to bow to his influence and that is what really mattered to them. For Caesar, the alternatives were unacceptable. To accede to senatorial demands was to accept a lessening of his honor; it was better to risk death. This chapter has charted a path leading inexorably to this moment. If Caesar had not become Caesar, someone else would have, probably Pompey. Therefore, structural problems made the demise of the Republic inevitable.

---

* *Imperator*: honorific title meaning Conqueror. It is the basis for the title Emperor.

## Fall of the Republic Timeline

| | |
|---|---|
| Tiberius Gracchus as tribune proposes controversial land distribution program and deposes his colleague | 133 |
| Tiberius killed by mob led by *Pontifex Maximus* | 132 |
| Gaius Gracchus as tribune proposes controversial programs, including citizenship for allies. | 123 |
| Gaius, attacked by senators, commits suicide; 3000 of his supporters killed and dumped in the Tiber | 121 |
| Marius reforms army, including dropping land ownership qualification | 107-99 |
| Rome's allies demands citizenship, revolt | 91-90 |
| Rome's first Civil War (Marius versus Sulla) | 88-82 |
| Sulla strengthens power of senate, retires | 82-78 |
| Pompey Magnus, successful and illegal commander in the civil war, is granted illegal triumphs | 80; 71 |
| Pompey, wildly popular, is given a special pirate command, unprecedented in scope | 67 |
| Pompey's eastern Command | 66-61 |
| Pompey, Crassus and Caesar form a pact | 61 |
| Caesar's command in Gaul | 58-49 |
| Crassus killed in Parthia | 54 |
| Civil War (Senate/Pompey vs. Caesar) | 48-46 |
| Caesar assassinated | 44 |
| Civil war (Anthony and Octavian vs. assassins) | 44-42 |
| Civil war (Anthony vs. Octavian) | 32-30 |
| Mark Anthony commits suicide | 30 |
| Octavian becomes first Emperor of Imperial Rome | 27 |

# Chapter Seven: Lions and Christians

*How did Christianity become the official religion of ancient Rome?*

Most people know that the Romans executed Jesus and are vaguely aware that Christians were persecuted during Roman antiquity. There are several good stories here. There is, of course, the life of Jesus. There is also the religion his followers created. And then there is the story which is most relevant to this book: the process by which Christianity, at first deemed a strange cult, became by fits and starts the official religion of the Roman Empire. So how does one get from a despised cult to the most potent force in the Roman government? This chapter will present that journey in steps. Each of these steps emphasizes how Christians as a community were perceived and received by their host culture—the Roman Empire.

## A Strange Cult* (c. AD 60-100)

The Romans didn't really notice the Christians at first. And why should they? For the most part, the Romans cared little for personal religious conviction except as it might affect public order or undermine the protection of Rome's gods. In chapter two, we emphasized *public* religion in antiquity, partly because we know a lot about it but more importantly we tried to demonstrated that practical and functional elements exist in all state-sponsored religions. We can take as an axiom that, as far as any state is concerned, religion exists to protect the community and to reinforce its

---

* *Cult*: The word, as currently used, has a pejorative connotation and is usually applied to a set of practices that seems abnormal or threatening. The term is appropriate here because, from the outside looking in, this was exactly how Christians were at first perceived by the Romans.

political legitimacy. We can see this emphasis even in the execution of Jesus. All the evidence would seem to indicate that, from the Roman point of view, the execution of Jesus was a routine matter, even if it might be considered a little heavy handed by today's standards. The Roman proconsul Pontius Pilate wanted to suppress anti-Roman expressions during the popular Passover holiday and he had no problem using Jesus' public humiliation and execution as a diversion for the mob. The board placed on his cross with the letters INRI (Jesus of Nazareth, King of the Jews) further emphasized the political emphasis that Roman authorities in Judea placed on the whole affair.

Meanwhile, the Roman empire as a whole was stable. Tiberius, the adopted son of Augustus, had become emperor fifteen years earlier, but by the death of Jesus he was an old man and had lost his taste for ruling. Tiberius isolated himself on the island of Capri and left the day-to-day problems of running the empire to his chief subordinate (Sejanus) and the Roman senate. The city of Rome was a bustling metropolis of a million souls. The public religion we looked at in chapter two continued to exist but the absence of the emperor reduced its significance and relevance dramatically. Its positions of authority were reduced to opportunities for the accumulation of individual prestige and its acts become empty rituals. Partly this has to do with the shifting focus of public religion from the community to the person of the ruler. Unlike the eastern half of the empire with its Mesopotamian and Egyptian influences, public religion in the West had never emphasized ruler cults and so this had to be introduced after Augustus became the first emperor. But it never really caught on. When the second emperor, Tiberius, abandoned Rome for his island retreat, the relevance of the state religion to everyday citizens in Rome was nil.

Perhaps in response to this alienation, Romans began developing a taste for religious options that were more personalized in emphasis and more exotic in shape. The cult of Isis provides an excellent example. Isis was honored for, among other things, her abilities to defeat fate and death. Although resisted officially by the emperor before Tiberius (Augustus), the emperor after Tiberius (Caligula), dedicated the first temple to Isis in Rome.

Mithraic ritual included ideas of rebirth and ascent to heaven. Christianity emphasized redemption and the permanent defeat of death. The obvious overlap in these thematic concerns in Isisian, Mithraic, and Christian ritual suggest that all of these imported cults resonated at some common level.

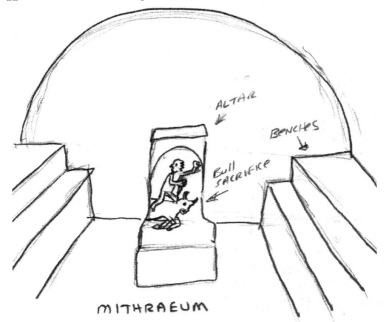

MITHRAEUM

A NUMBER OF THESE HAVE BEEN FOUND SCATTERED ACROSS THE ROMAN EMPIRE. MITHRA WAS BECOMING POPULAR AT THE SAME TIME AS CHRISTIANITY. THESE UNDERGROUND CAVERNS WERE ALL FILLED WITH RUBBLE AFTER CHRISTIANS TOOK OVER. SOMETIMES THEY BUILT CHURCHES ON TOP OF THEM.

Early Christianity differs importantly from Mithra and Isis however in that Christian tenets challenged an established orthodoxy and an entrenched Jewish elite (the Pharisees) prepared to defend that orthodoxy. It is important to note that the followers of Jesus did not imagine, at least at first, that they were founding a new religion. On the contrary, they argued that Jesus' ministry represented the fulfillment of promises made by God in Jewish sacred texts. But the existence of a Jewish leadership resistant to that

Lions and Christians  127

message created a competition of sorts between the conservative guardians of an old faith system and the challengers in what we might call the new Jesus cult. Thanks to the evidence preserved in the Christian text, *Acts of the Apostles*, we can see how this battle literally spilled into the streets and attracted the attention of municipal authorities. The dramas that unfold in that text illustrate the power of first impressions.

*Acts of the Apostles* is mostly about Paul the Apostle. Paul is universally given credit for carrying the Christian message outside of the Jewish community and he did this by de-emphasizing the dietary and other restrictions articulated in the primary Jewish texts of the Torah. Even so, Paul never stopped preaching in the synagogue, or to the Jews. If one reads *Acts* for insights about the travels of Paul, one sees a consistent pattern. Paul had an advance team that he sent to make contact with local Christians. When he arrived, he tended to visit the local synagogue, and preached there. If we take the text at face value, he returned there daily until at last, finally there emerged a complaint that he was causing trouble. He or his lieutenants were occasionally arrested but when everyone is bailed out, Paul promptly left town and repeated the process in the next town.

One of the most colorful of the stories in *Acts* involves a silversmith named Demetrius who worked in Ephesus. Ephesus boasted a huge temple to Artemis that is still regarded as one of the greatest wonders of the ancient world. Built entirely of marble, its columns were carved in relief and the temple covered a footprint of 100,000 square feet. It attracted pilgrims and tourists from all over the Roman world. Given what Demetrius says in this text, one must conclude that Paul had apparently been a regular presence in the temple precinct for months haranguing and preaching the gospel to temple visitors. Demetrius called a meeting of craftsmen and vendors in the theatre of Ephesus where he complained that Paul's proselytizing was hurting his business, the sale of votive statuary dedicated to Artemis. The meeting was well attended and threatened to turn into a riot with Christians, Jews, and Pagans shrieking at each other and chanting in vain attempts to drown each other out. These events apparently passed without serious incident, but if this was the first time a Roman passerby heard or saw anything to do with the Christians, his impression could hardly have been positive. If we are trying to locate where Christians stood in the consciousness of the ordinary Roman, then they were obviously and firmly in the category of troublemakers. What, if anything, might have been known about Christian ritual did not help. From the outside looking in, the Christians seemed to connect immortality with secret rites and ritual cannibalism. So, not only were they troublemakers, they were a very strange cult.

Even so, none of this would probably matter very much except for a huge fire that engulfed Rome in 64. Coincidentally, Paul had only just been released from a two-year house arrest in Rome where he had been facing charges for causing trouble in Jerusalem. We're not really sure where Paul was when the fire broke out, as he seems not to be directly connected to the drama concerning it. Nero was the emperor at this time and, as emperor, he would be vulnerable to criticism: did he do enough to stop it? Did he help those rendered homeless? Nero didn't help himself very much when he decided to build a new palace on the ground scorched by the fire. Rumors spread that he had actually *started* the fire to make room for his new palace. The truth of this is doubtful but Nero did have a genuine public relations problem on his hands and he decided to arrest some Christians to deflect the criticism: "Those pesky Christians: they did it!" The Christians' dicey reputation made them perfect scapegoats. There had been certainly Christians in Rome for some time and it is likely that their public profile had increased as a consequence of Paul's stay in Rome in the preceding two years. In any case, Nero rounded up some Christians, tortured them and subjected them to various kinds of gruesome executions. This represents a huge turning point in the history of the movement. Now Christians will be legally proscribed* *just for being Christian.* Whereas before this incident, they might be hauled in for causing disturbances or perhaps making treasonous statements about new kings, now they were subject to arrest merely for being Christian. Many moderns think that Paul was re-arrested and

---

* *Proscribed*: declared outside the lines of civil society, outlawed.

beheaded a year or two after the fire *on the basis of this new legal situation,* but the evidence is not clear.

Nero says no to Christianity

With Christianity now essentially illegal, the activities of Christians become almost impossible to trace in any detail over the next few decades. With Paul's death and the outlawing of the new religion, it seems probable that the Christian message would have collapsed back into Judaism but for two events that prevented this from happening.

The first was the death of James, brother of Jesus, around the year 62. There remains a lot of controversy about the exact relationship of James with Jesus as his very existence impinges on the virgin birth doctrine of Catholicism. There seems no real doubt that they were *at least* cousins, if not actual brothers. In any case, James was a figurehead in the Christian community in Jerusalem. Under his influence, the Christianity practiced in Jerusalem had a lot more in common with traditional Jewish beliefs than did the version preached by Paul in the rest of the empire. Were it were not for Paul's work it seems logical to think that James' stature and relationship to Jesus might have exercised a decisive influence over the future direction of the movement. The result would have been more of a reform movement than the revolutionary movement it did ultimately become. But this did not happen. James was murdered by the order of a court of Pharisees during a hiatus between Roman governors. This meant that the most logical person who might have nudged Christians back into the Jewish fold was gone. It is important to note that many Christians practiced their faith within synagogues well past the legalization of Christianity, nearly 300 years later.

The second event that pushed Christianity away from Judaism was the Jewish rebellion of 66. For some time already, various outrages against Judaism had been mounting in the minds of the Judeans. The Emperor Caligula's demand to put his statue in the temple of Jerusalem, the acts of rapacious and insensitive Roman governors, and the widespread impression among Jews that their officials, especially their king, were too cozy with the Romans—all of these stimulated the growth of radical anti-Roman groups like the so-called Zealots and the Sicarii. In 66 BC, Zealots overran a lightly held Roman garrison and then defeated a legion sent from Syria to destroy them. These early and dramatic successes emboldened all the radicals to think they could actually win independence from Rome—as it turns out, a colossal misjudgment. The Romans seldom forgave and never forgot. The future Emperor Vespasian and his son Titus returned with three full legions and a number of allies.

For the Romans, it was a long, annoying campaign to take back the province and the Zealots guaranteed the worst possible ending by summarily executing any Jewish officials who showed the slightest interest in compromise. The ultimate and inevitable result was a terrible siege and the deaths and slavery of many tens of thousands of Jews. Jerusalem and the temple were utterly destroyed. Probably the most famous episode in the doomed insurrection was the mass suicide of zealots and refugees at a fortress called Masada. Rather than be taken by force or surrender voluntarily, the defenders of the fortress chose instead to kill themselves, leaving the Romans a hollow victory when they finally breached the walls. The Romans were probably impressed. The story may illustrate the resolve and courage of the Jewish rebels but it also highlights both the hopelessness of the revolt and the waste of humanity it embodied. For our purposes, we note the revolt because it transformed Jerusalem's influence on the direction of Christianity in the post-Paul period. Whereas Judaism was a more or less respected religion of an integral people of the Roman empire before the revolt, it was now the religious practice of a failed revolutionist movement. The space this created encouraged Christian thinkers to distance themselves from the Jews. All of this was reinforced by two subsequent rebellions in Judea (in 115 and 135).

# Prosecutions not Persecutions? (c. AD 111-200)

Even though Christianity was technically illegal after the Great Fire there was neither obvious probable cause to arrest Christians nor any institutional constituency sufficiently motivated to cause them any serious trouble. The result is a long gestation period for the new religion that was only occasionally interrupted by locally initiated prosecutions. We really have no idea how many Christians there were 100 years after Jesus but there were certainly enough for them to be noticed by the Romans. The general impression of our Roman sources is that Christians were either atheists or that they were obsessed with foreign superstitions and magic. It seems odd to our ears to hear them accused of atheism but the accusation was flung because Christians paid no heed to the traditional gods whose job it was to protect the community. Even so, we know of only scattered instances before AD 200 where Christians were arrested and executed because there was no concerted effort by any of the Emperors to harass them before at least AD 250. Two pieces of evidence seem to illustrate the legal position of Christians in this period. The first is a pair of letters between a Roman governor (Pliny) and a Roman emperor (Trajan). The other is the diary of a Christian martyr (Perpetua).* These two episodes are separated in time and distance but they complement each other nicely because they describe the same process but from radically different perspectives.

The composite of the two stories suggests that accused Christians were routinely given an opportunity to deny their crime and were they to do so, it would constitute sufficient reason for release. One can easily imagine that many whose nerve was not steady enough to endure execution took this remedy and quietly disappeared from the pages of history. We have no surviving individual testimonies of this strategy, but this should not surprise us. There is nothing heroic in a failure of nerve. The surviving individual stories we *do* have, and Perpetua's is one of them, all feature the confident

---

* These episodes and the evidence for them are widely known and readily available.

embrace of voluntary martyrdom. Perpetua's story of her own experience is remarkable enough but its pathos is multiplied by the testimony of her death supplied by a witness to her death. One is impressed by the calmness with which she seemed to embrace her fate. One can also imagine the impression made on spectators in the arena. Executions were always public in the Roman world—how else might they be deemed a credible deterrent?—and promoters of public entertainment would sometimes employ condemned prisoners as throwaway props in miniature theatrical dramas. In a warrior society, a good death was a good thing to witness and the execution of Christians—at least the ones we hear about—gave witness to a unique inner power and confidence. In a strange sort of way, their executions became recommendations for their religion.

And so it proceeded in this way until the middle 200s. From the Christian point of view this period was most important because Christian intellectuals and writers began to refine and define their principles in a wider intellectual context, particularly that of Greek philosophy. Meanwhile, Christianity was in the process of developing its own internal orthodoxy This was made quite difficult by the fact that there little agreement was reached on which of the sacred texts were actually authoritative until after Christianity was legalized in the 300s. We need not spend much time on the details here but it is important to note that all of this argument about what was and what was not Christian only makes sense in an atmosphere of relative stability for the church as a whole. This stability went out the window in the middle 200s.

## Persecution and Blame (c. AD 250-300)

The Romans had a rough period from 235-284. There were more than twenty-five emperors in fifty years, some of whom lasted only a matter of days. It was a period of civil war, financial crisis, and invasions from without. Pieces of the empire were broken off while rival emperors raged against each other for control of the rest. Two things became clear to the Romans. First, it was obvious that the system of succession was broken. Second, and more to the point, the gods had withdrawn their favor from

Rome. The last emperor of this period, Diocletian, made a valiant effort to fix the systemic problems and to construct safeguards against pretenders and civil wars. He divided the empire into eastern and western administrative districts, designated rulers for each half and named their presumed successors in advance.* He enacted wage and price controls, overhauled the tax system, and he restored stability on all the borders of the empire. Diocletian and a few other emperors from the period of dysfunction also attempted to restore the protection of the gods.

Maintaining this favor was the central purpose of state religion, of course, and the perceived loss of divine favor normally instigated consultations of sacred texts, inquiries made of oracles, and repetitions ordered of familiar rituals. In the Imperial period, this would all be supervised by or on behalf of the emperor, whose own safety and legitimacy obviously depended on the approval of the gods. What this means in practice is that at least some of the emperors of this troubled period took pains to be seen seeking divine favor. Moreover, given that public participation in public religion had fallen off over the decades for reasons we have already mentioned, emperors had to employ some sort of coercion to ensure general compliance. This meant that Roman citizens were, in some instances, required to prove their attendance at public sacrifices to the usual gods. We have forty or so affidavits surviving from the reign of the Emperor Decius (250-1) attesting to this policy. It would appear from this evidence that individuals were required to appear at a local magistrate and swear under oath that they had made an appropriate sacrifice to the patron gods of Rome.

This changed the legal situation of Christians in a fundamental way. Until now prosecutions of Christians had been local initiatives spurred by

---

* The rulers of each half of the empire were now titled "Augustus," after the first emperor. The second in command was titled "Caesar" after, well... Caesar. Both of these names had already morphed into unofficial titles over the preceding century because each ruler wished to establish an adoptive family connection with these legendary figures. Diocletian made them official titles instead of adoptive surnames. This system of four rulers is dubbed the *Tetrarchy*, from the Greek, meaning four rulers.

local political situations. The process required an overt act by a citizen, a denunciation of some sort, to which local authorities could then react. Logically, there had to be some extraneous motive for an accuser to denounce a Christian, perhaps a petty grudge of some sort. That this did not take place on a regular basis suggests that Christians were not so outside the mainstream as we might imagine. But with this new Imperial policy the government had a motive and a means to instigate legal action on behalf of the whole community. And moreover, compliance with the Imperial policy meant Christians were asked to do something they could not in fact do: sacrifice to non-Christian gods. There is another way in which this period of persecution differs from earlier practice. With emperors now actively initiating anti-Christian policy, they began to be more systematic. Books were burned, buildings confiscated, leaders singled out. The last and most vigorous persecutor of the Christians was Diocletian. Had he not retired in 305, or had his policies been continued by his successors, it is not hard to imagine that Christianity as a movement might have stalled or even disappeared altogether. But it didn't happen that way.

## Constantine's Epiphany (c. 325)

Diocletian fell ill and retired in 305. He left behind the system of four rulers we mentioned above and a completely redesigned administrative structure. The structure would survive mostly but the system of four rulers would not. Constantine (the Great) would be the next successful emperor and in steps he extended his control over the entire empire, finally ruling it all by 325. Constantine embraced many of the reforms Diocletian had made and he introduced a few of his own, particularly with regard to the image of the emperor. He set up a new capitol in an old Greek city (Byzantion) near the entrance to the Black Sea and renamed it Constantinople. Whereas previous emperors at least pretended that the Roman Senate was relevant to decision making, once Constantine left Rome, he chose to ignore it altogether and he began to emphasize the connection of his power directly to higher authority. He and his successors set out to create an elaborate court culture that supported this impression.

What is most interesting for us here is the way he shaped Christianity to complete this process. He did this in steps that corresponded to his march to power. The first major step took place in a series of episodes spanning the years 310-12. In 310, Constantine reported a vision of himself receiving from Apollo a wreath of victory and with it the symbolic right to rule the

CONSTANTINE GETS
THE MEMO!

whole world. At the same time, we see Constantine's coinage suddenly emphasizing Sol Invictus as his partner. This choice was clever in that it resonated with traditional devotees of Apollo—a cult strong in Gaul—and provided a monotheistic emphasis to his divine sanction, something that might appeal to Christians. In 311, Constantine's dying colleague in the East, Galerius, issued an edict of toleration with respect to the Christians. In 312 Constantine reported a vision or a pair of visions instructing his army to display a Christian symbol as they proceeded into battle to take the city of Rome against his last rival in the west, Maximian. These roughly parallel acknowledgments of Christianity by the rulers, one east and one west, make it clear that Christians were in sufficient numbers to make them an important constituency.

Having won the battle for the city of Rome in 312, Constantine met his colleague and rival in the east (Licinius) the next year and together they issued another edict of toleration (frequently called the Edict of Milan, where it was announced). Christianity was now at least legitimate, but the absence of Christian symbols on the arch of Constantine (erected 315) or on any of his coins suggests that Constantine was not yet favoring Christianity to the exclusion of other religions.

The next phase of Constantine's Christian policy spans the years 320-325. In 320, Licinius announced a new policy, reneging on the religious toleration to which he and Constantine had previously pledged their support. Constantine, taking this as a challenge, girded once again for war. The decisive battles took place in 324, resulting in Constantine's victory. The war had significant religious overtones with Licinius representing the old gods and Constantine the new. Meanwhile, Constantine was being drawn into Christian doctrinal disputes. Some years before, Constantine had already played a role in suppressing Donatism, a variant on mainstream Christianity prevalent in Roman Africa. In 325 Constantine convened an empire wide council—the Council of Nicea—to put to rest a whole series of disputes and controversies within the church. These controversies included, among other things, the nature of Christ, the method of calculating the festival of Easter, which bishops had the most authority, and the thorny question of whether to re-admit apostates who had fallen away during the now-ended persecutions. Most scholars question whether Constantine had any personal stake in any of these questions; the consensus is that the disputes were political for him in the sense that disunity in the religious community implicitly undermined his legitimacy and effectiveness. This was especially important as he had already made his association with Christianity a key part of his court persona.

So, Constantine took a religion that was focused on the inner life of individuals and adapted it to work as a public religion. In so doing, he asked Christianity to perform all the roles of public religion that we detailed in chapter two. Religious figures did not see it this way, naturally. From their standpoint, Christianity had its own agenda, namely, to pave the way for Jesus' return. No doubt some Christian leaders interpreted the new protected status of Christianity as a step along that road and furthermore, that the protection was a sign of the submission of the state to Jesus. Inevitably, a conflict must arise between these two fundamentally different

of religion: shall the state serve religion? Or should   religion
in the same way that it had always done before? That conflict
.ɔ play a role in undermining a fundamental element of stable
...ɕty, a common notion of civil justice.

# Theodosius, Ambrose, and Hypatia: the End of Antiquity (378-415)

Many reference resources assign the year 476 special significance as marking the end of the Roman empire in the west. In that year, Romulus Augustulus, earning the dubious honor of being the last Roman Emperor in the West, was forced into retirement by his German military advisor, Odoacer. But Odoacer was little different from other barbarian rulers and pretenders who had already effectively held power in Italy both before and after 476. It was Odoacer's preference for the word "king" and his rejection of traditional Roman symbols that provides the symbolic break that historians really like. The fact is that since the year 395 the empire had *already* been split into two. In the decades before 395, the western empire had been beset by a number of invasions against which the resources of the west alone proved inadequate for resistance. The east, unwilling or unable to make up the difference, effectively abandoned the west to its own fate by the year 400. From the standpoint of Constantinople, the nominal capitol of the Roman Empire since Constantine, the decision to cut the west loose was a practical one. A convenient fiction was maintained that the west was still a viable part of a united empire and so relations between the two now-separate Roman Empires continued to exist long past the point where they had any practical importance. So what happened in 476 can be taken as the logical consequence of policies and decisions taken since 378. One such policy shift occurred in the relationship of the church and the Roman state.

In 378 the Emperor Theodosius came to power after his predecessor, the Emperor Valens, was killed in an ill-advised and catastrophic battle with the Goths. Theodosius restored some stability by reaching accommodation with the Goths, but at too great a cost. Historians like to criticize Theodosius for his policy of integrating the Goths and other barbarians into the Roman military but this sort of thing had been an integral policy since the beginning of Roman History. The real problem was that large numbers of Goths served in military units which were made entirely of Goths and led by Gothic commanders, and the soldiers were subject to Gothic Law, not Roman. It is hard to imagine a more wrong-headed approach to inculcating Roman identity and values.

For our part here, it is Theodosius' radical policies concerning Christianity that draw our attention. Step by step Theodosius made Christianity the official religion of the state and incrementally turned up the heat on any alternative. In a series of decrees, Theodosius adopted Nicene Christianity as the only state religion and banned pagan sacrifice. He did away with all the traditional pagan holidays or converted them to Christian ones. In the meanwhile, he surrounded himself with Christian leaders, prominent among whom was the Bishop of Milan, Ambrose. Ambrose was a radical and believed that Christianity must aggressively destroy its rivals; and under his influence the emperor agreed to sit by while mobs of Christians attacked pagan sites. He ordered the Temple of Vesta closed and the symbolic home fire of Rome extinguished. The temple at Delphi was pulled down on his orders, and he shut down the Olympics permanently. When in 388 a bishop led a mob to destroy a synagogue in the city of Callinicum, the emperor responded by demanding the bishop rebuild the synagogue at his own expense. But Ambrose pressured the Emperor to overturn his decision and look the other way. Christian radicals in the streets took this as a license to unleash all their passions on Jewish targets now, and a wave of destruction washed over synagogues from one end of the empire to the other. As far as Ambrose was concerned, love of God was sufficient motive to forgive any such violence. But what had happened to the rules of civil society? Where was justice? Here we see the fundamental contract exemplified in the stele of Hammurabi—the provision of justice—forgotten and, symbolically, a harbinger of the *real* fall of Rome.

Perhaps the most dramatic moment in all of this was the murder of Hypatia, a philosopher and astronomer in Alexandria. In 410-415, Hypatia found herself a symbol in a vicious dispute between the prefect of the city, Orestes (a sort of mayor), and the radical bishop of the city, Cyril. Alexandria was a large city divided among substantial Jewish, Christian, and pagan populations. The emperor, Theodosius II, was only nine years old in 410 and affairs were firmly in the hands of the Regent and Praetorian Prefect, Anthemius. Anthemius was sympathetic to the radicals and when reports came to the capitol that gangs of monks associated with Cyril were making life miserable for Jews and pagans in Alexandria—interrupting their gatherings, engaging in acts of destruction and violence, and so forth—he issued a series of decrees in the boy-emperor's name supporting Cyril. Meanwhile, the pagans and Jews in Alexandria demanded that the prefect protect them and their property and that he restrain the excesses of the Christian mobs. The Prefect Orestes had an impossible mission. When in 414, Anthemius either died or was fired from his position, things went from bad to worse. The leadership of the Eastern Roman empire was taken over by the fifteen-year-old sister of the emperor, Pulcheria, also a supporter of the radicals. Orestes was very much on his own. Meanwhile, Hypatia was a respected figure among the city elite and a natural ally of the prefect. Her public utterances against the excesses of Cyril's monks were taken as insult to Cyril and a challenge to his moral authority. Unfortunately, this backfired for Hypatia; although she was well known to the city elite, she was less known on the street and Bishop Cyril was easily able to portray her as a dangerous anti-Christian threat in his daily speeches to the mob. The details are obscure, but it appears that some of Cyril's supporters abducted her in the streets, stripped her naked, and they either dragged her to her death behind a cart, or literally ripped her limb from limb. In a relatively short period of time, thirty or forty years or so, many pagan temples and synagogues disappeared from the cityscapes of the Roman Empire or were converted into Christian churches. Others were abandoned and quarried for their building materials. It is impossible to overstate how different the rhythms of city life had changed in such a short time.

The death of Hypatia points to the *death of classical learning*. Artistic expressions leaned in a new direction; we call it Byzantine and it is characterized by the rejection of realism in favor of symbolism. Much of the old elite of Rome was absorbed into the church and they took their wealth with them. These are some of the obvious changes wrought by the new religion but something else, something not so obvious, was also different. The Roman empire had survived repeated disasters and invasions in part because, like any stable culture, its citizens and residents bought into the idea of a continuing community. Here we see a new idea of community developing, but one centered in the church as opposed to the physical city. What meaning is left in political citizenship? What investment does the citizen have in the idea of the state? A decreasing share to be sure and without this investment of self in the idea of being Roman, it is no surprise that Rome should fade away, which is exactly what it did.

As the ancient world disintegrated, cities became targets of violent depredation. The Sassanid Persians seized the great city of Antioch in 256, the Goths sacked Rome itself in 410, and the Vandals did it again in 455. What was once unthinkable to Romans—the ancient Romans called Rome the Eternal City from at least the time of Ovid—was now a real prospect: Rome might be no more. Augustine wrote his book, *City of God*, in direct reaction to those who wanted to blame the Christian God for these disasters, for not protecting his people. Was it not true that only a few years before the Goths sacked Rome that Theodosius had removed the statue of Nike from the Senate house in Rome? Was not the sacred fireplace in Rome extinguished on his orders? Augustine scoffed at these criticisms. To sharpen the point, Augustine listed chapter and verse all the failures of the pagan gods in their supposed duties. What then was the business of Christianity in this world? To prepare for the next.

## Christianity in Ancient Rome: a TimeLine

| | |
|---|---|
| Jesus born in the reign of the Emperor Augustus | 4 BC |
| Jesus crucified in the reign of the Emperor Tiberius | AD 27 |
| Paul begins proselytizing outside of Judea | 46 |
| Paul arrested in Jerusalem, later sent to Rome | 58 |
| Paul released in Rome | 62 |
| The Great Fire | 64 |
| Peter and Paul executed in Rome | 67 |
| Gospel of Mark (the earliest) written in Rome | c.70 |
| Pliny and Trajan correspondence | 112 |
| Christian canon of gospels and letters mostly set. | 140-200 |
| Martyrdom of Perpetua | 203 |
| First empire-wide persecution (Decius) | 251 |
| Last Empire-wide persecution (Diocletian). | 304 |
| Edict of Toleration. | 311 |
| Council of Nicaea (first comprehensive council)       . | 325 |
| First decree outlawing pagan ritual. | 341 |
| paganism tolerated | 361-375 |
| incremental steps taken to outlaw pagan ritual | 381-395 |
| First execution of a Christian for heresy (Priscillian) | 385 |
| Olympics suppressed | 393 |
| Virtual war on paganism | 395-476 |
| Death of Hypatia | 415 |

# The Beginnings of European Monasticism

Nothing really demonstrates the "otherness" of an developing Christian culture better than Christian monasticism. As we push our narrative past the end of the Western Roman Empire in the direction of the "Middle Ages," it is more and more the case that monks and monasteries become prominent elements of social organization. By the time we get to what some historians call the "High Middle Ages (c. AD1100-1300)," established orders of monks were everywhere. The lives and collective experience of medieval monks were well ordered, regular, and perhaps even banal. There were hundreds of monasteries sheltering many thousands of monks mostly living lives more comfortable and more secure than those of the average peasant. But it was not this way early on.

The *first* phase of Christian monasticism took place in a world in apparent decline. The Roman Empire, especially in the west, was structurally corrupt and increasingly incapable of defending itself. The predictable social anxieties generated by this sober reality played into both the individual experiences of would-be monks and their reception in the minds of those ordinary people who either met or heard of them. Although monks in the first centuries of Christianity had different lives and experiences, common threads in their lives tie them together in two really important ways. For us, they stand as cogent representations of an important moment in the creation of a European Christian culture and as emblems of a society in fatal decline. But for the ordinary citizen on the street in the AD 400s, they were both living symbols of the vast distance between God and men and a means by which God's attention might be brought to bear on human concerns. They came to this place by steps.

The earliest candidates for conversion to Christianity were prepared for that conversion by their readiness to believe in the miracles associated with Jesus. In the next few generations, before Christianity was legalized, the lives, the deaths, and miracles of the martyrs provided a contemporary testimony and vicarious re-enactments of the Passion. Once Christianity was legalized, this role was filled by the experience of Christian ascetics* and a new genre of literature arose in celebration, hagiography†, and this gave wide exposure to the phenomenon. Ascetics, like the martyrs before them, were epic heroes in a sense and their deeds and travails made convenient substitute narratives for the now dethroned epics of classical literature. Celebration of miracles was always a prominent feature of this new genre, just as it was in the story of Jesus with some subtle differences. Jesus performed miracles actively, as in turning the water into wine. The miracles of the saints tended to be passive in that miracles happened as a consequence of proximity. The Holy Spirit presumably suffused the body of the saint and is itself responsible for the miracle, not the saint his or herself. The presence of the Holy Spirit was always presented as consequent to levels of human suffering and deprivation far beyond the boundary of reasonable expectations and so by this repeated reminder in story format, the faithful came to see the saintly monks as necessary proxies upon whose intercession for divine favor they could rely. Church leaders who were not predisposed to asceticism themselves—this would be most—could nonetheless point to those who were and, eventually, to validate their authenticity. This acted in the long run to reinforce the church's efforts to claim exclusive authority in divine affairs. But there was no such monopoly, presumed or otherwise, in the early church. Nor were there any organizational rules governing proper monastic behavior. This left a lot of room for individual expressions of piety. We will now feature four early monastic figures whose lives seem to exemplify points made in this brief introduction.

---

* *Ascetics*: those who trade physical comfort for spiritual inspiration. The phenomenon has and does exist in many cultures and is not peculiar to Christianity.
† *Hagiography*: biographies of saints.

# St. Anthony of the Desert (251-356)

Anthony grew up a Christian in Roman Egypt during a period of active persecution although there is little reason to think he was himself victimized in the persecutions. But those ongoing persecutions, along with the instability of the period, must have been significant factors governing Anthony's view of the world. At eighteen his wealthy parents died and Anthony decided to take Jesus' admonitions to his own disciples seriously and he gave his inheritance away. Around the same time he fell under the influence of a local holy man who lived outside of town. By this time, there were any number of such individuals who lived on the peripheries of Egyptian cities; we know of some small communities of ascetics although we don't have much detail about them, mostly just a few names. As it turns out, Anthony was destined to become the best known of these, perhaps because he lived so long. It certainly did not hurt that his life was later featured in that new genre of literature called hagiography. Anthony's life exhibits characteristics that become important and formulaic elements in the first installments of that new genre. First, there his the reputation of dramatic deprivation and extreme solitude; for a time he actually lived in a tomb. For about twenty years, he locked himself up in an old abandoned fort and fed himself exclusively on what visitors brought him. Despite decades in virtual isolation in the desert Anthony became a well-known figure to locals. Just before Christianity was legalized he made an appearance in Alexandria where he attracted a lot of attention, as he seemed to be daring the authorities to arrest him. For whatever reason, they did not bother. When Anthony afterward returned to the desert, his growing reputation attracted more and more visitors and before long those who venerated him established a community of monks. His fame reached the Emperor Constantine in Constantinople who seems to have written to Anthony asking for a blessing. Later, the patriarch in Alexandria convinced him to speak on behalf of the Nicene Creed. Although Anthony didn't write anything down, his saying were collected by his admirers and later published. His remains have made a few stops and are now preserved in southern France.

# St. Simeon the Stylite (390-459)

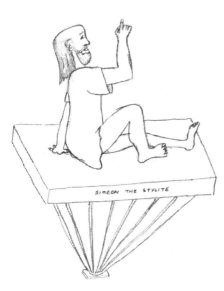

SIMEON THE STYLITE

Like Anthony, Simeon is famous for leaving town but in a different direction. Rather than leave town for the desert, Simeon shimmied up an architectural column and lived there for 39 years. He is sometimes called Simeon the Elder to distinguish him from imitators by the same name. Like Anthony, Simeon systematically deprived himself of any comfort. Early in his life Simeon developed a reputation for extreme deprivation even to the brink of starvation. At sixteen, he was thrown out of a monastery that he had joined because of the extremes to which he was then willing to go. I suspect his fellow monks believed his piety to be too much a prideful badge of honor. Later stunts included refusing to sit for long periods, shutting himself up in a tiny hut for months at a time, and imprisoning himself on a rocky outcrop in the mountains, all of which attracted a great deal of attention from pilgrims who flocked to see him. They regarded what seemed to be superhuman endurance as an indication of the presence of the Holy Spirit. Eventually, finding himself unsuccessful at finding solitude on the X-axis, Simeon tried the Y-axis and climbed a fifteen foot column he found in a ruin somewhere so as to escape his many admirers. Undaunted, they kept coming and not only did they bring him offerings of food but they rebuilt his platform to reach even higher. Visitors describe him as genuflecting endlessly in between visits from spectators, admirers, and pilgrims, whose consultations with the strange holy man were facilitated by a convenient ladder. His visitors are said to have included Roman emperors and a king of Persia. Simeon's escape from the city seems here more symbolic than real, but he fits the pattern nonetheless.

# St. Patrick (387-460)

Patrick was a contemporary of Simeon but lived on the other side of the Roman empire. He grew up a well-to-do Christian in Roman Britain only to be captured by Irish pirates when he was sixteen. After six years as a slave, Patrick escaped and returned to Britain. He returned to a different world, most especially the Roman abandonment of Britain. The last troops left in 410 but the Romans had been withdrawing in stages since before Patrick was born. In fact, it was because the Romans were leaving that the Irish were raiding the English coast in the first place. Reliable details are hard to come by in Patricks' life but we know that upon his return to England, he became a cleric and eventually returned to Ireland where he became a missionary and then a bishop. The widespread beliefs that he introduced Christianity to Ireland and banished the snakes are, sadly, without basis. Biologists seem pretty confident that there were never any native species of snakes in Ireland and we know of several other missionaries who visited Ireland before Patrick. He did however become one of several patron saints of Ireland and he inspired several hagiographies of his own. While we cannot know what was in Patrick's mind, it is hard not to conclude that the ebbing of Roman influence in his native land was an important influence in shaping his decisions and experience.

# St Benedict (480-547)

Benedict's life has an important similarity to that of Patrick in that he was a direct witness to Rome's decline. Born about forty miles from the city of Rome, he was attending school there around the year 500. Between 476 and 534, Italy was ruled by a succession of German kings who ruled from Ravenna. Meanwhile Rome had declined to a city of secondary importance. The culture in Rome had become ever more undisciplined and violent.

Benedict's hagiographer tells us that he was disgusted with the urban lifestyle and that Benedict abandoned the city at the age of twenty. Like Anthony, he came under the influence of a monk living near his boyhood home and under his influence, was convinced to follow that example. As always, reliable detail is scanty, but Benedict attracted the attention of many like-minded men and he was associated with a dozen or so separate monasteries in the hills around Rome, including his final and most famous one on Monte Cassino,* a hilltop halfway between Rome and Naples. Benedict's process of removal from the city mirrored the dissolution of the idea of Rome in Italy. In the 530s the emperor Justinian sent an army to retake Italy, which he actually managed to accomplish but only after two destructive sieges of Rome and the annihilation of Milan. In 546, Rome was re-taken by the Goths, taken back in 547 and lost once again in 550. By 554, Rome was again in Roman hands. Roman attempts to retake the city of Rome did more damage than the Barbarian raiders ever did.

The population of Rome dropped to a level it hadn't seen in a thousand years. Imagine the psychological impact on what remained of the Roman nobility: the greatest imperial city in the imagination of Europeans had, in a matter of decades, been reduced to a battered ghost of itself. Imagine the deserted buildings, streets and markets. And now look to the dozens of communities of monks in the hills outside of Rome preparing themselves for the next world. Many of these monks, including Benedict himself, were from the elite and as far as they were concerned their flight to the monasteries was not so much a disorganized retreat but a preparation for what was to come. Practically speaking I suppose, there isn't much difference. In any case, the Romans were nothing if not organized and it was here that Benedict drew up his famous "Benedictine Rule," essentially a handbook for monastic life in a communal setting.

Other monastic guides were already in existence but Benedict's rule seemed to trace a line of moderation in pious life. Benedictines were committed to a life of simplicity, manual labor, and biblical study, rather

---

* As a side note, Allied bombers trying unsuccessfully to destroy German artillery units in WW II destroyed this monastery site.

than the extreme asceticism typical of some foundations. We see already the future of medieval monasticism talking shape in Benedict's rule. One element that is worthy of emphasis for us here is the stress on independence. Each monastery was like a legal family in the sense that it was independent from any other family and its head, like the father in traditional Roman families, was the legal patron of the rest of the family and legal custodian of their property. As each monastery was an independent entity, each could and did set the standards for its own piety and severity of life. In practical terms, this means that a great deal of variation existed from one monastery to the next. In addition, there was nothing in the rule to prevent women from organizing themselves independently under Benedictine rules nor any presumption that the church was obligated to actively supervise them.

Each of these four lives provides a testimony to the decline of Roman civilization and to the centrality of the monastics in defining patterns of appropriate piety. Anthony was a survivor of the persecutions and lived most of his life intentionally separated from urban centers. Simeon was an extreme ascetic denying himself not only the accouterments of civilization but even the most basic of bodily comforts. Both Anthony and Simeon seemed to demonstrate the presence of the Holy Spirit and provided a vicarious conduit to that mysterious power. Patrick witnessed first-hand the disappearance of the border between civilized and uncivilized. This gave him a personal witness to the themes explored by St. Augustine in his *City of God*. Benedict provides a perfect culminating figure for this epoch. With the rules for civil society having been mooted by violence and civil decline, he and Patrick were in their different ways instrumental in energizing the institutional growth of Christianity. Patrick was an important figure in extending church influence in Ireland and Benedict took it upon himself to write a new set of rules, one that corresponded to a different and presumably transcendent plane of existence. That new set of rules will help shape the history and culture of the Middle Ages.

# Chapter Eight: Popes, Kings, and the Early Middle Ages

*What are the key developments of the Early Middle Ages (500-1000)?*

The Middle Ages represent a long section of European history. If one takes the traditional date that scholars like for the fall of Rome in the west (476) for the beginning of the Middle Ages and the Ottoman capture of Constantinople in 1453 as its end, it is almost exactly one thousand years. Obviously, a lot happens in 1000 years; so how does one represent such a long period in a sensible way? In the next four chapters we will emphasize major themes that highlight important trends and dynamics that stand out, but none are more important than the unfolding drama of popes versus kings. Try to see it as a conflict of two radically different visions for how society ought to work. The first vision is familiar and has existed in the mind of every king or queen who has ever claimed the right to rule: obey the king above all things! In this vision, religion played the same kind of supporting role that it had since Bronze Age Mesopotamia. However, in the Middle ages, a different kind of vision was born in the church. In this vision rulers were supposed to play a supporting role to the church, a radical proposition indeed.

The essential difference between the two visions is suggested by the title of that famous book we noted briefly in Chapter Seven, *The City of God*. Augustine wrote this shortly after barbarians sacked the city of Rome in 410. In those days most people believed, even some Christians, that devoted worship of the gods was necessary to protect the community from calamities of this sort. As we noted already, Augustine set out to prove that this was a fallacy, but he also went further than that. He argued that true religion had nothing to do with politics or material comfort. Instead,

.isted that the point and purpose of religion was to seek with God. Those who followed Augustine in the centuries to .ned that the state existed to protect and facilitate the vision of , and not the other way around. One can easily see that these two visi.... : mutually exclusive; they cannot both be true. The question then becomes: which vision will prevail in the long run? And in this question lies the central dynamic governing Medieval history.

When the Roman empire died its slow death in the west, all the institutions associated with it slipped inexorably into turmoil or disappeared altogether. The church, however, continued to exist although its power to effect events was dramatically reduced. It was simply not designed to manage the practical realities of the everyday world; it needed a functional state as a partner. Meanwhile, warlords and would-be kings came forth one after the other and claimed the right to rule, but the scarcity of resources sufficient to compel obedience made their claims largely bluffs. In addition, there were practical issues in running a state—collections of taxes, public records storage, expertise in law—none of this came naturally to illiterate warlords, however great their ambitions. For these emerging leaders, religion could serve its traditional role, to reinforce their claim to power, but more importantly the church was a logical place to look for practical help in running secular affairs because that was the only place to find literate and numerate talent.

Here we have a temporary symbiosis*: the church looked to political leaders for protection and assistance and new kings looked to the church for legitimacy and practical assistance. However, this can only be a *temporary* symbiosis because the fundamentals of the relationship ignore the principles so powerfully argued by Augustine. No king or queen would ever agree that the church could or should overrule him or her. Neither would any churchman agree that the church exists to serve the interests of the king or queen. At whichever point in the relationship one party or the other feels strong and confident enough to end the relationship, or change its terms,

---

* *Symbiosis*: a relationship in which all parties gain something important.

from that moment the cooperation will change fundamentally. One side must dominate the other; they cannot coexist as equals. This is the central story of the Middle Ages. It was a time when kings learned to fear popes, and popes to fear kings, because the vision of each represented an existential threat to the other. We know how it all turned out of course, but for a long time it was an open question, which vision shall triumph?

The chapter to follow will examine a series of moments illustrating the progress of this competition in its earliest stages. It is by no means a comprehensive list of such moments; there are many dozens along the narrative arc of the Early Middle Ages. One must always remember that the church was a collection of parts and existed, as it exists now, at multiple levels. Every city had *at least* one bishop and there were many hundreds of monasteries, tiny and large, dotting the countryside, each with its own management structure. Each of these parts of the thing we call 'the church' has its own agenda, its own imperatives, its own economy and its own personality. In the early Middle Ages, there were popes to be sure, but the church in its many parts was seldom obedient to them and never consistently. Meanwhile the secular structure had only the appearance of a functional hierarchy. From a distance it looked neat: kings at the top, peasants at the bottom, everybody sitting in a hierarchy of power. But counts, barons, earls, dukes—each and every lord of the land obeyed his king only reluctantly and sometimes not at all. And nobody cared much for the peasants. Any person in leadership, religious or secular, did what he could and obeyed when he had to. There was a lot of space between these options in the Middle Ages.

# Peppin the Short and Pope Stephen II (AD 754)

We draw our attention first to the part of Europe we now call France. The Romans called this area Gaul when they ruled it and it was a very well developed part of the Roman Empire. It should be no surprise that it sustained a viable political culture in the years after Rome fell. In the late 400s a dynasty of men called the Merovingians consolidated control over Roman Gaul and kept it until the mid-700s. The lands under their control came to be called *Francia* and these eventually extended across the Rhine into what is now Germany. The Merovingians were a large family and their history is characterized by a lot of squabbling and conflict between the various branches. Only a few of the family were strong or effective leaders and after a few generations it became clear that the real power was not in the royal family but in the military structure they created, especially the "mayors of the palace" they appointed to supervise the army, and is to these men we turn to get a sense of this moment in the Middle Ages.

The man we want to highlight is Peppin the Short, mayor of the palace from 741-752 but first a few words about his father, Charles the Hammer. The Hammer, previous mayor of the palace, led an army to stop an Arab advance into France in AD 732. This military victory brought great prestige to the Hammer's family, not to mention gratitude from the church that you might well imagine had regarded the Arab expansion with great fear and trepidation. On the other hand, the Hammer used the gratitude of the church to force the church in France to reward his soldiers in the form of leases of church lands at favorable rates. The Hammer's logic was simple: the church should pay for its own survival and commanders have always sought ways to reward their soldiers. The various French churches and monasteries were in no position to refuse. Keep in mind that there is not yet any functional hierarchy in the church, except perhaps at the local level. Local bishops did not fear the supervision of the papacy because the pope could not enforce anything he said. Even if the local church could have invoked the pope's disapproval, the pope had no power over the Hammer.

With this in mind we turn back to Peppin and the year 754. It was thirteen years since the Hammer died and more than twenty since the Hammer turned back the Muslim invasion. In this year Peppin decided he was no longer content with being the mayor of the palace. He wanted to be king. As he ran through his options it seemed like a good idea to seek the approval of the church; he thought to himself, "was it not a natural and traditional function of religion to confer legitimacy to rulers?" Alas, his plan failed when the churchmen he consulted demanded something in return: redress on those land distributions made by Pippen's father. In no way could Peppin renege on that deal, not if he planned to need soldiers ever again. So on to plan B: appeal to the bishop in Rome, the pope. Peppin's timing was good. It turns out that the pope in Rome had much to gain by acceding to Peppin's request. On a practical level, Peppin represented a successful military leader who might be helpful in giving the city of Rome protection from the latest variety of invaders, the Lombards. On a symbolic level, if the pope were to overrule the French bishops, this would demonstrate his claim that they were subject to him. Indeed, Peppin invaded Italy and expanded the lands under church control. The compensation for Peppin was that he was crowned king of the Franks by Pope Stephen in 752 and became the first of his dynasty (the Carolingians) to be called king. It was also the first instance in which a secular leader was crowned king in Europe by a Christian figure.

What is the significance of this moment? One first has to grasp that this was an uncertain and dangerous world for everyone. Rome in the west had long since ceased to exist except in the dreams of would-be kings. Peppin spent most of his life at war with his neighbors, his friends, and a few of his relatives as well. His claim to rule was not clear-cut; he *needed* the church to validate his authority. His use of the church signals a *weakness* on his part, *not a strength*. Why should anyone bend a knee to receive as a gift what one claims to own already? One does this only because one needs to, not because one wants to. From this point on, the church played a role in the coronation of all European rulers. But this is not as great a victory for the church as it seems. The papacy was ready to ignore the Hammer's policy toward the church. Why? Because the church was weak and feared the Lombards. The church needed a protector. The cooperation we see in this moment is a signal of the weakness of *both* parties. The story illustrates how weak are *all* the institutions of Europe in the 700s.

# Charlemagne and Pope Leo III (AD 800)

Our next medieval moment is in the life of Peppin's son Charlemagne (Charles the Great). Charlemagne was a very successful king who used the reorganized army of his father to expand his realm to include all of what is now Germany and France plus bits of all those lands that border these modern countries. Charlemagne surrounded himself with church advisors and took the same sort of leadership role, as did Constantine in fostering unity within the church. I am sure that he imagined himself a great king in the mold of Constantine, and like all great kings he looked to his legacy as a testament to his stature. He financed the collection and reproduction of thousands of ancient manuscripts, he started schools in the churches, he commissioned a unified liturgy for the church, he codified systems of law where none existed and recognized those that did. Like his father, he assumed the role of defender of the church and like all the Merovingian kings he used the church as an extension of his own authority.

In the year 800, Italian nobles unhappy with Pope Leo III's leadership of the church attacked him near Rome. Because of the relationship begun by Peppin, Charlemagne took this as an insult to his own authority and on Leo's request, Charlemagne traveled to Rome to set things right. When he arrived in Rome, he made it clear that an attack on Leo was an attack on himself; the Italian nobles that had been seeking to challenge Leo got the message and backed off. Afterwards, Charlemagne decided to stay in Rome for the winter. Christmas came and Charlemagne received communion from the pope in a special ceremony….only Charlemagne didn't realize how special Leo planned to make the occasion. Leo surprised Charlemagne by giving him a crown and a title of which he had never heard: *Holy Roman Emperor*. In fact. no one had heard of this title and for good reason: Leo had invented it. What did it mean? It added no lands to Charlemagne's kingdom, no tribute to his treasury, nor any soldiers for his army. So it must have been only a symbol. But of what?

Leo crowns Charlemagne

Scholars have wrestled with this question and there is no clear consensus because none of the people involved left us any evidence. We know from Charlemagne's biographer that Charlemagne was displeased and never returned to Rome. We are left to ponder the symbolism. Here is the Pope putting a crown on Charlemagne's head, a crown that corresponds to no physical empire. We are forced to consider that the title is something other than a physical empire; that it corresponds perhaps to a *spiritual empire* of Christians. If this were true, then Charlemagne had been made king of all Christians and he had received this from Leo the pope of Rome. Theoretically Leo, as pope, received his authority directly from God so logically then, the chain of command would flow from God to Leo to Charlemagne, at least as far as Leo was concerned. This was almost certainly why Charlemagne was angry: he had put himself in the position of publicly acknowledging that the Pope's authority exceeded his own.

In practical terms this meant nothing. Charlemagne was still the most powerful man in Europe and Leo was not in a position to demand anything of him. Although there is a power play of sorts taking place here, it is an entirely symbolic one. Nevertheless, an important precedent had been now reinforced. Pope Stephen anointing Peppin was the original precedent. Here Leo took the concept to a higher level, establishing that there was a kind of kingship that exceeded regular kingship and the papacy had the authority to confer it. But it remained for future kings and popes to test and refine the idea. As for Charlemagne, he tossed the crown and title into a drawer for thirteen years, at which point he gave them to his only surviving son, Louis the Pious. Meanwhile, Charlemagne remained the most powerful man in Europe.

# Otto I and Pope John XII: 962

Our third medieval moment took place 162 years later. A lot had happened in the meantime, mostly not good. The grandchildren and great-grandchildren of Charlemagne had carved up his empire and spent their lives squabbling and plotting to murder each other. The serendipitous appearance of Vikings raiding from the north provided mercenary forces and grist for the mill in this war of Carolingian cousins. By the early 900s there were so many Viking longboats tied up in Paris that one could nearly walk from one shore to the other, just by hopping from boat to boat. The resulting anarchy fed upon itself and the Carolingian dynasty collapsed altogether in the late 900s. An emblem of their collective incompetence is captured in a true story involving one of the dynasty's lesser lights, Charles the Simple. In 911 this hapless king handed what later became Normandy over to a Viking chieftain named Rollo. Charles also handed over his daughter Gisela, asking only that Rollo kiss his foot as a symbol of submission. Rollo refused and had one of his own men do it instead, only Charles ended up being flipped onto his rear, much to the embarrassment of himself and his entourage as the Viking warrior lifted the king's foot instead of kneeling to kiss it. Some authorities

"I THINK YOU DROPPED YOUR CROWN!"

KING CHARLES THE SIMPLE GETS NO RESPECT FROM THE VIKINGS IN 911 (BTW, VIKING HELMETS DIDN'T HAVE HORNS)

158

claim that Charles defeated Rollo, but it sure doesn't seem that way. In any case, the days of the Carolingian dynasty were numbered and a new French dynasty (the Capetians) emerged in Paris, scene of much conflict between French and Viking forces.

Meanwhile, across the Rhine river, a new power was developing. When the Carolingian empire collapsed in the early 900s, parts of the Carolingian administrative apparatus remained intact and its leaders were positioned to help create a framework of a new kingdom. The two main halves of the Carolingian empire went in two different directions and in this division one sees the birth of what will become modern France and modern Germany. Otto, duke of Saxony, was the strongest of the dukes on the German side of the Rhine and by force and persuasion he had made himself first among equals. But he could not call himself king, at least not according to German custom. Germany has an interesting history regarding kings. There really weren't any in German tradition. Historically speaking, German regional leaders would acclaim one of their own to facilitate cooperation on the battlefield, but this unified command had no civil component, nor was it hereditary. This ancient custom emphasized the presumption of equality among the chief men among the Germans and now it corresponded nicely to the political reality in Germany in the 900s. There really wasn't any one truly dominant power. Nevertheless, Otto sought some symbolic way that he might gain any advantage over the other dukes. He thought of that title, Holy Roman Emperor, which had been invented a century before, but since fallen into disuse. The more he thought about it the more he liked it. To claim that title would be to claim the authority of the church and the authority of god. Moreover, he could use the title to legitimize his bullying of church leaders in Germany to do what he wanted. And finally, it would make church officials in the territories of the other dukes technically answerable to him as opposed to their respective dukes. Otto was a practical man and when John XII, pope in Rome, contacted him he saw his opportunity.

John XII's lands in central Italy were under attack and he was desperate for help. Ever since the Carolingians had begun feuding with each other, they had neglected their protective relationship with the popes in Rome.

This left the papacy in an extremely vulnerable position. All the noble families in Italy wanted to control the papacy and at least some of those who earned, bought or stole the position in the 800s and 900s were truly scurrilous characters. None knew this better than John himself, a notorious womanizer fated to be killed by the husband of one of his lovers. And so John consented to conferring the empty title in return for Otto's protection of the papal estates. But Otto had other ideas. Otto marched into Italy and received his crown as holy roman emperor and, as promised, he dispensed with the enemies of the pope. However, he then proceeded to rule the pope's Italian possessions as if they were his own. He treated Rome as if it were now the capitol of his empire and John expressed misgivings; Otto fired him and appointed a new pope. It was clear to all that Otto was now the most powerful man in Europe and his control of the church was a big part of that.

What do we take from this medieval moment? We have just passed the lowest level of political stability since t the Roman empire in the west came apart. The Carolingian dynasty had disappeared and was replaced by two new ones one in France and one in Germany. Of the two, only the German dynasty successfully inherited a political connection to the Roman papacy. Because of this, the new center of political gravity moved to Germany. Only it wasn't called Germany then; it was called the Holy Roman Empire because of the title that Otto used. As for the church, its power had sunk to its lowest level since the legalization of Christianity in the Roman Empire. On the other hand, political leaders all over Europe understood how useful the church might be and control of the church became a desirable element in any successful ruling strategy. But, for the moment at least, Otto and his German successors controlled events in Rome. Now having sketched the outline of dynastic and institutional change in the former Carolingian empire, let us now turn back to the topic we opened at the end of the previous chapter and take note of important changes in the shape and role of monasteries in the emerging culture of the Middle Ages.

# The Reform Movement

By virtually any measure, the century that straddled the year 1000 represented a new low in European history. In terms of numbers, the population of Europe had been in decline for centuries. Much land in production in the Roman era had been re-claimed by the forest. Long distance trade slowed to a trickle. Secular leaders were impotent to protect their people from brigands, foreign or domestic. Religious foundations were regular targets for loot and extortion. Peasants were helpless against the ravages of thugs and outlaws. Monks were forced to dig up and hide the bodies of their saints to avoid their kidnap for ransom by Norse raiders. It was anarchy at virtually every level of society. The only institution with any sense of continuity was that collection of things that added up to what we call the church, and the church was mostly powerless to protect itself. For the individual living in those years it must have been easy to interpret all of this as portending the end of the world.

It should be no surprise then that the endemic anarchy stimulated a dramatically renewed interest in the monastic life. Best to prepare for the next life as this one was surely over. But unlike the situation facing the first generations of monks and ascetics, this time there were well-established monasteries already in existence. One did not have to found a monastery from nothing, as Benedict had to do; one could just knock on the door, and sign up. But something else was also different. Whereas the first generation of monasticism embraced a disciplined and simple life separated from the concerns of the world, the intervening centuries had relaxed the discipline of monasticism. Monasticism had become an integral feature of society and no longer a rejection of it. Centuries of noble gifts made many individual monasteries wealthy and this certainly undermined their internal discipline. In addition, families responsible for establishing or gifting monasteries generally felt that the monasteries were a permanent extension of their own family interests and made a habit of interfering in their management. The cumulative effect is that leadership positions of all well-endowed monasteries became patronage positions doled out to favorites of the nobility. The dynamics that had created monasticism in the first place, as exemplified in the lives of Anthony and Simeon and the others we mentioned in the previous chapter were diluted to the point of non-existence. But now a new generation, fired with some of the spiritual enthusiasm typical of the first generations of monasticism, rose up and sought to transform the old monasteries, to return them to their pure roots if possible, and to build new ones if not. This will come to be known as the Reform Movement.

# Cluny (910)

Would-be reformers were convinced that they understood that the essential flaw in the original Benedictine rule lay in the relative independence of any given monastery. Independence from worldly concern was always central to the idea of monasticism but, ironically, it was that very independence that had made them vulnerable to secular influence and, inevitably, to a corruption of monastic discipline. William I, Duke of Aquitaine, also known as William the Pious, was sympathetic to this problem and in 910 he was convinced to become the patron of a new order of monks proposed by Berno, a sixty-year-old monk who had already made a reputation in tightening discipline at a series of monasteries. The catch was that William had to forswear any interference in the order once it was established. William was amenable to this proposition and with his generous support, Cluny, located in the region of Burgundy (SE France), became the first of the great reform orders. To ensure Cluny's independence, William endowed the monastery generously and Berno set forth to create a formal hierarchal organization of monastic houses under the nominal control of the papacy but in actuality supervised personally by Berno and his successors at Cluny. The heads of all associated monasteries met periodically in Cluny and submitted to the authority of Berno who reported only to the pope, at least in theory. But in the 900s the papacy was a very weak institution and so this submission to the authority of the papacy was more a symbol of separation from secular authority than it was an organizational reality. However, when the papacy recovered and began to assert itself in the late 1000s, its authority over Cluny and the other reform foundations played a huge role in papal politics.

Anxious to curry favor with what was obviously an influential organization, other nobles supported these monasteries financially, just as they had always done, but the regional structure of the new system made it much more difficult for individual nobles to coerce or manipulate individual monasteries. The new system worked as intended. Berno's success encouraged many independent monasteries to enter Cluny's system and by the 1000s Cluny had become the richest and most influential of all European institutions. Their growing wealth encouraged the Cluny monks to hire laborers to support them, which allowed individual monks to devote themselves to prayer, at least theoretically. It also meant that Cluny monks were available to work as advisors to secular rulers and by the late 1000s reformer monks had even worked themselves into positions of influence on the papacy. Pope Urban II gave his speech launching the first Crusade at a Cluny cathedral in Clermont (1095) to an audience of Cluny reformers upon whom he relied to spread the word across Europe. Some evidence suggests that Urban was himself a Cluny monk. In any case, Urban endorsed the Cluny rules at Clermont and further decreed that no churchman could ever be subject to a secular lord. Herein are the seeds of a major power shift (more on this in chapter ten).

# Cistercians (1098)

The wealth of Cluny combined with a lack of commitment to manual labor as specified by the Benedictine rule created a problem for some monks, and competing orders sprang up to address this. The most famous of these was the Cistercian order, founded by a group of monks who left Cluny in 1098 to create an alternative. Named for the city where the new order was established (Citeaux), the Cistercians grew quickly and—perhaps ironically—became even more powerful than Cluny within just a few years. The Cistercian order was a synthesis of the traditional Benedictine emphasis on work and the structure of the Cluny reformed system. One significant difference between the Cistercian and Cluny systems was the lack of an overarching leader in the Cistercian system. Rather than submitting to the authority of a single person, as was the case with Cluny, Cistercian houses had independent abbots who met periodically in submission to a written constitution. There was no one all-powerful leader. This structure was less threatening to some secular rulers of Europe who for their part regarded Cluny's more monolithic structure with deep suspicion. The lords of Europe voted with their checkbooks and despite Cistercian dedication to simplicity and manual labor, their order became enormously wealthy. The Cistercians wielded influence in all the kingdoms of Europe, especially from about 1150 to 1200. Its most famous member was Bernard of Clairvaux, who found himself advisor to and mediator on behalf of the French Crown. The second Crusade (1147) was launched in large part by his influence over the King of France, Louie the VII, who needed absolution for having burning down a cathedral full of people in 1144.

# Norbertines (1120)

The Norbertines were another reform order founded in France. Like the Cistercians, the Norbertines sought more discipline than the Clunys but unlike the other reform orders, its members were priests whose public duties were carried out in nearby churches. The Norbertines often had female foundations associated with them. By this time, independent female foundations had largely disappeared and some accommodation had to be made for women wanting to enter religious orders. For their part, entering an order was the only realistic way in which women could assert and retain independence from men. In these dual foundations, the women were nominally subject to the authority of the male abbot, but in practical terms, the women largely ran their own affairs.

These reform orders all had much in common. The movement as a whole was born from the institutional weakness revealed in the chaos and anarchy of the 900s. We can trace in their development the creation of powerful organizational principles capable, potentially, of reorganizing all of society under the authority of a unitary church. The widespread networks of all reform foundations was a ready-made extension of church power and influence and because the three reform orders were present all over Europe, they provided a potential superstructure for a functional federal state. This capability faced no credible secular alternative, at least not yet. The only important question was whether the activist reformers could achieve the critical mass necessary to seize control of the entire church before a credible secular alternative might arise, as it was sure to do sooner or later. That critical mass came together in the middle 1000s.

# Henry IV and Pope Gregory VII: Three Days in the Snow (1077)

We fly forward now to our final medieval moment of this chapter. It was in the 1070s. Germany was still called the Holy Roman Empire. Two more Ottos, three Henrys, and a Conrad had all come and gone, each of whom used the same title, Holy Roman Emperor. Each of these men treated the church in Rome as an extension of their political and imperial authority and took an active role in appointing leaders of the church up and down the hierarchy from bishop to pope. But two new trends worked to undermine the power of this German monarchy, one from outside the church and one within. Outside the church it was always difficult for the emperors to control the other nobles because their power to coerce was limited. Keep in mind that the military potential of each noble in Germany was his own to command and the army of the Emperor was the combined army of all the lords. If the lords chose not to fight, the Emperor had no army, except for what he might cobble together from his own personal retainers and whatever mercenaries he could afford to pay. Meanwhile, inside the church, the vibrant reform movement we have just mentioned was in full sway.

As it turns out, what a beautiful irony! The German emperors, like the Carolingian rulers before them, treated the church as part of its ruling structure and made appointments to various church positions as they saw fit. But the people they were appointing were in many cases the reformers whose reason for existence was their rejection of secular authority. They were in every way adamantly opposed to kings interfering in the church. By appointing these men to positions of authority, emperors gave the church a stick that they could potentially use to beat the emperors. It all came to a head with Pope Gregory VII in 1073. Gregory was elected with strong support from the reformers and the people in Rome but without the input or consent of Henry IV, the Holy Roman Emperor, and this was the first time this had happened in a very long time. Henry was young, only 23, and his political position was very weak in Germany. From the beginning it was clear that Pope Gregory would not take orders from the inexperienced emperor and when Henry made some church appointments in 1075, Gregory reacted by threatening excommunication and deposition from his position as emperor. Henry went ballistic and responded by declaring the pope deposed! Gregory was not bluffing, however, and promptly followed through with his threat; he excommunicated Henry along with all the bishops Henry had ever appointed.

Here we have something new. For the first time, a pope is openly challenging the right of a political ruler to rule his own kingdom. From our standpoint we might sympathize with the Pope as it is hard to imagine that any modern political leader would argue a right to appoint church officials. But in this case, precedent argues the opposite: since the first embrace of Christianity by Constantine, political rulers had been managing and interfering in the structure and administration of the church. Gregory was the one changing the rules. His attempt to push Henry out of church matters represented a significant break with the past and all established precedent. As it turned out, Henry soon realized that he had overplayed his hand. Gregory was quite popular with the people—as were all the reformers—and much of the German nobility regarded Henry's embarrassment with glee and unconcealed ambition. German churchmen were split in their loyalties. Henry was forced to back down.

Henry came to see Gregory at Canossa, a castle in northern Italy, where he stood in the snow outside the gate for three days in penitential clothing, all the while begging for forgiveness. Inside, Gregory debated his alternatives: should he forgive Henry and assume he would be obedient in the future? Should he kick Henry to the curb and use him as an example? But Gregory did not have the nerve to follow through; after three days, Gregory relented and reinstated Henry with certain conditions, all of which Henry would later ignore. But the matter was not settled. Back in Germany, Henry's enemies, led by his brother–in-law Rudolph, took advantage of his weakened position and revolted. The pope, encouraged by this turn of events, switched sides and excommunicated Henry a second time. This turned out to be a huge mistake. Rudolf was not popular in Germany and the pope's apparently capricious change of heart pushed public opinion back toward Henry. When Rudolf died in 1080, the opposition to Henry in Germany melted away. Henry now turned his attention back to Gregory. It was payback time. He declared the pope deposed, appointed another more to his liking, and then proceeded into Italy to enforce the decision. This time, he had no significant opposition from the other nobles in Germany and his position among church officials was much stronger than it had been at any time since he had become emperor.

Several times Henry attacked the city of Rome, but he failed to take the fortified area surrounding the Vatican until 1084, and even then Gregory clung tenaciously to the fortified Castel Sant' Angelo.* He was finally able to escape when Robert (the Weasel) Guiscard, a Norman† warlord operating in southern Italy, approached the Rome to rescue him. Henry withdrew from Rome and monitored events from a distance. Things were tense in the city of Rome. The Roman residents resented the presence of foreigners in the city (the Normans) and when they rioted in protest. Robert the Weasel responded by ordering his men to sack the city. When the job was done, the Normans decamped from the city and took Gregory with them. Still technically pope, Gregory died in exile in Salerno while Henry's newly

---

* *Castel Sant'Angelo:* This formidable castle, located a short distance from the modern St. Peters in Rome, was originally the tomb of the Emperor Hadrian. Various popes as a fortress and prison used it over the Middle Ages.

† *Normans:* Ever since Rollo the Viking took over the part of France now named for them (Normandy), the Norse and Frank warrior culture blend became known as Norman.

appointed anti-pope Clement III* took power in Rome. Unfortunately, the story does not have a neat ending. Henry will be embroiled in more wars to keep his throne and two more popes confirmed the second excommunication against him. Nevertheless, the story does illustrate a turning point and an important axiom of medieval *realpolitik*.† For the first time, the church had acted proactively on the belief that kings were subject to the church. It also highlighted something else: if the church really wanted to play in the game of thrones, it required some form of coercion.

| Early Medieval Timeline | |
| --- | --- |
| Merovingian Dynasty founded by Clovis the Frank | 486 |
| Army typically commanded by advisors called 'Mayors of the Palace' (Major Domo) | 486-752 |
| Charles the Hammer, Major Domo, defeats Moslem incursion into southern France. The Hammer dispenses church lands to reward troops. | 732 |
| Peppin the Short, son of the Hammer, is crowned King of the Franks by the Pope; | 752 |
| Charlemagne: the greatest of the Carolingians | 768-814 |
| Pope Leo invents new title: Holy Roman Emperor | 800 |
| The grandsons and grandnephews of Charlemagne run the kingdom into the ground. | 841-987 |
| Chaos; Vikings and Castellans | 850-1150 |
| Otto revives Holy Roman Empire idea in Germany. | 962 |
| Capetian dynasty begins in Paris. | 987 |
| Reform oriented monastic orders created (Cluny, Cistercians, Norbertines). | 900-1100 |
| Clash of Henry IV and Gregory VII | 1073-84 |

---

* *Antipope*: At this and various other moments in the Middle Ages, two popes existed at the same. The modern church looks back into time and refers to popes it deems to be irregular or unapproved as "anti-popes."

† *Realpolitik*: a German word meaning practical politics as opposed to idealistic politics. It can be a pejorative in that it hints at politics without morals.

# Chapter Nine: Medieval Institutions

*What are the key Institutions of the Middle Ages?*

We have now crossed the year 1000 in European history and so we have entered a political and cultural environment *much* different from the one we saw in the Roman Empire. The Roman political model featured a *fully functional state* in which political leaders did not *pretend* to own the state; the medieval political model featured a *minimally functional state* that the leaders *did pretend* to own. In this new environment, all political power was essentially *personal* in that it was distributed from hand to hand up and down a pyramid of personal relations. The traditional term scholars have used to describe such a model is "feudalism" and this term can be applied generically to any political system that is characterized by such relations. While feudalism as a theoretical construct has a vocabulary, what those words mean in actual practice fluctuates wildly from place to place and from time to time. For this reason, some historians are moving away from using the word altogether. The reality is that political power in the Middle Ages was in a constant state of mediation within and between multiple hierarchies of power: those within the church, within the nobility, within the monasteries, within the cities, and even within the first great universities. To understand the interaction of these overlapping hierarchies is to understand the Middle Ages.

# Feudal Theory and Practice

The feudal model in theory is this: the king owns everything, either by right of conquest or by heredity. He distributes portions of what he owns to his trusted lieutenants in exchange for their loyalty, their availability as general officers in war, and access to their armed entourages. Let us call these leaders "dukes" (from the Latin *duce*, leader). The dukes take portions of what is allotted to them and re-distribute these to the leaders among *their* followers. Let us call those lower level leaders "counts" (from the Latin *compte*, companion). And so on, to the bottom where an individual knight (*miles* is the word they used, from the Latin for soldier) might control a hamlet with a few dozen peasants. Let us call the entire collection of figures between the king and the knights "feudal barons," nobles, or just plain lords. The king, the nobles, and the knights are all supported by the labor of their own local peasants. The purpose of the structure is twofold: first, to maintain a potential army for the king. And perhaps more importantly, to neutralize challenges to the king's authority by distributing just enough power and privileges to the lords to keep them happy. It is always an unstable system. Successful conflict under the king's authority means more plunder and power to distribute downhill. Unsuccessful conflict—or none at all—can result in the opposite. A *strong* king might theoretically rebuild the whole apparatus if he doubted its loyalty. A *weak* king would never be so reckless, as his followers would promptly defenestrate* him (or worse). In practice, all medieval kings existed in the space between these extremes and they spent much of their time managing the dubious loyalties of the hierarchies they nominally commanded. The cares and concerns of the peasantry were irrelevant.

---

* Defenestrate; literally, it is to throw someone or something out of the window (from the Latin *de fenestra*). History records a number of incidents of this nature, the most famous in Prague in 1618. In that incident a confrontation between Catholics and Protestant officials resulted in the Catholics being pitched out of a castle window some 70 feet to the ground below. The Catholics survived, by their own account through the intercession of the Virgin Mary. The Protestant account differs somewhat; according to them, the Catholics survived due to a soft landing in a pile of horse manure. The truth is somewhere in between.

By virtue of their capacity to coerce, ambitious men with swords forced the peasantry to support them, presumably in exchange for security. In fact, violence was most used against peasants. It was a protection racket, pure and simple. Knights, lords, and kings: they all ruled what they could *because* they could. Relations *between* these ambitious and violent men were usually cautious as no one really knew who was more powerful than whom. To some extent it was an elaborate game of bluffs.* Over time, what began informally as a collection of localized protection rackets crystalized into a closed nobility with titles, initiation rituals, and codes of honor. In the world of fantasy fiction and legend, Arthur's "round table" in the castle of Camelot represents that very thing. In Western Europe, the transition to a closed nobility was mostly accomplished before 1200. Even with the codes of honor associated with this new nobility, all so-called nobles routinely engaged in all manner of rapine and abuse of the peasant class upon which the entire social structure depended.

One quickly grasps that political legitimacy is not rooted in law, at least not at first. But once having attained power, all such rulers will proceed to do whatever they to use the law to render the position permanent. Let us take two different kinds of examples to illustrate the point. Shortly after King Philip Augustus of France took the throne of France in 1179 he began a policy of harassing Jews by arrest and seizure of their property. Two years later he evicted them from France and took all their land. Philip's biographer, a monk, records the incident approvingly and in some detail. According to his account, the policy was justified because Jews were kidnaping and murdering children and were desecrating Christian religious items they had taken as loan collateral. Of course, even if the monk believed it were true, the accusations were ridiculous, but such inflammatory accusations against the Jews had already become a common feature of medieval society (more on this in the next chapter), and lack of evidence was never an impediment to justice. The nebulous legal status of the Jews meant that they received this kind of treatment frequently, so frequently in fact that they found themselves back in France twenty years

---

* The model suggested by the character King Arthur in the opening skits of *Monty Python's Holy Grail* works well to illustrate the dynamic.

171

later (in 1198) by which time a special legal status was invented to regularize their exploitation: Jews and their property were now to be officially considered the property of the lord in whose lands they resided, in this case, King Philip Augustus'. This built on the principle established by King Louis the Pious in the 800s, that all legal cases involving Jews would thenceforth be heard by a special official appointed by him. With this legal nicety now in place, the king could dispense with the lives and property of Jews with no legal objections. And other rulers adopted the same legal posture.

In our second example, we leap forward 150 years. The male line of the French Capetian dynasty ended in 1328 when the three sons of Phillip IV failed to produce a male heir. However, there was a *daughter* of Phillip IV, Isabelle, married to King Edward II of England and mother of Edward III. By reckoning this as a direct line, Edward III should have inherited the throne of France through his mother, as she was daughter of the last French king to die with an heir. But the prospect of France falling under the control of the King of England inspired some French nobles to resist the claim, and they supported instead the claim of a *nephew* of Phillip IV— the future King Philip VI. Having been enthroned, Philip VI and his supporters referred for justification to Salic law, a collection of customs dating back to the Carolingian period, to argue that a son could not inherit through his mother. By this convoluted and archaic calculation, Edward's claim was conveniently dismissed. In 1340 the pope confirmed the interpretation. But Edward III insisted on his rights and went go to war over the question, at least nominally (*much* more on this in chapter eleven).

In the first of these examples an arbitrary seizure of private property was initially possible because Jews had few legal rights and the ubiquity of anti-Jewish rhetoric isolated them socially. Nevertheless, the action violated norms of property law and custom and so the king papered over his arbitrary power by resort to convoluted legal precedent. In the second example, the French feudal barons were sufficiently united in their opposition to reject Edward's claim out of hand. But rather than have the incident seem to be an arbitrary use of power—which is what it actually was—the new king claimed precedence in archaic law and the pope, resident at that moment in France, was happy to add his endorsement...more medieval *realpolitik*, I think!

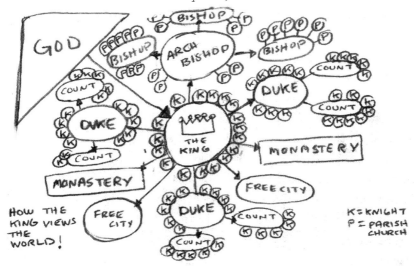

The tortured resort to Salic law and its adornment with papal approval was, like that of King Philip Augustus' ruling concerning the Jews, an *ex post facto* rationalization. Political leaders routinely resorted to these kinds of legal arguments whenever they seemed useful and ignored them when they were inconvenient. In any feudal system, and certainly in Medieval Europe, a tension always existed between naked power on the one hand and legally mandated power on the other. Stronger kings tended to emphasize naked power while weaker kings tended to emphasize the law. All kings exploited the space between these extremes.

## Ecclesiastical Power in Theory and Practice

Organizationally, there are similar dynamics at work in the medieval church. First, one substitutes pope for king, archbishop for duke, bishop for count, and so on, to identify the main outlines of the hierarchy. A second hierarchy, also with the pope at the top, consisted of the major monastic houses each of which reported directly to the pope. After Pope Gregory VII, popes routinely commanded obedience from their subordinates and could theoretically replace them at will. However, as with kings' men, such

HOW THE CHURCH VIEWS THE WORLD!

obedience was not always guaranteed and effective popes were careful to choose their battles. The currency of power was not physical violence; in theory it was the determination and dispensation of God's will on earth. But the rewards of power were more mundane. The various entities of the church held collectively as much or more wealth than did the feudal barons. Churches and monasteries derived direct income from tithes and ritual services, rents from properties, and customary dues, as well as labor from peasants on church lands. Even though the papacy claimed authority over all arms of the church, it had no accounting of local church finances and so there was ample opportunity for abuse of privilege and diversion of church funds.

These obvious invitations for abuse made positions of authority in the church highly desirable and provided opportunities not only for profit but for patronage. Whenever the leadership of a wealthy monastery should fall vacant or likewise the bishop's seat in the cathedral become available, a parade of ambitious and greedy candidates inevitably lobbied whomever might be useful and payments were frequently made, mostly without the knowledge or approval of the church in Rome. Throughout the Middle Ages, and despite the frequent protests, rulings, and edicts of pope after pope, senior church appointments were routinely influenced by kings and their proxies. From a purely practical standpoint, all secular rulers thought of church officials as extensions of their own power, especially in places where the feudal barons' loyalty was in question. The exceptional occasions where secular leaders appointed church leaders who turned out to be more loyal to the pope make for some of the highest drama in the Middle Ages.

The insinuation of secular power into the church was not a one-way street. Kings routinely appointed church officials into positions of secular authority and one frequently sees the unofficial influence of high profile religious figures in the orbits of kings. We note that Thomas Becket, while holder of at least several church positions, was Lord Chancellor of England to King Henry II from 1155 to 1162. In another example, we note that Abbott Suger, the prior of St. Denis from 1122 to 1151, was regent of the kingdom of France while King Louis VII and his wife Eleanor went on Crusade. In addition, for more than ten years during this period he was at the king's side advising him on practical matters. It is thus very clear that the church routinely exercised direct influence at the highest levels of political power.

The two separate hierarchies we have now introduced—secular and ecclesiastic—were bound together by practical necessity. The feudal nobility simply did not have the administrative capacity to intervene effectively in the lives of their subjects. Since the feudal nobility was functionally disinterested in the peasantry so long as the peasants paid their dues, the practical management of the people on the local level was frequently left to the church. And this trust was well placed because the church required the assistance of the nobles to maintain their own positions and privilege. It was not logical for the church to challenge the existence and practices of a structure that protected their own privileges. In fact, the further down the hierarchy of power one looks, the more closely aligned appear the interests of the church and the feudal barons. To the extent that peasants were inclined to complain about their condition, their religious advisors assured them that God had ordained their position. When those complaints reached the level of civil disturbance, church and feudal officials always acted in unison to suppress it. Only in the most rare of instances do we see examples of the church officially championing the interests of the peasants over those of the nobility. It is therefore hardly surprising, as we will see in the next two chapters, that popular discontent would push back against the church as well as the feudal barons. The church's cooperation in maintaining the structure of society was rewarded at every level with a steady stream of gifts from the nobility with which the church festooned the sacred rooms of churches and monasteries and created endowments guaranteeing the independence of canons and monks from the necessity of work.

# Peasants and Serfs

We arrive now at the largest and lowest class of them all, the medieval peasantry. The pejorative connotation of the term peasant—uneducated, uncultured, and unwashed—has its roots in the rhetoric of the period we are now examining. As things stabilized in the 1000s and 1100s, the noble class that had clawed its way to power with violence and extortion now redefined itself as an aristocracy of birth ordained by God. This was very useful as it removed any requirement to consider social inferiors as actually human or even deserving of equal or much consideration. The extent to which peasants were actually uneducated, uncultured, and unwashed was then taken as evidence of a station ordained for them by God rather than its consequence. It is hard for us to look around the side of this rhetoric as the voices of rural farm workers do not survive for us to hear. We can see however, that those who claimed social superiority were usually at least one and sometimes all three of these very same things (uneducated, uncultured, and unwashed); keep in mind that forks were not in use in Europe before the 1600s!

We have a common image of peasants living on or next to noble estates. They were tied in some permanent contractual relationship to the noble. The peasants either rented from the lord or were taxed by him; the difference is mostly semantic. What was due to the lord was usually in the form of work, although it might also be a portion of grain or other produce and eventually it was cash. The peasant was not free to leave the land and in many other ways was constrained. It was common, for example, that lords would control mills for grinding grain, require their dependents to use their mill, and take another portion of the grain as payment. The children of the serf were obliged to follow in the path of their father. We usually use the word "serf" to denote this kind of peasant although during the Middle Ages the word most commonly used was *colonus*. Serf comes from the Latin word (*servus*) meaning both slave and servant, and *colonus,* also from the Latin, means tenant farmer. The conflation of these meanings is a strong indication of the social implications of *having* to work and the deep roots for that implication. The institution of serfdom survived in Austria until 1848 and in Russia until 1861.

While it is true that all lords had peasants as serfs, and indeed monasteries usually did as well, it is not true that all peasants had lords. There was always a freeholder class that existed outside the direct control of nobles and alongside the serfs. In fact, the serf class was originally derived partly from this class of freeholders and partly from slaves settled on the land. What happened was that during times of instability or crop failures, some freeholders voluntarily gave over title to their land and promised to work it indefinitely in exchange for protection or perhaps as payment for a loan. Some excellent studies have identified the period around 1000 as the time when this transition took place. It is interesting to note the inverse relationship of the histories of serfdom and slavery. Slavery never disappeared in the Middle Ages, but its decline was matched by the growth of serfdom, suggesting that one institution had grown to replace the other. As the medieval economy slowly converted from subsistence to a cash economy, the trend was reversed and serfs were eventually replaced with tenant farmers with virtually no rights at all. There were other categories of farmer that combined the features of freeholder and serf. The most common of these were villeins. Villeins held and could pass title to their lands, but were required to pay some sort of feudal dues; most often labor at harvest time. This requirement was tied to the land, rather than the individual, so that a new owner would assume the responsibility as a condition of the land's title. The last category was cottager. Cottagers were similar to serfs except that they had no hereditary rights to the land. The only salient difference between them and tenant farmers is that cottagers paid in labor whereas tenants paid in cash.

# The Medieval City

For many years historians called the period from about 500 to about 1000 the "Dark Ages" and this has a lot do with empty cities. The aristocratic class that had maintained the city infrastructure in the ancient world had reinvented itself as an aristocracy of piety. Now they built monasteries and churches instead of forums and public baths. The city infrastructures fell into ruin. No one maintained the roads. Aqueducts that had been cut off in sieges of cities were not repaired quite simply because no one who could afford to pay for them was interested in doing so. Grain was no longer routinely carried long distance by ship because there was no navy to deter piracy. The collapse of an organized food supply guaranteed that cites could not support large populations. With the disappearance of the urban population so also went the demand for specialized goods and services. The rural economy reverted to subsistence agriculture and specialized skills slowly disappeared. The monasteries managed to preserve some of the accumulated wisdom of the ancients but the process was haphazard and much was lost in the depredations on religious targets that occurred in the chaos and anarchy of the post-Carolingian world (c. 900-1050).

Not all was lost however. The Romans built roads to last and even in disrepair they continued to facilitate some travel and trade. Ancient cities shrank dramatically, but those convenient to ports and river crossings never disappeared entirely. Many communities featured churches or monasteries at least and—as island refuges of literacy and numeracy—these institutions were in a position to perform some limited administrative functions necessary and useful to civil society, e.g., the adjudication of petty disputes and property record storage. There was still some money in circulation and long distance trade never completely disappeared, especially in spices and other luxury items. Even in the worst of times, iron making and stonemasonry remained important skills needed by the warrior class and wealthier churches, as both represented constituencies capable of paying for them. Castles and monasteries often sponsored markets for peasants and craftsmen and so provided focal points for the growth of micro-economies. So there was an outline of a structure around which medieval society could and did develop an urban component. But it did so without the active management, for the most part, of a noble aristocracy, *a key difference between classical and medieval cities.*

## The Rise of Medieval Guilds

Medieval cities existed in the space between the two dominant power structures of the Middle Ages, the feudal nobility and the church. Neither of these had a direct interest in the management of the cities except to the extent that they were a source of potential revenue, so the cities were left largely to their own devices. There was no police force, no fire brigade. Residents of the cities were on their own. If you lived in the city, you made your living by making something or selling something and the only way to protect yourself and your business was to develop modes of cooperation with others having similar interests. The various tradesmen organized themselves and made rules to protect themselves from disaster and from competition. The system evolved, for example, bakers banding together to buy grain in bulk and weavers doing the same with wool. Every occupation was thus organized from within to sustain and protect itself. These informal associations also provided social services; they self-insured for funeral arrangements, they celebrated life's transitions, they became contexts for public discussion. This is the beginning of the medieval guild system. Medieval guilds were also useful for feudal barons or church officials as it provided an authority structure with whom the nobles and clerics might deal in an otherwise unorganized city. Ultimately, it was recognition from these structures that boosted the guilds to the next level of development.

At first glance, medieval guilds look a lot like modern unions because they share a common vocabulary: apprentice, journeymen, and masters are terms representing levels of competence in both contexts. But that similarity is misleading in that modern unions are associations of *workers for hire* whereas medieval guilds were associations of craftsman *employers.*

179

Medieval guilds ordinarily exercised monopolies within the bounds of the specific citiy where they existed. That is, only individual members of the bakers' guild could make bread in a given city. But the price of bread was the same anywhere in the city. Moreover, all bakers paid their unskilled help the same wage. Merchants also formed guilds so that the manufacture of an item (perhaps dyed cloth) might be reserved to one guild, and the sale to yet another. There was no genuine competition between members of a guild, and it is largely for this reason that guilds have mostly disappeared in the modern world, except as atavisms.* They are out of place in a capitalist economy because they discourage competition and inhibit innovation.

Cities did grow, trades and crafts became more specialized, and therefore categories of guild proliferated. Where blacksmiths might make swords, nails *and* barrel hoops in 1200, by 1250 these would be done by three different categories of craftsmen, each of which was anxious to protect its specialized activity from competition. Naturally, conflicts developed and guild members frequently sought official status for their organizations and their rights. It was in the seeking of recognition that we see the guilds come into the surviving records. We have numerous examples where church or feudal officials of various sorts stepped into disputes and adjudicated rights and privileges. Practically speaking, all the most prominent and successful citizens of the cities were in the guilds. Naturally, when there was a wider problem in the city, perhaps the need to repair a city wall, a question of public sanitation, wolf attacks, or other such concerns to the community at large, the leaders of the individual guilds were the default leaders of an otherwise unorganized community and they acted in concert to address these problems.

---

* *Atavism*: a cultural tendency or holdover from the distant past (from the Latin *atavus*, ancestor). The word is also used in biology, as in the human tailbone.

# City Charters

Charters are contracts. Royal authority usually granted City charters, and they granted cities certain rights of taxation, established boundaries of legal jurisdiction, and usually recognized some level of independence from feudal barons as well as providing a framework of civil administration. There comes a point in the growth of every community when these matters must be resolved. A community applying for official status went through some sort of petition to a higher authority, usually the king. Guilds that were recognized either by feudal or church authorities held charters granting the privileges they claimed. City charters served the same function as charters granted to guilds, only on a broader scale. Although city charters did give power to cities, this did not actually lessen the power of the king. Quite the opposite. If a city accepted that a king could give a privilege, it implicitly admits that the king can take it back. For example, in the year 1200, the French King Philip Augustus revoked the charter of the French city of Etampes because it was illegally levying tolls and taxes on the church and local nobility. We also note that where charters were granted to cities, the leading guilds in the city were to some extent recognized in the city charter itself as central to the governance of the city. Here is a key to understanding the medieval European city. In the classical era, the hereditary nobility not only governed but paid for the civic architecture of the cities. But *in the medieval city, guildsmen were the leading figures and, other than the church, were the most significant contributors to physical expressions of community identity.* As the Middle Ages progressed, this class became more stratified and generated separate banker, merchant, and craftsman elites, and these fostered new forms of display resonant with their growing social prominence.

Medieval Institutions 182

# Cathedrals

Cathedrals were the most noticeable buildings in the medieval city.* Starting around 1100 and continuing through the Renaissance, cities across Europe began competing with each other to build the grandest church of them all. Hundreds of examples survive. In England, some notable examples include "Old" St. Paul's (in London) and Lincoln Cathedrals both begun in 1088. St. Paul's was destroyed in the Great Fire of 1666 and later rebuilt on a more modern plan. Lincoln survives and for over 400 years it sported the tallest spire in the world at 525 feet (it blew down in a storm in 1548). York Cathedral was begun in 1175 and retains bragging rights for having the largest collection of medieval stained glass in the world. It is also one of the largest churches in northern Europe. Salisbury Cathedral, built rapidly between 1200 and 1258, sports the tallest medieval spires in the UK at 400 feet, the oldest working clock in the world, and a rare original copy of the Magna Carta.

In France, there is of course Notre Dame of Paris, begun in 1163. It was the first cathedral to use flying buttresses. These were designed to prevent exterior walls from bulging outwards, an unfortunate consequence of design trends in France, which tended to emphasize higher interior ceilings. Amiens Cathedral, built 1220-1270, is the tallest *completed* cathedral in France with a nave ceiling of 139 feet and the largest interior volume of any medieval cathedral. Beauvais Cathedral's vault is even higher at 157 feet, but construction on the building stopped several times after the roof kept falling in, and it was never completed. Beauvais was begun in 1225 and construction finally halted in 1573.

Cologne Cathedral in Germany was begun in 1248 and finally finished in 1880. A medieval crane put on the roof in the 1400s was still in place when

---

* The term cathedral is a Latin borrow-word from the Greek *cathedra* meaning seat, as in the seat of the bishop. Although the church where the bishop presides may be an impressive church, not all impressive churches have bishops and so these do not technically qualify for cathedral status. In Italy, the term *duomo* (from the Latin *domo*, house) is also used but, technically, the *duomo* is the principal church in any given city, whether or not it has a bishop.

the work resumed in 1842, after a nearly 400 year halt in the work. It is the largest church in Northern Europe; it has the tallest spires (after Salisbury) and sports the largest front of any church in the world. In Italy, examples abound. The largest cathedral in Italy (setting aside St. Peter's in the Vatican) is the Milan cathedral. Construction began in 1386 and after 600 years of interruptions was finally completed in 1965. The oldest cathedral in the world is St. John of the Lateran in Rome. This building was the papal seat until the 1300s and was rebuilt numerous times due to fires and earthquake. In Florence, the Santa Maria del Fiore, begun in 1296, has the largest brick dome ever built. Cathedrals in Burgos, Toledo, and Léon are contemporary examples in Spain.

The main elements of cathedral construction were usually undertaken through church fund-raising efforts like the sale of indulgences and display of relics. Naturally, they provided long term sources of employment and in many ways helped to stimulate the local economy. Forests of lumber had to be cut for the scaffolding and mountains of stone had to be quarried and shaped. But there was more to the cathedral than just the shell. The doors, the windows, the carvings, the chapels along the sides: these were all decorative elements paid for by secular patrons, either local feudal lords or the guilds. We see for example that at Chartres the nave windows in the cathedral were purchased by individual city guilds. The construction of any cathedral normally took generations and decorative elements continued to be added right up through the modern period. A walk through a cathedral today is a walk through the history of a city from the cathedral's initial construction through the present.

# Guild Halls

Probably the second most important category of community building in the medieval city was the guildhalls. Its primary functions were as official meeting places and markets and every city with a charter had at least one. Always centrally located, they provided focal points for political, economic, and frequently judicial activities. Their obvious political importance made many continental European guildhalls targets of destruction in wars, but a few do survive, especially in the UK. The center of Brussels features Palace Square, where a number of rebuilt guildhalls dominate the view (they were originally destroyed by Louis the XIV's cannons in 1695). About thirty have survived in England, including the London Guildhall that has housed the London city government since the 1400s. In Windsor, England, just outside the entrance to Windsor castle, a guildhall there now houses a museum. Prince Charles married Camilla there. The original building dates to the 1300s at least. From 1400 to 1970 the building was used for municipal meetings and trials.

# Medieval Universities

One of the most important developments of the Middle Ages was the growth of universities. The oldest universities are associated with the cathedral schools of the Carolingian period but by the medieval period universities were self-governing. In this sense they had much in common with medieval guilds. The early stages of their genesis is obscure in that they only come into the records as the limits of their power and privileges are recognized by outside authorities which were, as with city charters, either secular or ecclesiastic. When this took place, mostly in the 1200s, universities became, in essence, corporations of scholars and students independent of the church. Their appearance was a predictable response to the requirements of developing royal and ecclesiastical bureaucracies. Over the long run, the universities churned out an important new non-noble and non-clerical class of scribes and clerks whose expertise and knowledge positioned them to challenge local power structures. In some cases, kings and popes used them as intentional counterweights to local monopolies on law and religious practice. The most important rights guaranteed to the universities was the privilege of their graduates to teach anywhere (*ius ubique docendi*). In practical terms, this grant represented an intrusion of royal power on a local level.

The growth of the university coincided with the rediscovery of important texts from antiquity in areas of law, science, and philosophy; for this reason they became important centers for their study. Course organization was usually centered on specific texts as opposed to subject matters, as it is now. The oldest surviving university, established in Bologna, Italy (1088), most likely came together in direct response to the rediscovery of the most important ancient Roman legal text, the Digest of Justinian. It is certainly true that the most important subject in the curriculum at Bologna was civil law. At first, universities had no physical infrastructures; these only developed over time. Their governing apparatus also differed from one city to the next. A common concern and a predictable influence on their organization was the problem of citizenship. Since citizenship was not a portable commodity in the Middle ages, students from outside the city were theoretically a kind of foreigner stuck in a sort of legal limbo and therefore subject to abuse as a non-citizen. But there is power in numbers; as a consequence, students associated with the larger universities found themselves able to negotiate a status commensurate with their growing economic importance. Although both students and their teachers formed unions of a sort, students in Italian settings ended up with much more power than did the teachers because Italian *teachers were usually paid directly by the students.*

In England, the universities were controlled and teachers paid by the king, although many students were housed by monastic orders. Oxford was in existence by 1096 and Cambridge by 1209. The real impetus for Oxford's initial growth was that in 1167 foreign students were expelled from Paris and the large number English students studying there needed somewhere to go. At the university of Paris (c. 1170), teachers were paid by the church, so the curriculum favored religion. In 1200, the French King Philip II put the student body under the direct protection of the church. Students shaved their heads, signifying their connection to the church, and on this basis they received a legal immunity from city jurisdiction. In Spain, the oldest institution is the University of Salamanca (1130). The University of Padua (1222) rounds out the list of the early universities and like its Italian counterpart in Bologna, was especially notable for the study of law.

Over time, medieval cites represented important players in the political gamesmanship of the Middle Ages. Ordinarily, kings granted city charters and so kings were inclined to see cities as political allies useful to offset the influence of local nobles and church elites. Favors granted by kings—for example, immunities from some taxes and the right to collect others—were used as enticements to guarantee a partnership against those other centers of power. From the cities' point of view, partnership with the king was useful for exactly the same reason. Eventually, as the medieval economy gained more momentum, the wealth of the cites provided the indispensable capital necessary for kings to create and maintain military forces with which they might dominate their nobles. Over the long run, the cash position of urban elites made them more politically important than the landed aristocracy. This was ultimately the most critical factor in the French Revolution. But that is a topic for a different book.

# Chapter Ten: The Rise and Fall of Christendom (1000-1300)

*How close did the church come to ruling Europe in the Middle Ages?*

One of the most important things to note about the unfolding of the Middle Ages in Europe was the very real possibility of the church actually becoming a state. In many respects it actively played this role. It intervened in dynastic disputes, it operated judicial inquiries, and it sanctioned capital punishment. It shaped civil law with respect to personal behavior, it sanctioned hostile military activity, and it collected taxes in virtually every political jurisdiction in Europe. From 1000 at least and well into the 1300s, virtually all European social relations and secular politics were conditioned by this dynamic. We will call that putative state *Christendom*. A caution is required: *there is not, nor has there ever been, a state actually called Christendom. It is only an idea* belonging to a time in European history when the papacy acted as though it were a state and believed itself to be responsible for the supervision of every living Christian. In this chapter, we will trace the rise and fall of that idea.

In previous chapters we described the evolution of Christianity from a strictly social phenomenon into an increasingly political one. When Christianity was technically an underground and illegal religion, its leaders were perfectly content arguing endlessly over the meanings of arcane texts and their religious implications. Not long after the church became legal it became clear that the church had a new role to play as far as it was concerned, but an old one as far as the state was concerned. It was expected to lend divine sanction to the Roman state. Divisions within the church naturally undermined its ability to confer legitimacy. It was therefore incumbent on political leaders like Constantine to encourage Christian leaders to resolve their disputes. This had always been a central concern of church leaders but the political imperative lent the disputes much more urgency. But there is nothing inherent in Christianity that presupposes a single canon of dogma. Quite the contrary: the proof lies in the tendency of Christianity to fracture and splinter in every context in which it has ever existed, except where the political environment tended to enforce one thread of Christianity over all others. Since leaders from Constantine to Charlemagne wished to use Christianity as a unifying force, they helped to create a church hierarchy that not only presumed the existence of a consistent canon of religious truths but also was motivated to defend it. Since uniformity of belief is not an organic development of Christianity nor was it a predictable outcome, it was only possible as a consequence of a partnership with the state. This partnership resulted in a hierarchal structure for the church with a presumed authority emanating from the top. This is step one in understanding the origins of Christendom.

Step two is the absence of a credible alternative state structure. With the possible exception of the period of Charlemagne's rule we see an unmistakable decline in the reach of secular power since the Roman Empire fell in the west. We are all familiar with the expression, "nature abhors a vacuum." And so in the existence of a political vacuum, we expect that *something* will rush in to fill it: some new political reality. We already saw this illustrated, for example, in the example of Otto of Germany and even more dramatically in the episodic confrontation between Henry IV and Gregory VII. The eventual outcome of that conflict was determined primarily by Henry's ability to mobilize an army but his success was complicated by Gregory's military support from Robert the Weasel. The implication is clear: if the church could succeed in wielding an effective means of coercion, it would have a realistic chance of being a state. The Peaces and Truces of God represent the first wobbly steps in that direction.

# Peaces and Truces of God (c. 1000-c. 1100)

Previously, we saw that the Carolingian dynasty lost its credibility when it was unable to defend its cities and monasteries from plundering Norsemen. But it wasn't just the Norsemen. The period from 900 to about 1100 featured a free-for-all among opportunistic warlords, holdover Carolingian officials and freebooting pirates. Vikings came in boats; local bullies came on horseback (we call these bullies "castellans," for the little castles they built). Life was brutal and for those at the bottom the only safety lay in submission to whomever seemed capable of providing protection. This was the key dynamic behind the creation of the medieval serf class. The pattern was this: a freeholder signed over his or her land to a warlord or a church official in exchange for protection and the guarantee of hereditary rights to residence on that same land. In essence, this was devolution of the state down to its largest remaining functional remnants. One easily imagines networks of villages near churches, monasteries, and castles separated by stretches of forest and undeveloped land. The forests and hills were the territory of outcasts and outlaws. Those least able to defend themselves were obviously most vulnerable. This meant that, practically speaking, lands or properties under church control were more vulnerable than those under some warlord's control if only because the church's power to enforce its protection was limited.

With this in mind we take note of a curious phenomenon, the co-called Peaces and Truces of God. These were a series of edicts issued by various local church authorities, usually bishops, in the 1000s, demanding an end to the widespread violence. These edicts were put forth with the cooperation of feudal lords in the context of large open-air meetings of peasants and were a direct response to the violence and anarchy of the period. Since the church was the motivating force behind these efforts, crimes against persons or property were punishable by penance and excommunication. We can hardly expect such punishments to be effective, and they were not. What was notable about the Peaces and Truces of God is that the church is for the first time using its influence to define and punish crimes in the community; it is *attempting to provide for justice*. You will recall that in chapter two we noted that justice is always an essential responsibility of any state. In chapter seven, I intimated that the fall of Rome featured an abrogation of that responsibility. In chapter eight and here again, we note that the collapse of Carolingian authority erased any expectation of justice. Now the church was reaching out to fill that goal and, in this sense at least, *acting as if it were a state.*

The Peaces and Truces movement, as we have already noted, was an abject failure. We have no reason to think that the Peaces and Truces had *any* effect on the violence. Nevertheless, the expression reappeared frequently in church rhetoric at every level of the church for the next 200 years. Its importance was not therefore in how well it worked but what it came to signify as an idea in the minds of church leaders. In the first instance, it signaled the widespread dissemination of the idea of a church with obligations akin to those of a state. Moreover, it implicated a widespread dissatisfaction with the normal apparatus of justice. We should not see this as a conscious decision to create Christendom. Instead we should see this as a step toward *the idea* of Christendom. The church was here saying to all of society, "Stop the violence or we will punish you!" Many were thankful for the effort, and had no particular reason to understand that they were crossing an important threshold.

# The First Crusade[*]

We recall Pope Gregory VII from chapter eight. His radical stance against the emperor Henry IV flowed out of the very shift we are now observing. In that story we saw the Pope resisting the coercive authority of the emperor and making an awkward attempt to assert his own authority. We note here that Gregory also favored the idea of crusade—holy war—against Moslem authorities in the holy land *and* he also called for crusade against Henry IV for appointing an anti-pope. Neither of these crusades actually took place but the idea of war on behalf of the church was a logical extension of his aggressive posture with Henry. Theologically speaking,

---

[*] A note about the crusade numbering system: first, there are many more crusades than numbers. French historians writing in the 1700s featured certain crusades as being more important than others; these received official numbers (the First, the Second, etc.) the others did not. The conventions they adopted mostly stuck. For what it is worth, the numbered crusades were all directed at Jerusalem or Egypt whereas some of the others were not.

however, it was a huge leap from standard Christian doctrine. 700 years earlier, St. Augustine had argued in favor the concept of just war but with an important distinction. In considering the dilemma of Roman soldiers who were Christians, Augustine had argued that a Christian could, in good conscience, take up arms in a war called by a legitimate political authority because a function of legitimate political authority was to defend against wickedness. Here, Gregory is going far beyond Augustine by equating legitimate political authority with the church. This theological leap is what made Christendom a truly viable idea.

Only twenty years after Gregory, another Pope took up the idea of Christian holy war, Pope Urban II (1088-1099). But this pope actually set a crusade in motion. Urban was a reformer figure whose early career was helped along by Gregory. But unlike Gregory, Urban was less inclined to direct confrontation with his secular counterparts. That said, Urban was much more effective in moving practically toward the realization of Christendom. On an organizational level, Urban moved to create an advisory structure of cardinals to help him rule. He appointed Roger I of Sicily, the son of Robert the Weasel, as a sort of papal lieutenant with both religious and civil powers. He granted Roger the right to act in the pope's name, even to appointing bishops, the very thing Gregory VII had tried to curb only a few decades earlier. This seems contradictory but Urban needed Roger to expand church influence in formerly Muslim Sicily as well as Byzantine-claimed southern Italy and he regarded Roger as a trusted vassal. These extraordinary grants of authority will become an issue later on when, as one rightly expects, Roger's descendants used them to their own advantage rather than that of the pope.

Urban's most significant contribution to the idea of Christendom was his launching of the First Crusade. That story began in 1095 when Urban was presiding over the first major council of his papacy in Piacenza, Italy. It was a well-attended meeting with thousands on hand including over 200 Bishops. Taking up the work of his mentor Gregory, Urban's main priority at the council was to denounce Emperor Henry IV of Germany and reassert papal authority over all church appointments. While there, he entertained ambassadors from King Philip I of France who came to protest what he regarded as an illegal act: Urban's excommunication of the French king for an illegal divorce and re-marriage. Also in attendance were ambassadors from Constantinople carrying with them an appeal from the eastern Emperor Alexius for assistance in his campaign against Turkish Muslims.

For Urban, this presented a chance to push the boundaries of church power in the direction promised by Gregory VII, his beloved patron. Ever since Gregory VII instability and conflict in the Muslim world had made travel increasingly hazardous for pilgrims en-route to Jerusalem and anecdotes concerning death and privation had become common. We know that Gregory had already established the principle that physical protection of pilgrims constituted a legitimate form of penance. Urban combined these separate elements, the plight of the pilgrims, the request from Alexius, and the political instability in the east and crafted a bold idea: why not send an army of pilgrims to recover Jerusalem from the hated infidels, an army of God, presumably under his command?

Urban crafted an appeal to the knights of Europe, that they become soldiers for Christ in a form of penance for their evil ways. His pitch, directed at the knights and warlords of France, was simple: stop all the fighting amongst yourselves, sew a red cross onto your tunic and come to the aid of your Christian brethren in Constantinople, rescue the abused pilgrims, and liberate Jerusalem from the infidels. In reward, Crusaders would receive absolution from all sins and, as a bonus, get to keep all the loot they could seize along the way. In March of 1095, Pope Urban left Piacenza for what turned out to be a sixteen-month speaking tour of most of the important cities and religious centers of France. Four months into this tour, Urban presented a key speech in Clermont, France, where for the first time, the idea of holy war was heralded to the public. What happened next was not anticipated by anyone, least of all Pope Urban II.

Urban surely imagined that an army of knights, blessed by him, would proceed to the east to complete his assignment, the rescue of Jerusalem. But before a legitimate army could be assembled, rabbles of peasants and soldiers began to coalesce along the roads headed east. Unraveling all the threads of evidence is really complicated, but it appears that these were mostly spontaneous, and in some cases we have no idea as to the leadership or origins of groups that fade in and out of our sources. Traveling in separate contingents, these unorganized groups came together in larger groups as they headed east until they became a virtual plague of locusts moving across Europe. Unprepared for the ardor of such a long expedition, this often-called "Peoples Crusade" looted food storage facilities and helped themselves to crops in the fields along the way. And why not? They were on a mission from God! This naturally meant confrontations with local authorities, the most dramatic of which led to the burning of the city of Belgrade. But the most disturbing element of this moving mass mayhem was what happened to the Jews along the way.

Like all effective rhetoric for war, Urban's speech dehumanized the enemy, in this case the Muslims. But the average European peasant wouldn't recognize a Muslim if one whacked him over the head with a Quran. On the other hand, everyone knew the Jews. They were denounced regularly in Catholic liturgy as the killers of Christ and they were buried in separate cemeteries. The question of blame has much to do with the ordinary rhetoric and custom of a church that habitually painted Jews as suffering an eternal penance for the death of Jesus. The legal proscriptions that had flowed from lawmakers since the time of Theodosius I (see chapter six) reinforced their status as outsiders wherever they lived. Physically set apart in ghettos, Jews were legally circumscribed in other ways as well. The rules varied from place to place but it was generally true that Jews were restricted from certain professions, in owning property, and in access to the legal system. But they were not entirely separate in their existence. For reasons rooted in biblical ambivalence about usury, Jews were encouraged to provide a service that Christians were discouraged from providing, money-lending. The predictable result was an enduring association of Jews with money lending; an association that was further reinforced by the very real likelihood that the only Jew with whom most people came into contact was a moneylender. Jews existed on the margins of European culture while at the same time holding a prominent spot in the Christian imagination as enemies of Christians. Especially in the early stages of this first crusade and to varying extents in all subsequent crusades, mobs chased Jews down, extorted money from them, demanded their conversion, and murdered many hundreds who refused. The areas hardest hit by these attacks were in the west of France and the east of Germany.

To the church's credit, many church officials made individual and local attempts to stem the violence and protect Jews who sought their protection but they were wholly unprepared for the task. It is important to note that violence against the Jews was never a considered policy of the church as a whole and that the city of Rome provided a safe haven for Jews during various periods of the Middle Ages; to this day a significant Jewish population exists in Rome. But this must be set against the virulent anti-Jewish rhetoric used by individual church leaders and the anti-Jewish rhetoric found in pre-Vatican II Catholic liturgy. With all of this, there should be little surprise that some of the holy fury unleashed by Urban's speech should fall on the Jews.

The first ragged contingents of would-be crusaders made it to Constantinople by August of 1096. A month or so later, they finally made it into territory actually held by Muslims. When it became apparent that this sorry lot of crusaders was poorly led and insufficiently armed, they were unceremoniously slaughtered. They had traveled barely 100 miles from Constantinople. Meanwhile, the army Urban had actually imagined in his speech began arriving in Constantinople during that winter and were all assembled by May of 1097. Emperor Alexius tried in vain to have these bona fide Crusaders accept his authority but that was never in their plan. Not that there was much of a plan. Although the assembled knights presented a credible military threat, there was no clear leadership and the organization of the expedition was haphazard at best. This led to all sorts of problems. Alexius promised to support the crusaders logistically at various points along their way but confusion and distrust wrecked the arrangements and the crusaders were left largely on their own. The march through Muslim territory became a debacle. A hostile countryside and haphazard arrangements for re-supply meant that the crusaders had to eat many of their horses and there are reliable reports of crusaders barbequing Muslim peasants along the way. Imagine how that played in the minds of the locals.

It was a further two years before the crusaders actually arrived at Jerusalem. The city fell to them in July of 1099 after a five-week siege and a bloodbath of epic proportion. As a side note, Pope Urban died a week or so later, unaware of the success of the venture. Despite epic mismanagement and colossal miscalculation the crusade was technically a success. Jerusalem was—for the first time since the Romans ruled—a Christian city. A kingdom of Jerusalem was declared to exist under the authority of the church but in reality this was only ever a nominal authority. Other crusader states were established in Antioch and Edessa and a number of other venues, each under the nominal authority of the pope but in effect each was an independent political entity. In no way was the papacy prepared or equipped to supervise the various crusader leaders who came and went over the next 200 years and no coherent policy was ever devised to rule the crusader states. Complicating the situation even more, many of the crusaders who were present to take the city returned home, as their pledges were fulfilled and they had never intended to stay. This left only a skeleton garrison to maintain control. It was only a matter of time before the whole thing fell apart…it took 88 years.

Does the crusade phenomenon mean that the church actually had an army? Not exactly; but it *does* mean that a major foreign war had been instigated on its authority and at its behest. It also means that the church was actively involved in the political ambitions of society's most powerful class. Finally, it means that the church had positioned itself to become a political superpower and a genuine rival to the kings of Europe.

# The Knights Templar

The Knights Templar are familiar to fans of costume drama, video games, and conspiracy theorists of various stripes. Their shadowy history has also been absorbed into the founding mythology of the modern Freemasons. They existed as a monastic order sanctioned by the church from 1129 until 1307 during which period they grew to be the most powerful and wealthy of a handful of monastic fighting orders. The most famous function of the Knights Templar was of course to be a fighting force and all who faced them feared them. But the Templars were more than just a fighting force. They existed to facilitate civilian pilgrimage to Jerusalem and in that capacity they provided financial services that were truly revolutionary, at least for Europeans. By 1150, the Templars were issuing letters of credit to pilgrims leaving Europe that could be redeemed at various places along the journey.* It was not only pilgrims that took advantage of this and so the Templars played an important role in facilitating long distance trade. But here we are emphasizing the importance of the Templars as evidence of the church as a genuine state power.

Thanks to active promotion by St. Bernard of Clairvaux, the dominant reform order of the 1100s, the Templars became a favorite charity for nobles seeking favor with the church and they became enormously wealthy as a result; this wealth eventually became a factor in their downfall, of which we will talk in the second half of this chapter. For our purposes here, the biggest moment in Templar history was in a series of papal pronouncements from 1139 to 1145 that elevated the Templars above all authority except that of the papacy. In 1139, Pope Innocent II issued an edict granting the Templars exemption from taxes of any kind. In 1144 Pope Celestine II granted the Templars extraordinary rights to enforce and collect their own taxes and in 1145 Pope Eugene III granted them the right of free movement across any political border in Europe along with total independence from any church authority except the pope. For all intents and purposes, the church actually had an independent power of coercion. This is an essential element of any state.

---

* The Arabs in the 900s and the Chinese in the 1000s were already issuing paper bills of exchange and letters of credit.

# God Wills It!

To get a handle on how people thought in the Middle Ages, one starts and finishes with this slogan: "God Wills It!"* The expression itself was probably invented in the 1100s in conjunction with various recruiting campaigns for the crusades but the philosophy underlying it provides a convenient contrast with intellectual currents both before and after the Middle Ages. When we look to the Greeks and Romans of antiquity—especially the Greeks—one of the things we admire is their interest in science and logic. It is easy to get carried away by this. It is true indeed that as the ancient world unraveled, the cities emptied and the rich, who had always been patrons of art and science, now gave their wealth to the church instead of to starving astronomers. Many learned tomes were carted off as booty to the Arab world and many others ended up in the libraries of monasteries. Many thousands more volumes disappeared when monastic bookshelves went up in flames as a consequence of Norse attacks in the 1000s and the religious fervor of Calvinists in the 1500s. We rightly bemoan the loss of this material and note correctly that elite patronage of non-religious scholarship in the Middle Ages was exceptional at best. But at the popular level, this loss meant far less. We are tempted to assume that all the lost knowledge, e.g., the advances of Euclid in mathematics, Aristarchus' in astronomy, and numerous other examples of sophisticated thinking, represented a general emphasis on science in ancient society. But at the level of society where most people lived, the bottom, little really changed. Most people have always been ignorant. *The real difference lay in the relationship of the leaders of society with science and reason.*

In classical antiquity, to be noble implied at least some acquaintance with science and philosophy because those frames of reference provided a vocabulary and an idiom that separated those who led from those who worked. When the ruins of antiquity were passed along to the Middle Ages, those frames of reference no longer mattered. The secular nobility was not lettered and the ecclesiastical nobility had its own idiom; neither had any

---

* In Latin: *Deus lo Volt!*

The Rise and Fall of Christendom  199

real use for science and therefore no impulse existed to subsidize it. Ninety percent of the accumulated wisdom of the classical world disappeared, much from destruction and probably more from neglect. But none of that mattered because the sacred texts, ordained by God, their truths stipulated by faith, were taken as the basis for all necessary understanding. Where the text was silent, no more need be understood than everything was... *God's will.* For those at the bottom, complementary impulses acted to underline those assumptions. What was new was always something to be feared. The complete absence of social safety nets guaranteed short and brutal lives whose ends might bring welcome relief. The combination of those two things—societal antipathy to change and a deep-seated fatalism about the real world—discouraged any resistance to the comforting notion that society was the way it was *because God wills it.*

## The Big Picture: European Institutions Evolve

The fight between the German emperor Henry IV and Pope Gregory VII had laid bare a fundamental conflict between two completely different visions of how society should work. But it was not just a matter of whether kings should kneel to popes, or popes should kneel to kings. The reformers who had risen within the church were vigorous proponents of their authority to order the spiritual lives of *all* Europeans, not just its leaders. This idea represents a much more intrusive, aggressive, and top down version of Christianity than had ever existed. It should not be surprising that the genre of hagiography evolved to conform with this shift. From the time of Anthony of the Desert through the 900s, hagiographical narratives tended to feature imitations of the life of Christ; afterwards, hagiographical narratives in the 1000s and 1100s were less about praise for exemplary behavior and more about moralizing and finger wagging. Those who damaged or challenged the interests of the church were overcome by the superpowers of saints or their relics and those who were generous to the church found themselves eulogized as saintly heroes. By the late 1200s, many narratives looked like official investigations into saintly credentials.* This clearly signals the church's intention to arbitrate the process of legitimizing definitions of piety.

After 1100 the papacy embarked on a vigorous program of reforms meant to further enshrine the independence and authority of the church. In 1122 and 1123 popes called the First and Second Lateran Councils. Hundreds of bishops and abbots assembled in Rome under the leadership of the popes. Many of the resulting provisions were concerned to consolidate papal policies in their fight to remove church appointments from the discretion of secular rulers, but they also attempted to impose more discipline on religious figures within the church. Both categories of reform were intended to enhance the power and relevance of the papacy. And the trend in this direction meant not only increased influence but also increased wealth. As we noted above, the increased wealth of the church was becoming more visible in the architecture of the church, especially after 1200, as we witness the race of cathedral spires into the skies of Medieval Europe.

The money to fund projects like cathedrals was available because of the economic boom of the thirteenth century (1200-1300). The climate was in a warm cycle so that crop yields were generally strong. The crusades stimulated the economy by forcing nobles to borrow against their landed assets in order to spend vast sums to finance their expeditions. As something on the order of eighty or ninety percent of all those who left on crusade never returned, this also provided an outlet for the endemic violence that had plagued Europe since the collapse of the Carolingian world. Long-distance trade was very healthy, due in part to the stabilizing influence of the Mongol empire to the East. With trade comes travel and the roads of Europe increasingly swarmed with traders and pilgrims. Population growth was strong and cities swelled as a consequence. An increasingly powerful merchant class arose to challenge for political leadership in the cities. This new class along with the already established

---

* *Processus canonizationis*: the official record of an investigation into qualifications of sainthood.

craft guilds helped finance and decorate cathedrals in a grand competition of civic display.

Not everyone benefitted by this prosperity or these changes. And the more obvious and ostentatious the expressions of wealth, the more obvious became the economic chains holding the peasantry and menial laborers in place. In the countryside most people still lived a subsistence life and many remained bound to the service of feudal barons. In an accelerating economy oriented more and more to cash transactions, those unable to escape the subsistence economy found themselves at a major disadvantage. This was not just a problem for peasants. It was common in the cities for domestics to be loaned shoes and clothing as a substantial part of their compensation.* It was not only a uniform signifying dependence on a particular family, but it was also a uniform signifying class. The accelerating economy thus produced an inevitable and very visible stratification of wealth, which, in turn, engendered ambivalence among lower classes concerning money and commerce. As it turns out, this had an interesting effect on patterns of popular piety and monasticism, both of which began to feature a rejection of wealth and material display. Some of this antipathy was turned against the church. Why should this be?

First, one must appreciate the communal threads tying together common society in the Middle Ages. As we discussed briefly in chapter two, all persons manage multiple levels of identity. For a Christian medieval peasant, we might say that his or her operative identities were: family member, village member, member of a Christian fellowship, dependent of the local baron, and finally, subject of the king. The relationship of a peasant to a baron was obviously not a relationship of equals and less so would be his relationship to the king. But all the other levels of identity tend to emphasize communal ties within a group of ostensible equals. A craftsman in the city would manage a similar set of identities: family member, *guild* member, member of a Christian fellowship, *member of a city commune*, and finally, subject of the king. The differences are not substantial, but they do matter. Craftsmen of like occupation came together in guilds

---

* The term "livery" comes from this. To be 'in livery,' is to be a dependent. It comes from the French *livrée*, something handed over.

and managed their affairs in common. They set prices, cooperated in the purchase of commodities, and set work rules to which all members were expected to adhere. It was a communal enterprise.

The city itself was also a communal enterprise in that many cities operated under a charter granted by a noble, perhaps but not necessarily the king. Some sort of governing council was usually recognized in these charters and most often the importance of the guilds and merchants was reflected in the allotment of political power. The result was in fact a limited version of representative government. As far as the king was concerned, the city was an entity very much like a lesser noble. A king could choose to grant special privileges, or to revoke them, as seemed convenient to his own goals. What happened *inside* the cities was of no more importance to him than was the welfare of the peasants on the lands of his other lesser nobles. The result was that cities were evolving into virtual islands of communal power in a sea of feudal relations.

Located prominently on these islands were the soaring symbols of church authority. As grand as were the mighty cathedrals and abbeys reaching for the sky across Europe, they were also obvious manifestations of wealth in a period of rapid economic growth and stratification. The acceleration of the cash economy was leaving many ordinary people behind, all of whom feared the bewildering changes they were forced to endure; all they understood was that it was all somehow related to money. As the church seemed to have a lot of that, it should be no surprise that it became the focal point of considerable social resentment at street level.

## Peter Waldo of Lyon (1140-1218)

So what happened when the economic boom of the 1200s distributed its benefits unevenly in a society with such important communal elements? Waldo, a wealthy French merchant, provides an excellent answer. Details on his life are sketchy but Waldo seems to have experienced some sort of epiphany around 1170 that caused him to give most of his fortune to the poor and to embark on a life as an itinerant preacher. His essential message was that one could not seek God and profit at the same time. The message resonated for the reasons we have already suggested and Waldo attracted a lot of attention. Waldo went further though and criticized the church directly, partly on matters of dogma, but most especially on the church's display of wealth and power. He is given credit for the first translation of the bible into the vernacular. The implications for the church's monopoly on the management of religious truth are obvious. In 1179 Waldo was summoned to Rome to explain his views. Pope Alexander III responded by forbidding Waldo from preaching and condemned some of Waldo's criticisms of Catholic dogma as heresy. Waldo himself was spared direct mention in that condemnation. Five years later Pope Lucius III took a stronger view of the matter by declaring any who supported Waldo to be ex-communicants. Pope Innocent III finally declared them heretics in 1215. By that time, the distinction meant little as Waldensians were already being burned at the stake including 80 who were burned in Strasbourg in 1211. The movement went underground. When it did so, it became virulently anti-Catholic. The closing of this viscous circle made them an even more important priority for the church and the further history of the Waldensians is marked by brutal massacres including one particularly heinous one in 1655 (the Piedmont Massacre). Nevertheless, despite the church's several attempts at extinction, the movement managed to survive (mostly by being absorbed by the Calvinist movement of the late 1600s).

# The Cathars (1200-1300)

The Cathars represent another expression of popular piety rising in opposition to the church. This movement flourished in the south of France, an area in which neither the papacy nor royal authorities ever had much direct influence. Like the Waldensians, Cathars interpreted material wealth as inherently evil, especially as it pertained to the church. But unlike the Waldensians, the Cathars were *always* anti-Catholic on certain fundamental matters of dogma. Cathars called themselves "good Christians" and rejected the moral authority of Catholicism as well as its sacraments. There was no individual founder or leader of the Cathars, as the movement had roots going all the way back to the early centuries of Christianity. Nor was there any centralized structure, although there was a hierarchy of merit. So far as we can tell, Cathars lived alongside Catholics without any friction at the local level. However, with the reformers in Rome so vigorous in their pursuit of orthodoxy of belief and obedience to Rome, it was inevitable that sooner or later the Cathars would draw their attention.

By about 1200, the Cathars had constructed an organization in the south of France that rivaled that of the Catholics. Increasingly alarmed by this trend, the church made numerous attempts to bring the Cathars back into the fold, all with little effect. One after the other, papal legates crisscrossed the region attempting to convince the Cathars of the spiritual jeopardy into which they had so obviously fallen. One of these legates was St. Dominic—founder of the Dominican Order—to whom we will return below. It did not take long for the church to realize the futility of the effort and they moved to change their strategy; they turned to the feudal barons. The barons in areas with a significant Cathar presence seemed to be good Catholics but they had no direct interest in whether the people should be Catholic or Cathar. On the other hand, *all feudal lords try to keep the influence of outsiders—be they kings or popes—to a minimum.* If there are no coins going into the church's collection box, the church is weaker and local money is not being bled off for the benefit of the church. It was therefore a win-win for the feudal barons in the south of France if their people were Cathars. From the standpoint of the church, the barons were tolerating heresy and were therefore complicit in their crime. From the barons' point of view they were merely providing passive resistance to an outside influence that might compete with their own.

INNOCENT III

Things took a mean turn in 1209 when a papal legate sent to confront one of these barons was murdered. Pope Innocent

III, hearing of this, immediately wrote to the king of France demanding he organize a crusade against both the heretics and the nobles who sheltered them. King Philip chose to give a limited approval to the crusade but for reasons unrelated to those of the pope. This began a twenty-year series of campaigns collectively called the Albigensian Crusade (named for the city of Albi, one of the areas of strongest Cathar influence). One would not think it wise for any king to approve a declaration of war by an outsider on his own subjects but Philip had his own problems and the crusade provided him a convenient way to deal with them. Philip had only just defeated King John of England in a contest for the control of the northwest of France and he was certainly interested in consolidating his power in the south, an area which continued to have significant feudal connections to the English. He also wished to reward his northern supporters.

When the Pope declared forfeit all the lands and titles of any nobles who should provide shelter to the heretics or should fail to assist papal legates, Phillip saw this as an opportunity to solve all these problems and gave his approval for a new crusade in the south of France. The combination of spiritual and worldly rewards on offer from both pope and king encouraged much enthusiasm on the part of crusaders. A dramatic proof of this enthusiasm was the siege of Beziers. A papal legate, Arnaud, a Cistercian abbot, commanded the crusader army investing the city there. According to a fellow Cistercian, when asked how to identify the heretics Arnaud responded, "Kill them all, God will know his own." After the city was taken, Arnaud wrote a letter to Pope Innocent III bragging that "today, your holiness, 20,000 heretics were put to the sword, regardless of rank, age, or sex."

The Albigensian Crusade did eventually result in the southern nobles, one by one, bending their knees to the king. On the other hand, the Cathars were far from extirpated and as far as the Pope was concerned, so did the continuing rationale for the crusade he had called. But destruction and loss of life in his own kingdom were not in the long-term interests of any king and when the remaining southern nobles finally submitted to his authority in 1229, King Philip of France withdrew his support for the Crusade. So the crusade was a success from the king's standpoint but not from the church's.

Even with the dramatic massacres at Beziers and elsewhere, the Cathars were not wiped out, at least not yet. The last of the Cathars were mopped up about a century later as the conquest of a much more deliberate kind of crusade, the Inquisition (on which, more below).

# Francis of Assisi (1181-1226)

Despite its vigorous war on heresy and on Waldensians and Cathars in particular, the church was not universally hostile to the phenomenon of popular piety. We see this in the example provided by the life of St. Francis of Assisi. Born to a successful merchant in Italy, Francis enjoyed the fruits of his father's commercial enterprise but gradually became disillusioned by the disparities of wealth he witnessed all around him. There is at least one story of him angering his father with an excessive display of generosity toward a beggar when he was still quite young. A serious sickness from which he recovered at 24 gave Francis the license to do something decisive. He embarked on a spiritual journey that featured the rejection of wealth in a number of dramatic gestures. At various times he lived among lepers, he mixed with paupers begging near churches, he gave away some of his father's clothing stock and finally, in a dramatic scene of mutual recrimination and rejection, he stripped off his clothes, handed them to his father, and then dedicated himself to a life of poverty. He was soon seen wandering the roads in Umbria, sleeping wherever he might with a small but dedicated group of followers.

In 1210, Francis sought permission from the pope to found an order of "lesser brothers" whose mission was to wander Europe, advocating greater devotion to God through the rejection of material possessions. Pope Innocent II was ambivalent, given the existence of heretical movements espousing the very same principles, and chose at first to give Francis only a limited approval. The next year, with his influence, Clare of Assisi founded a parallel order for women and not long after that Francis founded an auxiliary order for those supportive of the movement, but not so supportive as to give away all their possessions. Francis was ambitious in his mission and made attempts to travel to Jerusalem and Morocco to spread his message, and at one point visited a crusader encampment in Egypt. He supposedly took this opportunity to attempt a conversion of the Sultan of Egypt (a persistent legend suggests he succeeded, although it be unlikely). The Franciscan orders were enormously popular and grew astonishingly fast. But without the formal supervision characteristic of traditional monastic orders, some Franciscans veered too close to Waldo's ideas and Francis was forced to revise the rules to keep the movement in line with official church teachings. Some Franciscan leaders resisted these efforts. The controversies had mostly to do with the practical meaning of poverty, and some errant Franciscans were actually disciplined as heretics.

# Dominic (1170-1221)

St. Dominic provides another example. Dominic was a Catalan priest who, as a papal legate under Pope Innocent III, was one of those tasked to bring errant Cathars back into the Catholic fold. As was suggested above, mostly this policy was a failure and for his part, Dominic was smart enough to understand why. The church was a wealthy institution and that wealth was a deterrent to the message. He proposed to represent the church with a face of simplicity by founding an order of priests bound by an oath of poverty. The order would be funded, at least theoretically, by begging.  In its organization, Dominic sought a middle ground between the traditional discipline of the Benedictine rules and the informal approach of the Franciscans. Unlike the Franciscans, Dominicans would receive the formal training of a priest but, like the Franciscans, they would preach in the vernacular. Pope Honorius III (the successor of Pope Innocent III formally recognized the order. Eventually, the Dominicans became key instruments of Papal authority and outreach. To this end, they were responsible for establishing numerous Dominican colleges and convents in the centuries to follow.

In the shorter term, the biggest tasks that these mendicant orders took on—both Franciscans and Dominicans—was in the church's war against the popular but illegal Cathar movement. When the Albigensian Crusade collapsed after the King of France withdrew his support, the church was forced to change its strategy. Cathars would now be sought out village-by-village and person-by-person. The mendicant orders became the new front line soldiers of the war on heresy. And so starts the Inquisition.

# The Inquisition

The Inquisition represents one of the most notorious chapters in medieval history and for good reason. Its mission was to seek out and destroy heresy as defined by the reformers in Rome. From its inception in the early 1200s, the office of the Inquisition has interviewed tens of thousands of individuals, ordered the execution of thousands, and the torture of many more. The work continues, but under a different name, and under different rules. There is an office in the Vatican called the "Congregation for the Doctrine of the Faith" whose job it is to continue that work, albeit happily without torture or execution. Over the long run, the Inquisition has been without doubt the most intrusive and intimidating weapon the church has ever deployed. It officially came into existence because the Cathars still endured, despite the crusade that had been waged against them. In response to the persistence of the Cathars, local church officials held tribunals to investigate charges of heresy, but the rules and process they employed were inconsistent, and punishments were mostly mild.

In order to regularize what was becoming increasingly irregular in practice, Pope Gregory IX issued a series of guidelines over the course of his pontificate (1227-41). The first man to hold the title "Inquisitor into Heretical Depravity" was Conrad of Marburg*, who had been a papal legate working on behalf of Innocent III in the Albigensian Crusade. With the assistance of the Franciscans and Dominicans, he threw himself into his work with such zeal that complaints began flowing to Rome concerning his use of torture and abuse of procedure. In 1233, Conrad died

---

* *Inquisitor haereticae pravitatis*: was thenceforth the official title employed in papal archives.

mysteriously...hmmm. In the very same year, another inquisitor, the Dominican friar Robert le Bourge, made such an impression that he was nicknamed "the Hammer of Heretics" by French bishops whose loud complaints to the pope resulted in his suspension after only a year. But a heretic hunter's work is never done and the Hammer was back at work in 1239 when those very same bishops were forced by him to witness the mass burning of 183 Cathars in Champagne.

Pope Gregory IX had decreed death for unrepentant heretics and life imprisonment for those who repented, but these punishments were frequently commuted. On the other hand, property and titles were almost invariably forfeit. Since, for all practical purposes, arrest was conviction, the opportunities for spurious accusation and illegal gain were obvious. Sensitive to this possibility, Gregory took administration of heresy trials away from local authorities and put it mostly in the hands of the Dominican order. Further modification of procedure ultimately shifted the conduct of the executions themselves into the hands of secular authorities. In 1252, Pope Innocent IV issued an infamous edict: *ad Extirpanda* (for the extirpating). The gist of this papal bull was that it defined the extirpation of heresy as the prime duty of the state and institutionalized the use of torture in its investigation. Here we see a concrete example of the church using the state as an extension of religious authority, precisely the opposite as had been the case traditionally. At the same time, we see that the state has full authority to investigate and punish religious irregularities. The dreadful consequences of this convergence will be hundreds of years of religious war.

All the popes of the 1200s participated in creating an elaborate legal structure to carry out these policies. Church officials issued instruction manuals detailing appropriate investigative procedures and penalties and popes issued papal bulls in response to requests for clarification. The elaborate system of inquisition that resulted turned Italy into a virtual police state. In 1278, 200 or so Cathars were burned in the Roman amphitheater in Verona under the authority of a Franciscan inquisitor. So broad was the authority of the Inquisition that in 1308 it arrested an entire village in France, Montaillou, with a population of 250, and interrogated each and every adult. The chief inquisitor in that instance later became Pope Benedict XII, partly on the strength of his efforts as a scourge of heretics. Interestingly, we would have no idea of the scope of those particular proceedings were it not for Benedict carrying his personal records to Rome where they ended up in papal archives. Although this episode is widely regarded as the last and ultimately most successful campaign against the remaining Cathars, the happenstance survival of its records suggests there were many other episodes of which we are now ignorant.

Our modern sensibilities are profoundly bothered by what seems such a visceral reaction by the church to what seems from our perspective to be benign spiritual movements. But the Inquisition was more than merely a reaction to deviant belief; it was a reaction to popular resistance to the church's vision. What Waldo and others who preached poverty maintained was that their vision of piety was preferable and superior to that decreed by the church. This position represented a challenge to church authority and by extension an existential threat to the church itself—this was the real issue.

It is important to note that before the influence of the reformer popes, the church possessed no administrative capacity to enforce uniformity of practice, never mind of belief. Before 1200 each bishop ruled what was essentially an autonomous episcopal district. Attempts by papal reformers to enforce dogmatic consistency were in reality something new and alien. In most cases, the bishop was a figure with local roots and probably an integral part of the local nobility. Papal attempts to monitor and supervise bishops were bound to meet with some resistance on purely political grounds. We can note a parallel dynamic at work in the secular hierarchy. At the very same time the church was trying to extend its direct influence down through the church hierarchy, we also see kings doing the same with the feudal nobility. In both spheres similar conflicts arose. Outside agents and local supporters of central authority were met with fierce resistance from local forces defending the status quo.

Accusations of heresy were first used to break down this local resistance and only later was it directed to counter popular challenges to church authority. Scholars have noted that accusations of heresy in the period before 1200 were much more likely to be directed at local officials—some church and some feudal—and interpret it as a strategy useful for both popes and kings. It was only after this phase is over, by 1200 or so, that the rhetoric of heresy was turned systematically against expressions of popular piety. By that time, the theory and rhetoric of heresy was more refined and resistance to its use had already been swept away at the local elite level. At street level, resistance to official church pressure to homogenize religious belief and practice ironically helped shape expressions of popular piety. As we will see in the conclusion of this chapter, the last step in this process will be the deployment of accusations of heresy against the church itself.

## Meanwhile the Rise of Kings

In this chapter thus far we have seen a steady progress in the quest of church reformers to bring the church into compliance with their own vision. But what of papal efforts to compel the obedience of secular rulers? In many respects the church had its own way in the 1200s. Pope Innocent III was the most successful of the reformer popes in manipulating secular rulers, but even with his successes, things seldom went exactly as he wished. The first of the political challenges facing Innocent was the church's relationship with the German emperors. In 1201 he waded into a three-way dispute over who should succeed to the German throne. The most important rulers in Europe were divided on the question, each according to his own interests. Frederick was the candidate with the hereditary credentials, as he was the son of the former emperor, but Frederick was also in line to inherit the throne of Sicily from his mother. Innocent could not abide this choice because Germany and Sicily united under one throne presented too much of a threat to his own position in Italy, which was located squarely between these two kingdoms. The barons in Germany were split on the question and elected two different candidates, Philip of Swabia, uncle to Frederick, and Otto IV from a different family altogether. King Philip II of France favored Philip while King Richard I of England supported Otto. Otto was an eager candidate and promised to protect the pope's interests. He also struck a bargain with the English to protect

English rights to lands in France. From a purely political standpoint, Otto seemed the best choice for Innocent and so the pope announced him as his choice adding ominously that the papacy reserved the right to make future changes in who ruled Germany. This was a remarkable assertion of papal authority over secular rulers. However, once he was confirmed, Otto quickly reneged on his promises to protect papal rights by attacking papal lands and he announced his intention to recover Sicily. Innocent responded by pivoting his support back to the previously jilted Fredrick.

Meanwhile, King John succeeded King Richard in England and immediately became embroiled in a religious controversy of his own. Kings of England had always had a hand in choosing the highest-ranking churchman in England, the Archbishop of Canterbury. The custom had evolved such that the king nominated and the pope confirmed. But in 1207, Innocent rejected John's choice and John, feeling insulted, reacted by seizing church lands in England. The result was an excommunication for John that was not lifted until 1213. John eventually bent his knee to the pope; but only after he agreed to become his vassal, and to pay restitution for damages. John's problems were just beginning. Most of John's revenue-producing lands were actually in France and so technically he was also a vassal of the king of France. For his own part, the French king preferred to rule those lands directly and he did all he could to interfere with John's rights. John decided to invade France to protect his claims. Otto supported the English because a weakened France, his near neighbor, was in his interest. Unfortunately, this contest went badly for both King John and Otto. Badly defeated at the battle of Bouvines in 1214, Otto lost all his support at home and Frederick was crowned emperor in Germany. John was chased out of France and lost most of his possessions there. When he returned to England, John was then faced with a revolt of English barons tired of financing his wars in France. The rebels were successful in seizing several cities, including London, and they forced John to sign the famous Magna Carta, which placed certain limits on royal power. Although John repudiated the document shortly thereafter, the Magna Carta stands as a potent symbol pointing to future and genuine constitutional limits on royal prerogatives. As for papal power, these disputes reveal the extent to which church politics presented serious problems for secular rulers in the middle 1200s. That will begin to change however, when we cross the year 1300 and meet Pope Boniface VIII.

# Demons as Pets: Pope Boniface VIII and King Philip the (not-so) Fair

ONE OF THE SCURRILOUS ACCUSATIONS FLUNG AT BONIFACE VIII WAS THAT HE KEPT DEMONS AS PETS!

Pope Boniface VIII was quite the controversial pope (1294-1303). Some said that he purchased his papacy for 7000 gold florins although this accusation is probably hyperbole and most likely originated in the nasty feud he and his family had with the Colonna, one of the more powerful families in Italy. It was certainly true that Boniface's predecessor, Pope Celestine V, was convinced to resign — something unprecedented— and apparently spent the last months of his life as a miserable hostage locked up by Boniface. But whatever the circumstances of Boniface's ascension, he was most famous for the dispute in which he found himself with King Philip IV of France. Philip, like all kings in Europe, was always short of cash and, again like all kings in Europe, he tried to find ways to cut into church revenues. Over the course of several years, pope and king exchanged a series of increasingly acrimonious letters and threats. Meanwhile, Boniface made numerous, mostly unsuccessful, attempts to manage relations with other leaders in Europe, succeeding only in alienating virtually everyone. In 1302 Boniface tried to put an end to his problems with Philip by issuing a document called *Unum Sanctum,* in which Boniface decreed that everyone, including kings, was subject to papal authority. This was and is the most sweeping and direct statement of papal power any pope has ever issued.

But Philip was not impressed by this bravado and he ignored the pronouncement; he instead attacked the pope's legitimacy, undermining the pronouncement indirectly. He convened a conference in Paris (1303) to which he invited representatives of the three so-called estates of medieval society: church, noble, and (urban) commoner. To this group he presented a bill of indictments that featured a variety of fantastic accusations including murder, incest, not to mention heresies of various sorts and finally, consorting with demons. Philip's closest advisor, Nogaret, read out the charges but it is likely that the Colonna family actually authored the outrageous accusations as they had much reason to hate the pope, including the physical destruction by him of their home city, Palestrina. But the bottom line is that Boniface, having no great diplomatic skills, had alienated too many powerful individuals both inside and outside of the church; few were inclined to offer their support.

When Boniface heard of the charges made against him he scoffed and excommunicated everyone who had anything to do with the matter. He certainly had no intention of standing trial! But Philip was not yet done. He dispatched a band of mercenaries under the joint command of Nogaret and Colonna family members to arrest the pope at his private palace in Anagni. Presumably, they intended to haul him back to France where he would stand trial for heresy. Nogaret and his confederates literally seized the pope and treated him roughly while they ransacked his palace over the course of several days. This ill-considered delay gave local Italians sufficient time to rescue the pope. Severely shaken by the ordeal, Boniface returned to Rome where he died barely a month later. This whole episode illustrates how out of synch had become the separate rhythms of power in the spheres headed respectively by pope and king. While royal power was still on the ascendant, papal power had clearly not kept up. In the next chapter we will cover the sequel to this story, wherein the church divided into separate Italian and French factions. But first, to close this chapter, let us look to the end of a vital symbol of medieval papal power, the Knights Templar.

# The Destruction of the Knights Templar

Earlier in this chapter we heralded the creation of the Knights Templar as a potent symbol of the papacy coming into existence as a kind of state. Now we will notice their destruction and propose it as a symbol of the moment when that status was no longer tenable. The demise of the Knights Templar is an episode full of drama and mystery from which conspiracy theorists and Hollywood screenwriters take repeated inspiration. Philip's seeming victory over Boniface had knocked the church back a few steps and those cardinals assembled to pick Boniface's replacement did so with that recent drama very fresh in their memories. They were torn: on the one hand, the circumstances of Boniface's election to pope, his scorched-earth policy against the Colonna family, and his obvious overreach against the French king, had all turned out to be counter-productive; on the other hand, Philip's dispatch of mercenaries to Italy to seize the person of the pope— certainly a contributing factor in his death—was an injury the church could hardly forgive. The complex circumstances called for an assertive but diplomatic pope, one capable of restoring the dignity of a papacy under attack. The conclave that met to decide the question ended up choosing one of the few cardinals consistently loyal to Boniface (Pope Benedict XI). Benedict, as master of the Dominican order in 1296, had taken the lead in squelching criticisms made of Boniface concerning his legitimacy and was the loudest voice supporting Boniface in the crisis with Philip.

This might seem at first look to be a strange choice, but it turned out a good one. In a move worthy of a medieval Kissinger, Benedict excommunicated Philip's advisor Nogaret and all those involved with the seizure of Boniface *while at the same time un*-excommunicating Philip. Meanwhile he acted as though Boniface had never issued *Unum Sanctum* at all. On balance it seemed a reasonable and clever compromise. Benedict was essentially deflecting Philip's guilt and allowing both Philip and the papacy a face-saving way of patching things up. All of this might have worked to preserve at least the appearance of the dignity and power of the church except that Benedict died before a single year had passed.

The cardinals were then deadlocked for another year over their choice of successor. This gave the French king plenty of opportunity to lobby the cardinals, many of whom were French. They finally settled on Pope Clement V who, like Benedict, had strong ties to Boniface VIII and was French and not Italian; again, a seemingly sound choice under the circumstances. But Clement immediately embarked on a series of actions that strengthened the French king. He chose Lyons in France for his consecration as pope and he created nine new cardinals, all French. He explicitly repudiated the edicts Boniface had made against Philip while allowing an investigation into the heresy charges that had been made against Boniface before he died. He eventually absolved all those who kidnapped Boniface VIII. With these actions, it seemed that King Philip of France had put the papacy into his pocket. And he proceeded under that assumption. The king then turned his attention to the Knights Templar.

In the two centuries since the order had been created, the Knights had become the most potent symbol of papal power, and become extremely wealthy in the process. The whole idea of monks strapping on swords may seem a bit odd to us and in fact the idea took some criticism in the years after the order was created. But thanks to the influence of Bernard of Clairvaux these criticisms had mostly faded. The church had already relied on Augustine's "just war" arguments to validate the church's active promotion of "holy war" and it was, after all, only a small logical step to extend the idea to a permanent order of holy warriors. Even more, the idea appealed to many sons of the warrior class, especially those unlikely to inherit land or titles, as a way of making a virtue of their limited resources.

The Knights Templar had a reputation for suicidal fearlessness and indeed, one of their tenets was that retreat was not allowed except under direct orders. This made their presence on any battlefield something of note, however small their numbers. In one famous example, the Battle of Montigisard in 1177, a contingent of 600 knights, half of whom were Knights Templar, destroyed the better part of an army of 26,000 Muslim warriors because Salah al-Din, the Moslem commander, did not take the small force of Templars seriously.*

Although their mission as holy warriors is what makes them famous now, the order actually was more important as an economic enterprise. The order had become wealthy mostly through donations, some of which were enormous, as e.g., a bequest by Alfonso I of Aragon, of a third of his kingdom in 1134. Although that will was contested, it does give a sense of the upper limit of donations made only a few years after the Templars were created. In 1192 the order purchased the island of Cyprus from Richard Lionheart, future King of England, and then sold it back a year later. Their wealth, their network of forts across Europe and the Holy Land, and their total independence from secular control made them, in effect, a multinational bank. Nobles on crusade could commit their assets to the order to manage while on crusade and could draw against those assets wherever Templars were based. Eventually, Italian trading families from cities like Genoa and Venice took over international banking but did so more or less on the model developed by the Knights.

By the time of Boniface and his conflict with the French King Philip IV, the Templars were already in some disarray. The fall of the Crusader fortress of Acre in 1291 marked the end of the crusade in the Levant in practical terms, which meant that the order's ostensible reason for existence was mooted. Understanding this, the Master of the Templars, Jacques DeMolay, visited Pope Boniface VIII when he became Pope in 1294, to gain his approval for yet another attempt to retake Jerusalem from the Muslims. The resulting expedition was a total failure as it resulted in the loss of an important Templar fort in Antioch. Cyprus was now as close to Jerusalem as the Templars could get. This failure, along with DeMolay's association with Pope Boniface, portended disaster for the Templars.

There were many reasons why King Philip of France would have despised the Templars, but the biggest was that he owed them a lot of money, thanks to loans his father had received from them. Moreover, the

---

* In 1187, Salah al-Din had his revenge. After destroying a Crusader army of perhaps 20,000 at the battle of Hattin, he went on to retake Jerusalem that same year.

collapse of the crusading mission made the existence of what was effectively an independent army politically dangerous. To what mission might they now turn? The Templars had already supported a coup on Cyprus and they owned a lot of land in France. The last thing Philip wanted to see was the Templars to do in France what another order of fighting monks, the Teutonic Knights, had already done in Prussia: create its own state.* And then, there was the Templars' symbolic importance for the independence of the papacy, to whom they were still directly tied. On Friday October 13, 1307, Philip arrested large numbers of the knights in a carefully coordinated effort. The charges involved, mostly offenses against religion, heresy that is, and their details were fantastic: idol worship, ritualized homosexual activity, and profaning of Christian symbols. All the charges made against Boniface a few years earlier were included and over 100 confessions were obtained under torture. The trial, convened under papal authority, found that *individuals* were guilty of heresy, but not the order itself. Of those who confessed under torture, 54 later renounced their confessions only to be executed as relapsed heretics. The three highest-ranking Knights were found guilty upon confession and given clemency. However, two of these three, including Jacques DeMolay, the Master of the Order, later renounced their confessions and were burned at the stake as relapsed heretics in 1314.†

Documents have recently turned up in Vatican archives that indicate that shortly after the trial Pope Clement V gave absolution to all those who confessed, but this had no effect on the fate of the organization. Despite having found no fault in the order itself, the pope officially dissolved it in 1312 and ordered that its assets be distributed to other monastic orders. This catastrophic collapse left many questions unanswered. No reliable

---

* After more than fifty years of bloody struggle, the Teutonic Knights established what eventually became known as Prussia. They were ousted from Prussia in the 1500s but the legacy of their warrior zeal persisted for centuries

† DeMolay is rumored to have called out a curse from the very flames, that both Clement V and Philip IV should die with the year. They did indeed die within a year, but the curse itself is probably apocryphal. It does make a good story, however.

records survive describing any orderly transfer of Templar assets. What happened to their ships? Where are their archives? What happened to all the money? There were thousands of Knights Templar, but only 56 were executed. What happened to the rest of them? Tantalizing clues lie everywhere and theories abound. There is every reason to believe that Philip stood to benefit the most by the demise of the order and one has to think he ended up with the lion's share of the loot, but there is no way of knowing for sure.

This marked a major moment in the fortunes of the church. If we agree with the proposition that the Middle Ages were characterized by a genuine struggle between two different leadership models for Europe, then it would seem that the Middle Ages were over because one of those two models had been mortally wounded. It is fair to say that from about 1100 to about 1300 the church claimed and exercised a power far greater than any time before or since. After 1300, the Pope's opinion and support continued to be important, but they would never again be decisive.

| Christendom Timeline: c. 1000-1300 | |
|---|---|
| Peaces and Truces of God | 1000-1100 |
| Henry IV versus Pope Gregory VII | 1070s |
| Papacy of Urban II | 1088-99 |
| First Crusade | 1095-1099 |
| Knights Templar founded | 1129-1307 |
| Jerusalem re-taken by Muslims | 1187 |
| (so-called) Third Crusade | 1189-92 |
| Papacy of Innocent III | 1198-1216 |
| (so-called) Fourth Crusade | 1202-4 |
| Albigensian Crusade | 1209-29 |
| Franciscan order founded | 1210 |
| Magna Carta | 1215 |
| Dominican order founded | 1216 |
| Inquisition began | 1229 |
| Papacy of Boniface VIII | 1294-1303 |
| Knights Templar disbanded | 1312 |

# Chapter Eleven: The End of the Middle Ages (1300-1450)

*Why was this period so clearly both an end and a beginning?*

Historians love to draw lines through the lives of empires and civilizations and give the resulting segments names. Sometimes the rationale for where those lines should be drawn is obvious. The end of the Middle Ages is certainly in this category. If one examines the period from about 1300 to about 1450 it becomes obvious that Europe was clearly in a space between two fundamentally different eras. The Hundred Years War (1338-1453), for example, was begun by knights in shining armor but decided ultimately by the use of cannon. Criticisms leveled at the church before this period had no real effect on its powers and prerogatives but by 1400 the papacy devolved into just another political power in Europe. The climax of that process featured three popes locked in a tragi-comic drama of mutual excommunication. Economic changes at work for some time reached a critical mass that made nonsense of medieval social categories and undermined confidence in the idea of a God-ordered universe. The implications of these changes were not lost on a peasantry whose social position was firmly anchored in that fundamental assumption. Their long simmering resentments erupted in significant violence (1338-1381). Meanwhile, the Black Death, after first appearing in Europe in 1347, swept back and forth through Europe taking with it something like half of its population. Profound social changes attended. One sees all the assumptions governing medieval society coming under siege, and the outlines of a new society emerging. The chapter we begin here will by necessity treat these events sequentially, but at the same time it must be clear that all these narratives crisscrossed and took place at the same time. As we mentioned in an earlier chapter, people seldom relinquish familiar modes of thought or action willingly, even long past the time when these habits of thought or action make sense or even work very well. Something dramatic must usually happen for people, or the social systems created by people, to embrace truly fundamental change. War and pestilence do that job in much the way that an earthquake releases pent up energy and tension. The result of an earthquake is a changed landscape. But it is not the earthquake that provides the energy for change; it is the inexorable movement of the tectonic plates deep below the surface of the earth. And as is also true of an earthquake, not all structures fall down; those structures that *do* fall down tend to be those that are the weakest. So in the aftermath of an earthquake, a patchwork of structures will exist: a mix of stronger versions of old structures alongside the creation of new ones. And so as we look to this period (c. 1350-1450) and we observe the trauma we also try to understand the fundamental direction of the significant changes that were underway.

# The Babylonian Captivity, a.k.a. the Avignon Papacy (1309-1376)

The most important assumption governing Medieval Society was the primacy of the church in matters both spiritual and temporal. In the previous chapter, we took notice of a pope beaten and abused by agents of a French king who had the temerity to accuse the pope of consorting with demons. We noted the near-simultaneous destruction of the Knights Templar, the most potent symbol of the church as a ruling authority. The collapse of papal authority that these two episodes reveal augured in a period of weakness, ill repute, and corruption that lasted well into the 1500s. The church, the single most defining institution of the Middle Ages, found itself transformed from an object of fear to one of ridicule and disdain. We treat the climax of that drama here.

The real trouble began with Clement V (1305-14), the pope with whose assistance the Knights Templar were taken apart. When Clement was first elected, he never bothered to move to Rome, and by 1309 he made this official by summoning all the cardinals to his side in Avignon, France. Avignon was at that time a possession of the king of Sicily. The feeble excuses Clement put forth for this decision were that the Lateran Basilica in Rome was in disrepair and that factional strife in Italy was out of control. Both were of course entirely true but one wonders whether these were reasons for the absence of the Pope *or the result of it.*

One notable development of the papacy moving to Avignon was an effort to enhance its physical prestige, a trend of which his successors approved with much enthusiasm. Clement sponsored elaborate court rituals, entertained ambassadors, and festooned his surroundings with lush decoration. This process paralleled what was happening in royal courts all across Europe. Kings were increasingly intent on creating transcendent images of themselves as rulers answerable to none and the papacy followed this cue. In the same way as secular rulers, the popes became prominent patrons of the arts. To finance the cost of this effort, Clement and the popes who succeeded him at Avignon created and fostered bureaucracies to manage patronage within the church and centralize the collections of revenue. Those appointed to high-church office were expected to pay for the privilege and soon the papal residence at Avignon really did resemble the halls of kings. Clement V's successors were said to eat from plates of gold. Needless to say, rumors of this sort did much to depreciate the reputation of the church as a *spiritual* institution. Clement, in a parallel effort to enhance the church's role as the arbiter of God's will, focused on the suppression of heresy in southern France; it was his influence that instigated the last stages of the eradication of the Cathars mentioned previously. You may recall Pope Benedict XII's rise in the church after his inquisition of an entire city. Benedict was one of the Avignon popes (1334-1342).

Over the course of this period, one can trace a decline in papal influence in the diplomatic troubles of the papacy. Some of the Avignon popes did think of returning to Italy but conflict with the emperors in Germany and the outbreak of plague in 1347 froze the papacy in place. In 1348, Queen Joanna of Sicily sold Avignon for 80,000 *Florins** to Pope Clement VI (1342-52) and so it appeared more and more that the move to France had become permanent. Over the next twenty years an impressive edifice was built to house the growing papal bureaucracy, much of which still exists. Meanwhile, the Hundred Years War between France and England was going on and the papacy could not help taking the French side. This naturally resulted in alienation from the English. Pope Gregory XI (1370-1378) employed English mercenaries against some of the city-states in Italy and found himself in disrepute for atrocities they committed while in his pay. By stages then, the popes in Avignon managed to alienate virtually everyone.

Nevertheless, Pope Gregory gathered up his cardinals in 1377—much to their collective surprise—and returned to Rome. Only he died about a year after arriving. The College of Cardinals, mostly French of course, despised Rome and for good reason. It was falling apart. Even the Lateran palace in Rome, home of the papacy for centuries, was falling apart. They missed their villas in the south of France. But here they were, in Rome listening to the Italians clamoring for an Italian pope. But the French cardinals *really* preferred a return to Avignon and that meant if not a French pope, at least a weak one. A dilemma!

Their eventual choice, Urban VI, seemed an ideal candidate. Born in Naples and trained as a monk, Urban had risen in the church hierarchy in Avignon before being appointed Archbishop of Bari, in Italy. The Naples connection was an especially shrewd move by the cardinals given the strong connections between Queen Joan of Naples and Avignon. Urban seemed not to be a politically connected and they believed him easily manipulated. This turned out to be wrong—very wrong. The French cardinals left Rome after the conclave and returned to Avignon. Meanwhile Urban stayed behind and announced a series of reform measures designed to curb the

---

* *Florins*: gold coins originally issued in Florence. Their consistent quality made them a coin of choice across Europe for large-scale commercial transactions for several hundred years. It contained 3.5 grams of high quality gold. At $47.00 per gram, the price of gold in mid-2013, one coin was worth $165.

privileges and excesses of the cardinals who had just left. Alarmed at this unexpected development, the cardinals spun around, returned to Italy and called a meeting at Anagni, inviting the pope to join them. By way of reminder, this was the location where Pope Boniface VIII had been arrested and abused in the months before the papacy moved to Avignon in the first place. Perhaps wishing not to repeat that unpleasant history, Urban demurred.

The cardinals, not to be outmaneuvered, declared the election of Urban invalid and a few weeks later appointed another pope, Clement VII. Clement's qualifications are note-worthy and suggest what measures the French cardinals believed might be necessary to solve the problem of a now dual papacy. His most recent appointment was as commander of mercenaries hired by the papacy to fight Florence. He is sometimes called the Butcher of Cesena for a massacre committed by mercenaries under his command. This pope and all who followed him in that line are now in retrospect deemed anti-popes by the church, but at this moment, that future had not yet been written. Meanwhile, the other *official* pope was making things even worse. Proving himself a political bungler, Urban alienated Joan of Sicily, which led to her murder, and indirectly to his being chased out of Rome. Soon Urban found himself an exile in Genoa where, hearing of a plan by his cardinals to arrest him, he had several of them

executed. In 1388, he set out for Rome at the head of a small army but, on the way, he fell off his mule and injured himself mortally. At least he died in Rome. Meanwhile, Clement moved back to Avignon. Each pope was succeeded by another, and so on, perpetuating the split until 1417.

The crisis in the church could hardly be more obvious. Numerous attempts were made from within and without the church to mend the schism. In 1409, under virtually universal pressure to resolve the controversy, the two popes and their cardinals were invited to meet at Pisa, in Italy. Although neither pope showed up, twenty-four of their combined cardinals did along with 500 or so senior church officials from all over Europe. Over the course of three months, the assemblage worked up the courage to fire both existing popes and appointed yet another, Alexander V. But this just made the controversy even *more* complex; instead of two popes excommunicating each other, now there were three.

# Wycliffe and Hus

This drama represented an existential crisis for the papacy. Critics howled in derision. John Wycliffe for example, Oxford scholar and theologian, had begun to question the legitimacy of a king-like Pope even before the schism. Wycliffe believed that spiritual power should be kept separate from temporal power and those in the church should remain poor in emulation of the apostles. Wycliffe supported the nationalization, as it were, of all church property. In 1377, he published an extensive criticism of the church when there was still only one pope, Gregory XI. Gregory, then engaged in an expensive war against Florence, reacted virulently and directed the energies of the church in England to seek Wycliffe's destruction. But this required the assistance and cooperation of the English government and the timing was bad. The English King Edward III had just died, leaving his ten-year-old grandson on the throne. Wycliffe took his case to the parliament and laid out in detail not only his critique of the church but also the radical notion that decrees of excommunication should be appealable to the king. Many in attendance were sympathetic, including the young king's mother. But before a decision could be made, news came from Italy that Gregory had died. Those who attempted to refute him had to be satisfied by what was essentially a house arrest from which he escaped without much fuss. News of the papal schism gave Wycliffe further encouragement and over the next seven years he published a series of pamphlets whose net effect was to dismiss any claim or practice of the church that was not explicitly supported by the Bible. He also began the first translation of the Bible directly into English.

In 1384, Wycliffe died and was buried in consecrated ground. He had been saved from the fire of inquisition by a church in schism and political confusion in England. However, his ideas lived to fight on without him. In Bohemia, a principality of the Holy Roman Empire, a man named John Hus took up the fight. Hus was an ordained priest and doctor at the University of Prague in 1406, where he put his hands on a eulogy of Wycliffe that he proceeded to read out from the pulpit. Hus was a favorite of both the archbishop and prince of Bohemia, which gave him a little license. But Hus' admiration of Wycliffe and the protection of him by the archbishop and prince drew the attention of one of the schismatic popes, Boniface IX, who ordered the university to reject Wycliffe's ideas. Hus acquiesced at first but continued to be a champion of Wycliffe's ideas in private. Meanwhile, the university did its best to stay neutral. But the council of Pisa with its election of a third pope blew things apart. Upset over the university pronouncements to stay aloof from the church controversy, several thousand students and professors walked off the campus and decamped to Leipzig where they founded a new university. The new Pope Alexander (pope three of three) ordered Wycliffe's writings to be surrendered and excommunicated his supporters. This caused rioting in Bohemia as Wycliffe's arguments were very popular in the Holy Roman Empire because of long term conflicts between German leaders and the papacy.

Meanwhile, Pope Alexander died and was replaced by John XXIII.* Given his colorful career, perhaps we should stress his pre- (and post-) pope name, Baldasare Cossa. His family featured a cast of Neapolitan

---

* John XXIII is, along with Alexander V, his predecessor, now deemed an anti-pope. The church does not acknowledge Anti-popes and, consequently, there is *another* John XXIII, pope from 1958-1963. Curiously, when I toured Notre Dame cathedral in Paris a few years ago, I found a little chapel along the southern side that displayed a case of miniature likenesses of all the Popes. Our *original* John XXIII was among them! Somebody obviously missed the memo!

pirates; two of his brothers had been executed for that very crime, and when Baldasare became pope, he had at his disposal the loyalty of several criminal networks in Italy. On the positive side, he was a cardinal in the church and was one of those present in Pisa when his predecessor was chosen. Oh, and he was made priest the day before being made pope. But all things considered, it was Baldasare's less noble attributes that were his main recommendation. If only he had been successful! Alas, after being driven from Rome by the allies of one of his rival popes, it became clear that another solution was necessary to the pesky problem of papal proliferation.

# The Council of Constance

When Baldasare failed in his attempt to establish himself in Rome, the new prince of Bohemia, Sigismund, weighed in once again. For his own part, he was an ambitious man with dynastic connections to several of the principalities comprising the Holy Roman Empire. He planned to be Holy Roman Emperor one day. The process by which this happened was twofold. Although there was a presumption of hereditary right, nominees for the position needed first to be elected by a council of German lords and then anointed by the pope. In this way the legitimacy of the Holy Roman Emperor was intimately tied to the legitimacy of the papacy. For this reason, Sigismund obviously needed the papal controversy solved. There were other issues as well. The situation in Bohemia was tense with rivalry between Czech and German factions. We saw some of that in play in the breakup of the University in Prague into two rival universities, one German and one Czech. Sigismund wished to silence John Hus not only because he criticized the church, but also because he had become a vocal symbol of Czech resistance to German influence in Bohemia. Hus had to go.

Sigismund convinced Baldasare to convene another council; it came later to be named the Council of Constance. The potentially disastrous consequences of creating yet a fourth pope had to be foremost in Sigismund's mind. Baldasare's apparent primacy in papal authority—he was picked by cardinals associated with both of the other popes—meant that he was the logical pope to convene the council, and he agreed to do so, although he obviously expected that the process would feature an unambiguous endorsement of his own authority. For this reason, of the three popes, he was, in fact, the only one to show up in person. Hus was also convinced to attend after Sigismund promised him safe passage to the conference. He should have read the fine print, however as, a few weeks after arriving he was arrested. Obviously the safe passage promised "to the conference" didn't apply once Hus actually arrived "at the conference." Baldasare, intending to put him on trial for heresy, tossed him into a Dominican dungeon. When Sigisimund protested at this obvious breach of etiquette, the Dominicans holding Hus blithely replied that promises made to heretics were not technically binding.

The first item on the agenda was the writings of Wycliffe, on much of which Hus had relied in his own intellectual growth. When Wycliffe's writings were declared heretical in May 1415, the inquisitors turned finally to Hus. After months imprisoned in a dank cell and given poor rations, Hus was finally put on trial in June 1415. Although he asserted his willingness to be convinced from scripture of his error, he was otherwise obdurate, and he was sentenced to die a heretic. Even as the firewood was stacked around him, he was given opportunities to confess. He refused and was burned. But Hus' ideas were not forgotten; Martin Luther would repeat many of them a century later.

Meanwhile, John XXIII (Baldasare) realized that the Council would not legitimize him and in March of 1415 he fled the proceedings, only to be indicted *in abstentia* for crimes against God, man, *and* nature (heresy, murder, and incest were prominent items on the list). Gregory XII, one of the other popes judiciously offered his resignation. Conveniently forgetting the logic of asking Baldasare to be present in the first place, Sigismund used Gregory's authority to lend the affair a new whiff of legitimacy. Before accepting Benedict's resignation, Sigismund asked him to re-convene the Council under *his* authority. This would ensure the legitimacy of all his own acts. Benedict XIII—the last papal holdout—was declared a heretic and deposed in 1417.

Once Hus was gone, other issues occupied the council attendees. The council acted essentially as if it were a pope. It entertained ambassadors from Poland, Lithuania and the Teutonic Knights in a conflict the knights had termed a crusade against pagans. The council established that Polish and Lithuanian pagans had rights and could not be forcibly converted unless they brought harm to Christians. They legitimized the Brethren of the Brothers and Sisters, a new movement of popular piety centered in the Netherlands. Finally, they chose a new pope, Martin V. In 1420, the new pope Martin ordered the remains of Wycliffe exhumed, burned, and his ashes tossed into the river.

Why was this council so much more successful in accomplishing its goals than the previous one in Pisa? I think perhaps a clue lies in the notebooks of one of the attendees, a certain Ulrich of Richental, a resident of Constance. Ulrich, having apparently much leisure at his disposal, kept a journal in which he recorded many details, including and especially a list of attendees. They came from the church: 300 bishops, archbishops, and cardinals as well as nearly 300 abbots attended. They came from the nobility: nearly 2000 were princes, dukes or knights. They came from the universities: nearly 800 doctors of medicine, law, and theology as well as 1500 university masters were in attendance. Thousands of commoners: merchants, bankers, and guildsmen came. So thorough was Ulrich that he even took the time to count the prostitutes (there were 700). By his count, a total of 72,460 persons over the course of three years attended 45 official sessions and listened to over 300 sermons. The thoroughly representative nature of the assembly made the whole enterprise simply impossible to ignore.

It was a remarkable moment. This was Christendom turned upside down, almost literally. The vision of a Christian commonwealth superintended by the Pope in Rome was giving way to a society organized by political and economic imperatives with spokespersons empowered from multiple levels of society. For centuries the church had resisted expressions of popular piety as contrary to a religion ordered from above only to give way to that pressure now. The construction of Christendom had been predicated on a monopoly of religious authority and now that monopoly was forever broken. In this respect then, the Middle Ages were clearly over.

# The Black Death (1347 and so on...)

What became known as the Black Death struck in the middle of the schism we have just now described. Also known as the Bubonic Plague, this very nasty disease swept through Europe dozens of times from 1347 through the 1700s. In its first pass it killed between one third and one half of the entire population of Europe. And it returned frequently. The populations of some cites, especially in Italy, have even to this day barely recovered. Sienna, for example, with a modern population of fewer than 60,000, had about that much before the plague arrived in that city in 1348. Where there are good records, we see the disease reappearing on the average of every 15 years or so for the first century and reappearing occasionally for the following two centuries. Giovanni Boccaccio, a Florentine writer and poet, provides our best first-hand account of the plague. The book he wrote was a fictional account of a group who fled the city of Florence to wait out the disease in the countryside. The preface to that book provides an excellent description; not only of the disease itself, but also of the enormous strains it put on social mores.[*]

The disease presented obvious visible markers and these gave it its most popular names. The term "bubonic"[†] refers to swelling in the lymph glands (in the neck, armpits and groin areas) that appear as a usual symptom of infection. The "black" in Black Death refers to the color of those swellings. This was not the first time the disease arrived in Europe. It, or some earlier variant of it, had already struck the Roman empire in the 500s and some related strain of it crops up periodically in the modern era. The plague kills within a matter of days. It is caused by a bacterium peculiar to fleas that are themselves partial to certain kinds of rodents. The plague most probably originated in central or east Asia somewhere, and was carried west on the trade routes. Genoese traders who sailed on their rodent infested ships back and forth between the Black Sea and the Mediterranean finally introduced it to Europe.

---

[*] *Mores*: standards of social behavior as defined by traditional practice.

[†] *Bubonic*: from the medieval Latin word (*bubo*) for a pus-filled swelling in the groin area.

Sicily was the earliest likely arrival point in Europe. When people started dropping dead, Sicilians reacted in a predictably...well, medieval manner. The citizens of Messina sought emergency assistance from Saint Agatha, whose relics were held in a nearby city, Catana.* They marched to Catana and demanded that her relics be handed over to save their city. Apparently Agatha preferred to stay in Catana, so her custodians refused to facilitate her emigration. The situation was a bit tense but a compromise deal was finally struck: the archbishop of Catana offered to dip Agatha's relics in water which might then be used to sprinkle and purify the ground in Messina. Sadly, the measure failed to check the spread of the pestilence and further measures were deemed necessary.

This drama played itself out all over Europe in various ways and inspired many to participate in one of the most colorful manifestation of popular piety we associate with the Middle Ages: the Flagellant movement. The term comes from the Latin *flagellare*, to whip, and here it refers to those who would whip themselves as penance for sin. On the assumption that the plague was intended as a divine punishment, many Christians embraced the opportunity to inoculate themselves from the plague by beating and tearing their own flesh. There are earlier examples of this sort of thing as a self-

imposed penance by individuals but what is new here is its re-invention as a mass offering of a *vicarious* penance for the sins of others. Troupes of flagellants processed through the streets of medieval cities, chanting and whipping

---

* *St. Agatha*: a Christian martyr who died in the persecutions associated with the Emperor Decius in 251. Although she is and has been widely venerated, little is known of her life. Among the tortures she is said to have undergone was the cutting off of her breasts. She is for that reason now a patron saint of cancer.

themselves in a frenzied interaction with city-dwellers. At first they were welcomed nearly everywhere since so many people were convinced that corruption in society *and the church* had caused God to send the plague. To welcome the flagellants was itself a variety of penance.

Such spontaneous and dramatic manifestations of popular piety created problems for a church that was conceptually committed to managing the spiritual lives of its members. The church could not logically approve of the movement, as its existence suggested that the church was not the last word on what was, or was not, an effective penance; the whole notion was contrary to the direction the church had taken since Gregory VII. But practically speaking, the lack of any central figures associated with the movement made it difficult for the church to react effectively and this impotence was compounded by the death toll the plague wreaked on church personnel. Popes made vain efforts to ban the movement (Pope Clement VI in 1349, and Gregory XI in 1372), but the movement persisted into the 1400s, especially in Germany. The result was an ongoing social phenomenon with no clear direction. Participants in their processions sometimes numbered in the thousands, but eventually the prospect of delirious strangers inciting city residents to unpredictable acts of mass piety inspired many sober-minded civic authorities to shut their gates against them. In the final analysis, it was not the papacy that curbed the flagellants, but civic authorities sensitive to disruptions in public order. This hints at the waning influence of the church and the increasing importance of city-based institutions at the end of the Middle Ages.

Given the state of European medicine in the 1300s, it will be no surprise to learn that no one really understood how the disease was actually transmitted or contracted. The church's official antipathy to human autopsy had made serious and systematic study of either human anatomy or the physical progress of the disease virtually impossible. Serious advances in medicine at the university level were also limited by medieval adherence to ancient Greek ideas about bodily "humours," something even modern American doctors believed in until the eighteenth century. Ancient medical theory held that humours were levels of moisture and heat, a proper balance of which was necessary for health. Bleeding was the most frequently prescribed response to a diagnosis of out-of-balance humours.[*] The medical faculty at the University of Paris decided that an unusual conjunction of the planets Jupiter, Saturn, and Mars had somehow corrupted the air and threw off the balance of humours. Doctors were obviously clueless. The only truly effective responses emphasized quarantining those already afflicted. In Pistoia, Italy, for example, we know of various municipal edicts meant to control its spread. Attendance at funerals was strictly limited, travelers and imports from cities known to be infected were turned away, and only gravediggers licensed by the city were permitted to bury victims.

In the hysteria surrounding the progress of the disease not all saw it as a divine punishment. Some were quick to suspect sorcery and premeditated murder. The Jews, already a marginalized population in Europe, became a predictable target for such accusations. In 1348, Jews in the Swiss canton of Chillon "confessed" to participation in an elaborate plot to distribute packets of poison received from some mysterious Spanish rabbi. In communities across Europe, this wildly fantastic notion found ready purchase. In 1349, according to the medieval historian Königshofen, 2000 Jews were rounded up in Strasbourg and burned to death, their property expropriated, and Jews as a class banned from residence in that city for a further 100 years. This is merely one of hundreds of documented attacks on Jews deemed responsible for the Black Death.

Clearly one would expect a huge impact on the economy as some cities shut their gates to travelers, and as both secular and church leaders fell as casualties, and as virtually every segment of society withdrew from normal patterns of intercourse. Wages and prices fluctuated dramatically in response to serious disruptions in patterns of supply and demand in land, commodity, and labor. Numerous studies have been undertaken to consider the extent to which the plague caused these kinds of changes as opposed to merely accelerating changes already under way; there is by no means unanimity in their conclusions. Nevertheless, it is possible to understand the

---

[*] *Bleeding*: a medicinal practice consisting of intentional draining of blood from the body. The location of the incision was the key variable, as blood drained from one place as opposed to another would vary in color, constancy, and temperature.

plague's effect in the metaphor I suggested at the top of this chapter, that the plague was an earthquake, and as with earthquakes in general, one expects stronger versions of pre-earthquake structures to survive while weaker ones would not. The resulting patchwork of new and old social relations explains the inconclusive evidence and the divergence of views on direct plague effects. In any case, the direction of change—however uneven its progress—was toward free tenancy relationships between landowners and agricultural workers and away from presumptions of hereditary land rights. In practical terms, this left peasants increasingly vulnerable to dispossession and to some extent it separated them from their customary access to undeveloped lands where tradition allowed them foraging rights.

# The Hundred Years War (1338-1453)

The Hundred Years War is a misnomer for at least two reasons. It certainly lasted more than 100 years. And it was really two major wars separated by a long and troubled truce. The ostensible issue at the start was whether the crown of France belonged to those descended from cousins of the French king who died in 1328 with no living children, or to the descendants of his sister.* The purely technical issue, at least at first, was whether the crown could pass directly through the female line. If it were so, then King Edward III of England, son of the sister in question, had a legitimate claim to the throne. But of course, there was a lot more to it than that.

English and French claims in France had been entangled since William the Conqueror, Duke of Normandy took the English throne in 1066. That drama was replayed, after a fashion, in 1154 when Henry Plantagenet, also Duke of Normandy, ascended to the English throne. The illogical result of these events was that because kings of England were also dukes of Normandy, they were technically vassals of the kings of France, at least with respect to Normandy. This was further complicated by Henry II's marriage

---

* Charles IV ruled France 1294-1328. His first cousin Philip VI who ruled 1328-1350 succeeded him. Charles also had a daughter who was born two months after his own death: **Blanche of Orleans**

to Eleanor of Aquitaine, countess and duchess of extensive French lands in her own right. When King John of England, son of Henry II and Eleanor, came to the throne in 1199, his most important revenue producing lands were those he inherited in France. But John's various blunders and missteps (mentioned in the previous chapter) gave ample opportunity to the kings of France to annul these claims.*

The long and short of all of this is that by the time Edward became King Edward III of England in 1327 at the age of fourteen, his French lands had been reduced to a tiny chunk of Aquitaine. Meanwhile, the young king also inherited a troublesome war with the Scots. The combination of his youth and these circumstances encouraged the French King Phillip VI to attack English interests in every way he could. He wished, were it possible, to sweep away all English claims in France forever. French ships were sent to raid English coastal targets in support of the Scots and Philip used this diversion to confiscate what was left of English Aquitaine in 1337. But young King Edward did not roll over; he chose this moment to press his claim to the French throne in a bold countermove in this real life "Game of Thrones." And there were many powerful interests in France that supported his gambit. The wool trade in Flanders and the Netherlands tied the economy of those regions firmly to England, a key source of the wool they required for their looms. Clumsy attempts by the French to undermine that connection pushed these regions into even greater sympathy with the English. For Edward, the wool trade was a key source of taxation for the English crown that did not depend on his troublesome nobles at home in England. All of this made Flanders and the Netherlands natural allies of England and likely supporters of his bid to retake French lands.

---

* Hence the nickname some have given King John: John *Lackland*. For John's military blunders, he also earned the epithet, John *Softsword*. Poor John; he cannot catch a break. Even now he is doomed to a comic book status in Robin Hood stories until the end of time...

# Act One: The Battles of Crecy and Poitiers

The first big action of the war took place near Sluys, France, in 1340 and happened, technically, at sea, although the victory was largely due to archers aboard English ships facing Italian crossbowmen on French ships. The daylong fight evolved into a bloody melee of hand to hand fighting and resulted in the total destruction of the French fleet with practically no losses on the English side. The mismatch between crossbows and longbows was a harbinger of things to come. Although the battle guaranteed English control of the cross-channel trade so important to his Flemish and Dutch allies, Edward was in no position to follow up with a full-scale invasion of France; this would have to wait. The English crown was virtually broke and many of the English nobles were not much interested in solving that problem (perhaps a bit of *schadenfreude* was at work).* As a result, Edward spent most of his time developing alliances with individual French nobles while mercenary companies that he had hired wreaked havoc and terrorized smaller settlements in France. The strategy was based on hard lessons the English had learned from the Scots, who had for some time become adept at this sort of warfare, only at English expense.† It was a relatively cost-effective way for Edward to pressure the French into negotiations, which were, as it turned out, not forthcoming. Meanwhile, Edward made plans for

a more ambitious invasion but it was not until 1346, eight years after the war had started, that Edward could proceed to France at the head of an army.

Edward and a force of about 12,000 landed in Normandy and marched northward, pillaging the countryside in a more ambitious version of the strategy he had been employing all along, taking

---

* *Schadenfreude*: pleasure derived from someone else's misfortune. In this case, the English nobles preferred that the English king be broke as this meant it was more difficult for him to give them a hard time.

† Portrayed semi-fictionally in the Hollywood epic, *Braveheart*.

smaller cities as he progressed. He probably intended to meet Flemish allies marching southward. Meanwhile, Edward tried in vain to avoid a large French force that was then moving to cut him off. Although he ended up being forced to fight a battle he did not really want, Edward nevertheless had the twin advantages of choosing the battle-site and having sufficient opportunity to make preparations that might offset his numerical disadvantage (the French were twice his number). The English, with a full day to prepare, dug ditches and made other hazards intended to slow the advance of the French. When the French finally arrived, they moved to attack immediately and in their zeal threw all caution to the wind. They began the attack with Italian crossbowmen sent out in front of the French knights. But, in their haste, the shields intended to provide cover from English longbows were left in the rear. Clouds of arrows launched by the English from long range decimated the Italians and, when the Italians seemed to signal their intention to surrender, the French knights stationed behind them cut down the survivors.

The French knights then proceeded to charge the English lines but the dead, wounded, and fleeing Italians on the field in front of them impeded their progress. Over and over again, sixteen times in all, the French nobles charged with the same disastrous result every time; each charge wilting under the sustained fire of thousands of arrows. The blind Prince of Bohemia, a cousin of the French king, led one of the doomed charges. In a bizarre concession to the inherent idiocy of such an idea, the blind prince's horse was tied to those of two other knights. Unhappily, all three were killed. For the French, the battle was a tragedy of epic proportion unequalled in its ignominy, at least until the next major battle between English and French. Edward, flushed with victory, advanced unopposed to capture the port of Calais, an acquisition that would ensure English control of the English Channel for the next 200 years. Meanwhile, a supporting Scottish invasion of northern England failed miserably. Edward, now released from a distracting war in Scotland, was suddenly in an excellent position to pursue his war in France.

As it turned out, the Black Death intervened and put the war on pause. Ten years passed before the next major battle, the battle of Poitiers, in

1356. The outcome was similar to Crecy but the defeat was compounded mightily by the live capture of the French king, John II. With John in custody, Edward now faced his son, the Dauphin* Charles, now ruling as regent for his imprisoned father. The Dauphin wisely avoided direct conflict with the English Army, which it seemed incapable of beating, despite the overwhelming odds provided by French numbers. On the other hand, with limited forces in the field, the English were unable to take any large cities. A sort of stalemate existed, which convinced Edward to sign the treaty of Bretigny in May of 1360, with quite favorable terms for the English. The French recognized an expanded English Aquitaine in exchange for English concessions elsewhere in France. The French also agreed to pay three million pounds of silver in ransom, one million down and two to be paid later†. For these concessions, Edward renounced his claim to the French crown while John returned to France to raise his own ransom. John left two of his sons as guarantors of the ransom. When one escaped, John, true to his word, turned himself in and he spent the last few months of his life in captivity. The Dauphin, now Charles V, officially succeeded him in 1364.

# Act Two: Disarray and Confusion, 1369- 1415

During the decade or so after the peace of Bretigny, France and England engaged in a war of proxies in Castille, the northern regions of Spain. For the most part, this did not go well for the English. Meanwhile, Aquitanian resistance to English tax collectors created financial problems for the English. Naturally, the French king, Charles V, was happy to see the English unable to collect their taxes and he did nothing to help, although he was technically obligated to do so as Edward's feudal lord (in France). The

---

* **Dauphin**: the presumed successor to the French crown. Meaning literally dolphin, it refers to the province of Dauphiné and the dolphins displayed on the prince's coat of arms.

† Both French and English currencies changed quite a bit in these years. The French created a new coin, the franc, to pay the ransom. It was worth a pound of silver.

son of Edward III, the so-called Black Prince, tried to force the issue by declaring war on the French in 1369. However, his death after a protracted illness in 1376, followed by his elderly father's death a year later, left his ten-year-old son on the English throne (King Richard II). The boy-king was obviously unprepared for what faced him; from the first he was battered by problems on every side. It began with a political standoff in England between the English nobles and the King's uncle, John of Gaunt, and a few years later yet another war broke out with the Scots. Meanwhile, the English lost control of most of their gains in France. By 1380, the English position in France had been reduced to a single city, Calais. Finally, In 1381, Richard was forced to deal with a peasant revolt (more on this below). Richard's popularity plummeted.

Meanwhile, things were just as confused in France. Charles V died in 1380, leaving power to his eleven-year-old son, now Charles VI. The four uncles of the young king seized the opportunity to plunder the treasury for their own benefit. The political backbiting that took place behind the French throne eventually evolved into a civil war dressed up as a renewed war with the English. When Charles was twenty-one, he dismissed his uncles in an attempt to regain control but began soon thereafter to display alarming episodes of insanity. Having an obvious incompetent on the throne made for even fiercer behind the scenes intrigue, especially between the king's brother Louis, Duke of Orleans and the king's uncle John, Duke of Burgundy. Louis's father-in-law was Duke of Armagnac and the feud of the resulting factions is frequently referred to as between the Armagnacs and the Burgundians. All this French dynastic intrigue, punctuated by the occasional assassination, provided new opportunities for expansion of English interests in France. When King Henry V of England took the throne in 1413, he began immediately to build bridges with the Burgundian faction, in the hopes of at the very least, wining the unpaid balance (about half remained) of the ransom of John II. In 1414, Henry sent ambassadors to King Charles VI demanding the return of all formerly English lands in France, and—clearly thinking long term—Charles' daughter as wife.

# Act Three: A New Kind of War
## 1415-1453

Needless to say, the demands were not met and Henry invaded France with a small force in 1415. His plan was to meet up with the Burgundians and together march on Paris. But delays in preparation, bad weather, and time wasted besieging the port city of Harfleur forced Henry to scale down his plans and so he turned for Calais to wind up the campaigning season. Even with all the delays hindering the advance of the English, the French were still slow to respond. As Henry marched north toward Calais, the French were content to block his progress and force him inland away from the coast with its possibility of resupply; they were biding their time, waiting for the remainder of their army to arrive. Time obviously did not favor Henry's position and he knew it. The English morale was desperate. Many of his men were sick, probably with dysentery. Every day that passed meant a stronger French force and a weaker English one. After a forced march of over 200 miles, Henry decided to provoke a battle while he still had some viable options. This was the battle of Agincourt.*

Three-quarters of the English force consisted of archers, all commoners, and so worthless for ransom. Their fate would be slaughter in any defeat. The French, on the other hand, were mostly noble men-at-arms, anxious to redeem the honor lost in previous contests with the English. When the battle took place, many of the French leaders insisted on standing in the front rank because of the dishonors they had endured in previous battles. These opposing mindsets, desperate English resistance against irrational French eagerness, may have had much to do with the outcome of the battle. As in the previous major battles, the English chose the field of battle. And as also in the previous major battles, Crecy and Poitiers, the archers made the difference. Arrayed on the wings behind a network of stakes in the ground and in blocks interspersed between men-at-arms deployed elbow to elbow, the archers were positioned to rain death upon French forces long before the contact necessary for men-at-arms to engage in hand-to-hand

---

* Forever made famous by Shakespeare in Henry V.

combat. The French charge against the wings—a failed attempt to drive the archers from the field—was turned back and the heavy mounted knights found themselves running into the tightly packed ranks of their own men advancing on foot into the gap between the two armies. The resulting confusion, exacerbated by clouds of smoke from first generation cannons, turned the middle into a horrible killing field onto which was launched flight after flight of deadly English arrows. Witnesses who were present describe a horrific carnage featuring heaps of bodies and a ground rendered muddy and slippery by wet soil and French blood.

As in the previous contests, the French outnumbered the English by a large margin, but the narrowness of the field of battle made it impossible for the French superior numbers to work effectively. The reports of the battle all indicate that when the two armies did collide, the English were initially pushed backward. This should have been decisive. But the French had advanced in too-closely-packed a formation for effective use of their weapons and they found themselves advancing over the bodies of their fallen comrades. The soft ground favored the English who were not wearing armor. Even so, superior French numbers should have prevailed. They did not, at least in part because the French broke off contact when news came that the English had begun executing French prisoners, whose numbers were swelling dangerously. The English kept only the high value prisoners and executed the rest. After the battle the English marched off unmolested.

# Cannons

Although without apparent effect at Agincourt, a revolution in war-making technology was underway: the development of useful cannons. We can credit the introduction of cannons in the west to a chain of transmission from the Chinese, to the Mongols, and then to the Arabs, from whom Europeans most likely gained the knowledge. We know that Europeans knew at least something about gunpowder before this: Roger Bacon of Oxford mentioned gunpowder in his writings as early as 1216. Even so, it was the Chinese who first made viable offensive weapons by creating gunpowder that exploded rather than merely burning. The Mongol conquest of China and the destruction of Baghdad in 1258 opened up a highway of cultural transfer between east and west that affected Europeans in dramatic fashion. An introduction—or at the very least, a significant boost—to cannon technology had an obvious impact but we can also find on that list such items as compasses, paper, the plague, and eventually moveable type. Gunpowder had been in use in China for some time before the appearance of the Mongols in the 1200's but the Mongol threat seems to have instigated a new urgency to its military application.

In any case, the Mongols carried the technology west and although the train of transfer is not settled, probably passed it to the Arabs. Arab cannons were certainly used in Spain in the mid-1200s. We have an account by a Florentine banker, Giovanni Villani, that English cannons caused some devastation at the battle of Crecy in 1346 but Villani was in Florence being convicted of financial misconduct at the time. If there is any basis for his report, that basis was relayed by the survivors of the Genoese crossbowmen who had been so rudely treated early in that battle. In any case, such cannons as existed at that early stage of development were impractical to move around and so were of little use either in siege warfare or in open field battles. Despite reports of cannons in various battles of the 1300s there is no contemporary evidence of their destructive capabilities. That all changed quickly during the 1400s. The French blasted their way into Italy with just a few cannons in the late 1400s. Already by 1453, the Ottoman Turks had a weapon so big it took sixty oxen to haul it into position, three hours to load, and its report could be heard ten miles away. With this and other cannons, it took only six weeks of bombardment to destroy the walls of Constantinople, a city that had survived unscathed for a thousand years.

# Joan of Arc

Meanwhile, cannons were finding their way into the action in France. But cannon technology was one thing, but one has also to know how to employ the technology. The critical moment in this learning curve coincided with the appearance of a French peasant maiden, Joan of Arc. When she entered the story, the French war effort had been paralyzed by the disaster at

Agincourt. Those French who had stayed neutral or who had allied themselves with the English were clearly on the ascendant. The sixteen year old dauphin, the future King Charles VII, tried to survive by separating himself from his insane father by arranging an alliance between himself and the Burgundians but this prudent move was undone by the assassination of the Duke of Burgundy in 1419. The Burgundians then took Paris and handed it over to the English. Under intense pressure from all around, the insane King Charles VI signed the treaty of Troyes in 1420 in which the children of the English King Henry V and Charles VI's daughter Catherine of Valois would inherit the French crown. The claim of the sixteen-year-old dauphin was declared null and void. It all looked pretty good for the English. For all practical purposes, Henry V had won the war. He controlled more than half of France and if his son and daughter-in-law should have a son, that son would be King of all France and England. But the young dauphin had other ideas, and fought on, although not especially well. Mostly he took refuge in Southern France as the English expanded their presence in Northern France.

Now enter Joan. In the midst of a long English siege of Orleans in 1428 and 1429, this illiterate peasant maiden made two attempts to see the Dauphin, claiming she had a divine mission to drive the English from France. On the second try, she won the opportunity after correctly predicting a French defeat on the very day she made her request. Intrigued, Charles consented to her appearance and was further impressed by her recognition of himself despite his attempt at disguise. He granted her the opportunity to accompany an army headed for the siege at Orleans. There is some scholarly debate about Joan's actual role at Orleans. We can hardly expect that the noble leaders present at the battle would willingly give her neither much authority, nor much credit should she be successful. Her own words, in letters dictated by her and in the transcript of her later interrogations, are ambiguous enough to support

244

different narratives. Her proclaimed visions from God had the effect of turning the war into a holy war and this certainly appealed to those defending the city. It seems that at the very least her presence provided a significant morale boost for the French forces whose record in the war had been mostly miserable. Her well-known and frequent exhortations to "attack, attack, and attack" had some practical effect. As it turned out, barely a week after her arrival at Orleans, the English siege was broken and everyone regarded Joan's presence on the field as instrumental.

The most logical explanation for the success probably lies in connecting her exhortations with an increasingly aggressive use of cannon technology, an experiment still very much in progress. But Joan's apparent success garnered her much support among the French war leaders and they supported her bold plan to relieve Reims, a city under siege deep behind English lines. Reims was the most important symbol of French royal history as it was the location for all coronations of French kings. Charles VII had not yet been crowned. A French victory there would provide an opportunity to establish himself as the legitimate king. But Reims had exactly the same importance to the English, as Henry wished to see his own young son, technically Dauphin of France according to the treaty of Troyes, crowned there as well. The French set off quickly along the Somme river, aiming to take all the bridges along the way.

Joan was a potent symbol associated with Charles VII and was instrumental in his coronation and to devalue her was to undermine Charles VII's legitimacy. The English decided to have her tried for heresy by French prelates upon whom they could count. It was therefore a political trial first and foremost, even if the issues being argued were religious. Her interrogation record has survived and is a fascinating document. Truth be told, there is little evidence of any religious controversy in her actions or words and her answers as recorded suggest that she was keen to avoid heretical pronouncements. Some of those present claimed the record of her interrogation was altered but we cannot know for sure. The only clear doctrinal issues stemmed from her claim to have heard from God directly and her habit of wearing male clothing. Indeed, one is struck by the number of times her interrogators returned to her clothing choices.* In any case, she was burned at the stake May 30, 1431, a year after her capture.

Joan's dramatic moment on the stage of history coincided with another period of weakness and indecision on the English side. King Henry V of England had died ten years previously, leaving Henry VI, yet another boy

---

* The problem is that if women were women, then according to God's will, women should wear women's clothing. Since Joan was doing something inherently male, being a warrior, she was acting, and dressing, in contradiction of God's will. This might be taken as evidence that she was inspired by the dark forces of Satan who existed to subvert God's will, instead of being by inspired by God, which is what she claimed. This is all complicated by the likelihood of rape at the hands of her jailors. Clearly, male clothing would have helped her defend her virtue but her practical insistence on wearing it while imprisoned was taken as an obstinate defiance of God's will.

king, on the throne. Squabbling among the English nobles translated into incoherence in both war planning and diplomacy. On the French side, many of those nobles who had been allied with the English switched sides. It was only a matter of time until French cannons blew up all the remaining English forts. In 1453, the last battle was fought, although France and England remained technically at war for another two decades. After 116 years of death and destruction, the English were left with Calais and a sliver of land in the south.

The Hundred Years War provides fascinating tales of medieval battle, royal politics, intrigue, and insanity. It is replete with dramatic turns of fortune, inspiring moments of heroism and rhetoric, and it was punctuated by entertaining examples of both stupidity and cupidity. It is also, like all wars, a bloody testament to the arrogance and presumption of political leaders who have always regarded the lives of their lessers as a currency meant to be spent freely—and gratuitously—in pursuit of the accumulation of…honor and privilege. But this war does more than merely lay bare the madness of all war; it reveals and points forward to ideas of nationhood and political identity that belong to subsequent eras. A century of warfare that began within a common French speaking nobility evolved into one between separate English and French nobilities. Before the war, one cannot reasonably talk about France and England as nations; they were fluid collections of individual realms. The expenses of protracted warfare stimulated the construction of ever more intrusive forms of taxation, a precondition for strong central government. The increasing reliance on expensive cannons only hastened this transition. Medieval cavalry was rendered obsolete by the use of artillery, first in the form of arrows, and then more decisively, with cannonballs. In so doing, the traditional divisions of medieval society—those who pray, those who fight, and those who toil—broke down. Modern warfare democratized combat. Neither arrows nor cannonballs required nobility to operate them. Nor did they care whose bodies they penetrated or shattered. What honor was there to be had in war now fought from a distance and from behind barricades? It is the same question posed by the ancient Spartans who, for their own part, eschewed archery as a combat unbefitting warriors with honor.

# Peasant Revolts

Over the same period we have been considering, four major outbreaks of public disorder took place in Europe. These most famous episodes happened in Flanders in 1323, France in 1358, Florence in 1378, and England in 1381. Historians call these disturbances Peasant Revolts. This convention is perhaps unfortunate as it obscures the much more complicated issues to which these outbreaks were frustrated responses. In only the English example is the conflict explicitly understandable as resulting from peasant complaints. In the French example, the conflict spread to the country only after beginning in the city. The Italian example had nothing at all to do with the peasantry; it was a conflict between levels of privilege and status within the city walls. The Flemish example was really a conflict between city government and royal government. Thus, each revolt had a unique narrative and although there is no direct connection between them, as a group they do reveal common elements of social and economic change that was taking place across Europe. Each one represented a serious challenge to outmoded medieval institutions. Three of the four represent challenges to royal authority and the fourth is a challenge to the authority of the medieval guilds. Let us take each in turn.

# The Flanders Revolt (1323-1328)

Medieval Flanders was centered in what is today Belgium. Like the Netherlands, it is primarily a Dutch-speaking area and has always existed in the spaces between France, Germany, and England; much of its political history developed as a consequence of its relationships to these more powerful neighbors. Throughout most of the Middle Ages it was technically subject to France, but that subjection was more nominal than real. The region was a textile-producing powerhouse buying huge quantities of wool from its neighbors, especially the English, and it featured a number of autonomous cities run by powerful textile guilds and an emergent merchant elite. Technically independent of aristocratic control, the obvious prosperity of these cities represented a cash cow that the counts of Flanders and French kings were eager to milk, and this led to much conflict. Because of their connections to the wool industry, the English were much interested in all of this as well. The intersection of these different political and economic interests encouraged city authorities to play each against the other. It was a dangerous game.

In 1302, a popular rebellion against French taxes broke out in the Flemish city of Bruges, resulting in the death of the French garrison there; this was followed by an embarrassing defeat of a French cavalry by an urban militia using maces and spears. To avoid the problem of guarding prisoners, the Bruges militia executed them all, including the French commander. The battle is called the Battle of the Golden Spurs for all the spurs collected from the French dead. Full Flemish independence resulted, but it only lasted three years, after which the count of Flanders, Robert III, steered a middle course between the English and French kings. He did this primarily by maintaining a friendly economic policy with the English while renewing obligations of fealty to the French King. This delicate balancing act lasted until his death in 1322; his successor, Count Louis III, immediately announced his intention to turn away from the English along with the collection of new taxes for the recently crowned French king, Charles IV.

Louis obviously had no real understanding either of the economic dynamics at stake or how his policy shifts would be received, because he arrived from Paris with no army to support him despite rumors that Flanders was on the verge of renewed revolt. The announcement of the new taxes, on top of recent bad harvests, and a history of relative Flemish independence inspired several larger land owners in the countryside outside Bruges to conspire with the mayor of Bruges to revolt. Apparently surprised by all of this, Louis was forced to negotiate a peace. But this was disingenuous and intended merely to buy time. At his first opportunity

Louis arrested some city leaders and in the resulting scuffle one of his men killed a commoner. Still without adequate military support, Count Louis found himself arrested and tossed into a dungeon. The new king of France, Charles IV, vacillated, then arranged the release of Louis and finally a peace in 1328. Count Louis, obviously harboring a grudge, convinced the *next* French King Philip VI to crush Bruges and the other Flemish city elites and with his help finally did so. The mayor of Bruges was executed in Paris, and Louis remained a faithful ally of the French until his death at the battle of Crecy in 1346.

What is the significance of all this? On the level of the particular, the callous disregard by the French for the economic connections of Flanders to England guaranteed that when Edward II announced his intention to fight for the crown of France, he found in Flanders much sympathy and support. On the macro level, the conflict lays bare the fundamentally different social, political and economic imperatives between the late medieval and early modern landscapes.* On the one hand there was a feudal nobility whose collective self-image was defined by membership in a noble warrior caste. This caste had little or no cognizance of the economic dynamics of the urban economy because in their world-view non-nobles only existed to support the nobles. On the other hand, an emergent urban economic elite challenged the traditional hereditary elite for partnership with national leaders. The inclusion of this episode in the category of peasant revolts is ludicrous of course; peasants may have played a part, but their interests were never at stake. Still, the term does highlight the dismissive and reactionary attitudes that feudal leaders reflexively displayed to the pressures of social change. We see this again in France, just a few years later.

---

* When we speak of the modern period, we refer to the period from about 1500 until the present. The *early* modern period is that from about 1500 to the French Revolution (1789), dividing the modern period roughly in half.

# The *Jacquerie* (1358)

This French revolt near Paris in 1358 is named for a peasant tunic worn in the period (called a Jacque). Like the collective connotation of the term peasant revolt, it was a derisive term meant to emphasize the low class of those in revolt.* The context of the revolt is the period shortly after the battle of Poitiers, when the ransom for the king's recovery was being raised. All the north of France was in turmoil. While the paralyzed French crown obsessed about the war with England, the French nobility squabbled and schemed in the power vacuum that resulted. French nobles were more interested in rebuilding chateaus that had been burned by the English than they were in anything else. City dwellers were resentful of new taxes and tithes, and the peasants were especially incensed at being forced to rebuild and defend noble refuges while English mercenary companies regularly ravaged their own lands. The dauphin, resident in Paris, was enormously unpopular and Paris roiled in turmoil with his presence.

Rebellion erupted in Paris under the leadership of a clothing merchant, Etienne Marcel, who seized the city gates and, after murdering the marshals guarding the dauphin, organized a new city government. The dauphin found himself, for all practical purposes, Marcel's prisoner. Marcel appealed to Charles II of Navarre—an ambitious noble with eyes on the French crown—for military support. Although from the Pyrenees region of France and Spain, Charles of Navarre also had extensive lands in the north and west of France. Charles accepted Marcel's invitation and entered Paris with his soldiers. This sealed the fates of all concerned. Charles was playing his own game and would be in the last resort loyal to his own class. In this now three-way struggle, Marcel's position was doomed because his murder of the nobles guarding the Dauphin made it unlikely he would ever be trusted by the French nobility. In the midst of all this excitement, somehow the Dauphin escaped the city and joined his few supporters outside. Soon both

---

* And so it was, in a manner of speaking, the t-shirt rebellion, similar perhaps to the *sans-culottes* (the guys with no fancy-pants) who fought the French Revolution of 1789.

Charles and the Dauphin were pillaging Parisians suburbs to put pressure on each other and on Marcel.

Meanwhile, Guillaume Cale, a peasant famer, raised an army in the northern countryside from disaffected peasants who had heard of the uprising in Paris. Marcel declared his support for Cale and, in for a penny, in for a pound, led a force of a thousand or so Parisians out against a fortress (Meaux) held by nobles about 25 miles from Paris. The Parisians were routed with little difficulty. Meanwhile, Charles of Navarre showed some of his true colors when he answered an appeal from the northern nobles to fend off Cale's newly raised peasant force. In a cruel gambit, Charles convinced Cale to leave his army to discuss terms. Cale was immediately clapped in irons and subsequently beheaded. Cale's leaderless army was then easily destroyed. These twin disasters for the rebels came within days of each other, followed by inevitable reprisals: for the next two months, peasants were slaughtered indiscriminately. Marcel was killed at one of the city gates in July. In the aftermath, heavy fines were assessed on all towns that supported the uprising. In retrospect, here at least we have a peasant revolt that actually involved peasants, although the peasants joined the game after it had already started. The peasants rose in support of an uprising that actually began in the city, revealing some of the same dynamics we saw in the Flemish revolt.

## The *Ciompi* of Florence (1378)

Now we turn to Italy where, twenty years after the *Jacquerie*, we have another uprising that occurred in a city. This revolt is named for unskilled textile laborers in Florence, Italy. *Ciompi* were wool carders, textile workers who straightened wool fibers. But the revolt was not just of carders, it was of all the unskilled laborers in Florence. The name stuck because the first important leader of the revolt, Michele do Lando, was a wool carder. The dispute was rooted in the prohibition of unskilled workers from guild membership. The discrimination was compounded by the fact that in Florence, as in many other cities, membership in a recognized guild was a prerequisite for political office. Florence had a three-tiered class system based on occupation: there were major guilds (*arti maggiore*), minor guilds (*arti minore*), and unskilled non-guild workers, among whom were the *ciompi*. Unskilled laborers played no role in government and, predictably, their economic and social position was tenuous. In June of 1378, infighting between the major and minor guilds gave the unskilled workers an opportunity to demand inclusion and reform. They seized government buildings and by July forced the ruling council of the city to grant them guild status, the abolition of corporal punishment, and tax reform. To enforce these changes, the *Ciompi* organized their own citizen militia under the leadership of Salvestro Medici.

The result was a brief—very brief—flourishing of democracy. While these events had been unfolding in Florence, relations between the northern Italian cities and the papacy had plunged to an all-time low. Florence had spent a fortune defending itself in a bitter and brutal war and was broke. By August, the financial pressures pushed the major guilds to close ranks; they went after the *Ciompi* leaders and undid, step by step, all the reforms benefitting unskilled Florentines. Notably, the Medici switched sides and were instrumental in restoring the original guilds to their previous dominance. Salvestro's role in this drama portended a new era in Florentine politics: the rise of the Medici. His cousin, Giovanni, was the founder of the Medici bank and the political dynasty associated with it.

In retrospect, this revolt really gets to basic economic changes underway at the end of the Middle Ages. Notice that the prime locus of this conflict was in the structure of labor relations and not between the feudal nobility and everyone else. In the Middle Ages, craft guilds developed to create and protect production and skill monopolies. Aside from the economic roles they played in the lives of individual craft categories, they also provided structure to the management of overall city life. But as medieval cities matured as social and economic organisms, inevitable stratifications appeared along economic lines. Meanwhile, the increasing velocity of the continental and world economies sharpened competition across all social boundaries. At the city level, this translated into conflict between skilled and unskilled labor, to the point that it became ever more indicative of class divisions than the hereditary lines between noble and commoner. We see this in Italy first because the feudal nobility in Italy was never as powerful as it was elsewhere, at least in part because of the presence of an assertive papacy. Nevertheless, these were problems that grew and became predictable features of the early modern period.

## English Peasant's Revolt (1381)

This revolt, also known as Wat Tyler's Rebellion, is the best known of the peasant rebellions and, once again, we have some actual peasants involved. It began in 1381 consequent to attempts by King Richard II to enforce war taxes. In this way it bore a resemblance to the tensions instigating the *Jacquerie*. King Richard had been king of England four years, despite being only fourteen, and there was little confidence in his ability nor much trust in his advisors, especially on the part of his uncle, John of Gaunt, reputedly the richest man in England. This wasn't just about new taxes, however. Peasants in England had been complaining of labor laws passed to restrict the growth in their wages since the Black Death, thirty years earlier. Nobles needing labor for fields made empty by the disease or by peasants fleeing to the city had been increasingly forced to compete for labor with city employers working in trades that paid better. Complaints made by nobles to King Edward III in the 1350s resulted in reactionary laws that restricted rights of movement and suppressed wages back to pre-plague levels. With wages artificially held down by this pressure, the new taxes announced by Richard became a straw that broke the camel's back.

It all began in May when an English tax collector was turned away empty-handed by angry Essex villagers. A judge sent to investigate the matter was then beaten up. News spread quickly of this defiance and, emboldened, peasants anxious to put their case to the king gathered in Essex and Kent and marched off to London. It was now mid-June. Wat Tyler was the leader of a group from Kent; Jack Straw of one from Essex. When the men arrived in London, there was at first little damage done by the marchers except to property owned by the more unpopular of the king's advisors. The king actually met with the leaders, who presented him with a number of demands, including and especially the abolition of serfdom. Meanwhile things started getting a little tense around the city. A group of rioters forced their way into the Tower of London and two key financial officials of the king were beheaded. Elsewhere in the city, Richard Lyons, Warden of the Mint, a notorious usurer,* and close associate of John of Gaunt, was also arrested and beheaded. These attacks on royal officials sealed the rebels' fate. The very next day Wat Tyler was murdered in a confused meeting with the king. In a rare display of prudent leadership, King Richard seized the moment and defused the situation by promising all sorts of concessions. Sadly, it was a ploy: when the revolt was over, all concessions were canceled. Meanwhile, the countryside was in uproar. But without leadership or coherent program the revolt was quickly and brutally suppressed.

So what is the significance of this pattern of rebellions? If you paste it all together, one sees an economic and social system in a moment of major stress and flux. The rise of cities and city governments presented major challenges to the feudal aristocracy. The pendulum of urban politics in Flanders swung predictably back and forth on the basis of economic interest; it was all about the wool trade. The English example opens a window on the breakdown of medieval serfdom. The Italian example highlights problems created by the medieval guild system. Originally created to protect urban workers and foster economic monopoly, guilds had evolved into mechanisms to enforce social and political privileges. The violence exposes to our view the relentless stratification of labor that took place in the transition from the medieval economy to a capitalist one and incidentally provides us an early illustration of the prime locus of revolutionary economic change—the urban economy.

---

* *Usurer:* someone who makes an exorbitant profit from high-interest loans. This was a common scam enforced by unscrupulous tax officials.

## End of the Middle Ages Timeline

Last of the crusader states in the Levant falls   1291
French King Phillip IV convenes *Estates General*
to indict Pope Boniface VIII                      1302
Knights Templar suppressed                        1307-12
Clement V moves papacy to Avignon.                1309
Flanders peasant revolt                           1323
Edward III, King of England                       1327-77
Battle of Sluys (Hundred Yrs. War)                1340
Battle of Crecy (Hundred Yrs. War)                1346
Black Death strikes Europe                        1347
Battle of Poitiers (Hundred Yrs. War)             1356
Jacquerie revolt in France                        1358
Treaty of Bretigny (Hundred Yrs. War)             1360
Richard II, King of England                       1377-99
Pope Gregory XI moves back to Rome, dies          1377
John Wycliffe under 'house arrest'                1377-1384
*Ciompi* revolt in Florence                       1378
Schism in the church: two popes       .           1378-1417
English peasant revolt        .                   1381
Council of Pisa elects a third pope               1409-1417
John Hus' writings condemned by new pope          1409
Henry V, King of England                          1413-1422
Council of Constance solves multi-pope problem.1414-1417
Battle of Agincourt (Hundred Yrs. War)            1415
Treaty of Troyes (Hundred Yrs. War)               1420
Joan of Arc burned at the stake                   1431
English lose Paris (Hundred Yrs. War)             1436
Moveable type introduced in Europe                1450
English lose all but Calais in Hundred Yrs. War 1453
Constantinople falls to the Ottoman Turks         1453

# Chapter Twelve: Columbus and the Modern Mind

*What was so modern about the age of Columbus?*

In the previous chapter we looked back upon a society experiencing irresistible pressures of change. All the organizing principles and assumptions that had long governed medieval thinking made less and less sense with each passing decade. Now, we can turn around and face in the other direction, toward the present. Of course, we know what is to come. And although those who lived in the late 1400s did not know their future, they did know that their world was changing. The geographic center of European identity was shifting away from the Mediterranean to the Atlantic. The intellectual complacency characteristic of the Middle Ages was jolted by the rediscovery of ancient knowledge, by first hand reports of the sophistication of China and, soon, by the discovery of vast new lands in the Americas. But something subtler was going on as well. The European mind at the end of the 1400s was deeply suffused by a sense of drama. This is not unique to the Renaissance era by any means; the dramatic mindset of the Middle Ages was rooted in fatalistic notions about God, fate, and the limitations of humanity. But the post-medieval mindset was different in a very important way. Rather than featuring the *limitations* of mortality, it seemed to emphasize its *potential*.

This is a modern notion. Not modern in the sense of up-to-date, but modern in the sense of tending to reshape tradition or even reject tradition altogether. Changes in fashion and the proliferation of handbooks on behavior signaled the dawning of the possibility of self-creation. This was only possible because the categories of caste predominant in the Middle Ages as exemplified in the three estates (priest, warrior, and commoner) no longer neatly signified prestige or station. The papal philosophy that had so strenuously strained to define, order, and enforce all societal norms had been largely tamed even as the demons it had unleashed in the Inquisition would resurface to haunt the witch trials of the early modern era. European society remained a dangerous and ugly world in so many ways, but the possibility of a metaphorical escape from traditional social categories was real, at least in the minds of the Renaissance man.* A space had opened that allowed for the individual to exist as *an idea*. This is how we will portray Columbus here. He represents the possibility of escape. We nominate him here as "the first modern man." But before we look at Columbus the man, let us look at his world.

## Justice and Public Spectacle

The first thing we notice is that everything seems so dramatic! One of the most vibrant expressions of the Renaissance sense of drama lay in its rituals of justice. In chapter two we argued that all political legitimacy was intimately rooted in the notion of justice, and logically we would expect that the conduct and management of justice would be exercised in public. And to some extent, there was always room for public participation in or a least witness to the process. Never was this more so than in the Early Modern period (1500-1789). Important changes had already taken place in European culture that shifted the role the public played in the witness and process of justice. To begin with, over the course of the Middle Ages, there was a transition from a system of accusatorial justice to an inquisitorial one.

---

* *Renaissance*: we talk of this as if it were a specific period of time, but it is more a set of principles than it is a period. The term is French, meaning rebirth, as in the rebirth of interest in old forms. At first the old forms, in this case the aesthetic principles of the ancient Greeks, are celebrated. Then they are reinterpreted. The *European* Renaissance began in Italy in the 1300s and spread northward through the rest of Europe over the next 200 years. Nowadays, when we speak of a Renaissance *Man*, it tends to connote someone interested and competent in a variety of both classical arts and modern sciences as were many learned men of the Renaissance. That sort of notion is mostly out of fashion now as experts in the modern era tend to focus on a much smaller number of competencies.

Accusatorial systems proceed from the accusation of an injured party and an inquisitorial system proceeds from a process of official inquiry. In the accusatorial system, the injured party and the public participate in the determination of guilt; trial by ordeal. By whatever method this was achieved—by walking through fire, immersion in boiling water, floating, holding hot irons—the process called for an interpretation that could be and certainly was affected by audience reaction. If the witnesses deemed the process to be satisfactory, the permission to punish was then conferred to the political authority and the punishment was then, in most instances, carried out immediately. We note that trial by ordeal declined through the Middle Ages but did not disappear entirely until the Renaissance.

The inquisitorial system, on the other hand, separated guilt determination from punishment in both place and time. The process by which guilt was determined was brought indoors and left to experts who were, of course, city officials assisted by learned scribes. In this system there was no room for the public to determine guilt nor was it given an opportunity to doubt the legitimacy of the process itself. The public's role was not passive however; the public witnessing of the execution and participation in the procession to the site of its denouement were themselves acts of validation. But these merely framed the *real* drama which lay in the moments *just before* death; and the more suffering, the better the drama.

It is hard for us to see beyond the apparent sadism and inhumanity of a huge crowd gathered to witness bodies cruelly mangled and torn, but it was not actually as much a detached and disturbing voyeuristic moment as we might think. In fact, it was a chance for the victim to change his ultimate fate. And this was a matter in which the witnessing crowd played a very real and important role. Would the criminal confess and seek the opportunity of redemption in the next world...hundreds pressed their bodies to the edge of the execution site in anticipation. Active interaction in the form of chants and cries to repent were encouraged by the crowd's physical proximity to the condemned and to the place and means of execution. A truly satisfying execution occurred only when the condemned begged forgiveness of God at the last moment, thereby exchanging in an act of free will the certainty of hell for the inevitability of heaven. The presence of clergy was necessary, of course, to validate the statement of contrition. Meanwhile, only the criminal's body suffered. *

---

* Contemporary woodcuts from the period emphasize the interaction of the attending crowds with the executioner. There have been a number of sociological and anthropological studies of this phenomenon and the best of these highlights the existence of a series of late Medieval and Renaissance manuals on the art of dying (*ars moriendi*). The best of these was written by Jean Gerson (1363-1429), who was, coincidentally, the most important theological figure pushing for the Council of Constance and an end to the three-pope problem. With the invention of moveable type and the engraving process facilitating woodcut illustrations, a series of subsequent editions of his book reached and impressed a wide audience.

The evolving Catholic doctrine of purgatory reinforced the outlines of this experience and helps us to interpret the moment. Although early Christian writers referred to a cleansing fire that filtered and washed away the sins of the faithful entering heaven, the doctrine was not formally articulated until the Councils of Lyon (1245 and 1274), the Council of Florence (1438) and finally the Council of Trent (1545). The doctrine was essentially a product of the Middle Ages and Renaissance. Developed in concert with the church's long-term centralizing efforts, it was *intended to reinforce the church's role* of indispensable mediator between men and God and, metaphorically speaking, as heavenly gatekeeper. A key doctrinal pronouncement by Pope Clement V in 1312 forbade the denial of last rights to condemned prisoners and, in so doing, Clement formalized the church as an active participant in the execution ritual. However, an *unintended consequence* of the doctrine was *to shift power to the individual* with respect to salvation.

The church has always maintained that the path to heaven or hell was a matter of choice. True contrition evinces a choice for heaven and the only question remaining is the length of the time (in purgatory) deemed necessary to purge the soul. But it is also true that suffering in this life can be an offset to that sentence of purgatory. All of this added a sense of intense drama to a good Renaissance execution. We certainly note that the more dramatic the means of execution, the more likely was the contrition. But the more painful and drawn out the punishment, the shorter the time in purgatory, and likewise was reduced the distance to communion with God. The execution was therefore not merely the excision of evil from the community but also a drama of repentance and salvation. So a truly satisfactory execution had to be as painful, drawn out, and theatric as possible.

No surprise then that executions tended toward the gruesome. The most dramatic of these and the one reserved for murderers was "the wheel." The doomed criminal was first tied down and immobilized over a lattice work of wood. A wagon wheel was then brought down sharply upon the larger bones of the limbs, breaking them all one by one. Between ankle and knee, between knee and hip, between wrist and elbow, and so forth; eight fractures in all. The limbs were then threaded through the spokes of yet another wheel, which was hoisted aloft to exhibit the mangled and twisted body in public well past the moment of death, an event that, despite the grievous injuries, might be delayed by days.

Meanwhile, through and through the medieval mind swirled other levels of drama. Starting in the early 1400s, we see a proliferation of books that sought to prove the existence of demons. There was widespread access to and interest in these books by learned men; all were perfectly credulous of the fantastic testimony they catalogued. Heavily dependent on interviews with accused witches, investigators were especially interested in documenting carnal unions between demons and witches. Carnal knowledge was considered the most intimate and therefore reliable category of testimony. To have sexual congress with a demon *proved* that the demon exists. If demons existed, so must their opposite, and by this method might be proved the existence of God—or so the logic went. But even if the premise is weak, it is nevertheless a logical premise and it portends a reordering of the relationship of human reason and faith. This is an indirect testimony of confidence in the power of the individual mind and *the idea of the individual infuses the essence of the modern man.*

## Post-Medieval Fashion and Manners

We can see a complementary trend at work in an increasing obsession with costume and manners as indications of identity. If one believes in a permanent transcendent identity, how one dresses or acts is mostly irrelevant. There is no reason to dress appropriately, or speak or act appropriately—whatever that means—because however one acts or dresses, one is what one is; one cannot be other than what *one is*. Conversely, if one can vary one's identity by dress or costume, then personal identity is not fixed in any existential sense. One is, or at least might be, what one *appears to be*. Once this conceptual horizon is crossed, it is inevitable that *appearance* will surpass *substance* as the most salient indication of identity. Modern historians of fashion and costume note that clothing styles changed very slowly before the 1300s. Clothing customs tended always to reinforce social boundaries. The crusades brought increased and regular contact with other cultures but this had little effect on clothing design except in the growing use of silk. Between 1300 and 1450, this all changed. All sorts of creative distortion of body shapes and variations in fashion began appearing. Men's fashions changed initially through tightening and shortening the pants. Hairstyles followed, and soon the changes were happening so quickly that modern historians can frequently date images within very small bands simply according to clothing and hairstyles.

By the middle 1400s, authorities reacted and began regulating these trends because they tended to obscure social boundaries. Laws performing this function are called sumptuary laws; in Europe before 1300 they were mainly intended to mark criminals, Jews, heretics, and lepers as outsiders to civil society. After 1300, they were established in response to the growing affluence of the urban merchants and guild elites, who were, despite their wealth, still considered commoners by the nobility. For example, in 1430, the duke of Savoy promulgated a set of laws dictating, among other things, appropriate modes of dress according to status. He listed 39 categories of person and specified clothing restrictions for each one. The most restrictive of these laws focused on the ten lowest social categories, signaling an obvious anxiety in higher classes that lower classes might be masquerading outside of their presumed station.

We see the same assumptions about clothing and identity showing up in portraiture and personal behavior. After 1450, portraits of individuals were much more likely to include views of the torso and legs than they ever were before. Modern studies of the costs of commissioning portraits and the clothing worn in them shows clearly that the cost of the clothing far exceeded the cost of the paintings in which they were featured. Just as in clothing, social mannerisms came to convey meanings in ways that seem familiar to us now, but not so much to those who lived before 1400. It would never have occurred to a noble in the year 1200 that putting his fingers into a common bowl was an indication of low class behavior. By the year 1500, there were dozens of popular writers publishing handbooks on education, behavior, table manners, and dress. Alberti, della Casa, Castiglione, and the most popular writer of his day, Erasmus, all made contributions to this genre. All of this goes to the same point: individuals increasingly found it within their own competence to define themselves even as they might resist the ability of others to do the same.

# Rediscovery of Ancient Knowledge

An important factor undermining the medieval mindset was the increasing ubiquity of evidence that medieval society fell short in comparison to ancient and other societies. A major byproduct of the crusades and the repeated opportunities for cross-cultural exchange was the unexpected return of Europe's own past. For centuries after Europeans lost interest in scientific information concerning the universe and our planet, Greek and Roman tomes that explored these topics sat on shelves in Arab libraries. Bit by bit this information crept back into circulation in Europe. Ptolemy's *Geography* represents a great example. A Roman citizen named Claudius Ptolemy published an atlas of the world based on ancient knowledge in the AD 100s. Our earliest evidence for its existence is in a mention by an Arab writer who described it around the year 1000. His comments indicate that the copy he saw contained maps. It first reappeared in western hands when a Byzantine monk named Maximus Planudes found a copy of it in 1295. The maps were no longer there, but Planudes redrew them from information found in the text. He made a copy and this copy made its way to Florence where it next appeared in its first Latin translation around 1410. By the 1470s, numerous editions were extant and after 1480, most of these had maps, presumably based on Planudes' reconstruction. The by-then-widely-circulated map, its many errors notwithstanding, was a remarkable document and Ptolemy's ideation of the world immediately became the default for all unexplored parts of the globe. Meanwhile, the Arabs had been publishing sophisticated critiques of Ptolemy's *Geography*, some of which were translated into Latin by the 1400s.

The astrolabe provides another excellent example of classical knowledge circulating through the Arab world and then making its way back to Europe. Invented by the Greeks around 150 BC, the astrolabe was originally designed as a primitive calculator for astronomic calculations.

Arab mathematicians then adapted astrolabes in the 900s to facilitate direct readings of stars and planets to determine correct prayer times and relative directions to Mecca. However, it was already clear to the Arabs by the year 1000 that it was also useful in determining latitudes and therefore suitable to facilitate navigation. By 1300, a complicated text on the astrolabe was circulating in Paris. A few decades later Chaucer wrote an essay on the astrolabe, based on an Arab writer (Messahalla) whose work had turned up, and other editions soon followed. By the 1400s, astrolabes and the knowhow to use them were available all across Europe. As it turned out, the timing for the arrival of this knowledge could not have been more perfect. Along with this technical knowledge was circulating a new genre of literature, the travelogue. One of the most popular, and earliest, examples was that of Marco Polo. Well over 100 different manuscript editions of the book survive. Polo's book, dictated to a cellmate in prison around the year 1300, is filled with tails of the true and the fantastic.* Some modern scholars doubt its authenticity but this is not the majority view. Polo's descriptions made it painfully clear to European readers that a civilization more advanced than Europe existed on the other side of the world. His descriptions of the huge cites, bustling marketplaces, the strange customs and marvelous inventions of the Chinese stimulated much interest, especially in the possibility of bypassing Muslim control of the overland trade routes.

# The Portuguese

Meanwhile, the rhythms of the world economy were also in flux. The Mongol Empire collapsed in the 1370s and the overland trade route known in western parlance as the Silk Road became more dangerous, driving up the costs of travel. In 1453, the Muslim Turks took Constantinople, the only western gateway to the Silk Road that was not already controlled by Muslims. The Turks, vehemently anti-European, placed tight restrictions on

---

* Marco Polo returned to his home city of Venice in 1295 after a 24-year trip to the Far East. Venice was then at war with Genoa and when the Genoans took Polo's ship, he was tossed into a prison for several years. It was during this time that he produced his famous memoir.

trade with Europe. The existence of a vast Muslim world standing between Christian Europe and the riches of the Orient constituted a challenge that excited the zeal of all European rulers. The real draw of course was the wealth of the Far East. Marco Polo's vivid descriptions of Chinese cites far greater in size and grandeur than those of Europe and the obvious profits of spice and silk were powerful inducements to sponsor trade missions. The widespread belief in the existence of the fabled Christian kingdom of Prester John encouraged the belief that an alliance with friendly powers on the other side of the Muslims might be possible. These events inspired some Europeans to consider alternate trade routes and the creation of alternate trade empires. The most successful of the early players in this new game were the Portuguese. Portugal was one of the kingdoms founded in the long war between Christian and Muslim lords in the Iberian peninsula (modern Spain and Portugal). Like all those kingdoms—Leon, Castille, Aragon—Portugal was founded in the fire of crusade and the Portuguese nobility carried the mindset of a powerful God who dispensed gold and glory to those who fought in His name.

The Portuguese were no fools and their rulers understood that Christian zeal was not enough to make Portugal great. In 1415 Henry, a prince of the Portuguese Aviz dynasty, seized a caravan trade terminus (Ceuta) located across from the Straits of Gibraltar. Young Prince Henry was twenty-one and, as fourth son of the king, unlikely to succeed to the throne. So Henry took as his personal mission the creation of a Portuguese empire in Africa (and potentially beyond). With his father's encouragement and the financial backing of the Order of Christ,* Henry sponsored exploration of the African coastline and the islands off the coast. Historians have for years suggested that Henry founded some sort of school for navigation and maritime technology but this is probably overstated. Henry was instrumental, later in life, in establishing the University of Lisbon. In the short term, however, his influence was more focused. He employed

---

* *The Order of Christ*: When the Knights Templar Order was taken apart in 1312, King Dinis of Portugal reconstituted those resident in Portugal under this new name several years later. They became one of the most important military assets of the Portuguese monarchy. Their connection to the papacy was severed in 1789, but they continued to serve the monarchy until its end in 1910.

mapmakers and ship builders, and generous extension of Portuguese patronage brought together useful technologies. For example, Abraham Zacuto, a Jewish astronomer from Spain, published a comprehensive set of astronomical tables in 1478. The book was translated into Latin in 1481, and into Portuguese by 1496. This eventually became instrumental in navigation as it allowed for navigation based on sun observations, instead of the North Star, which was useless as one approached the equator. Henry's

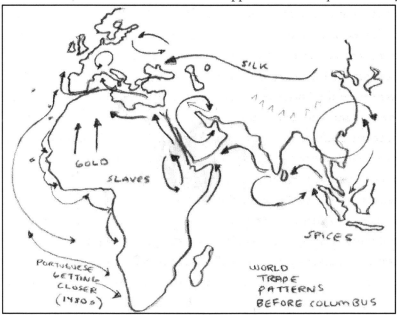

early ships employed the triangular lateen sail, which was common in the Arab world. These were especially helpful in going upwind. Henry's designs combined these with traditional European square sails, which were more powerful but primarily useful for downwind travel. Portuguese efforts integrated by steps all the elements of what was then state-of-the-art ship building and navigation techniques, which soon paid off. By 1444, Portuguese explorers working their way down the coast had advanced beyond the Sahara desert where the profits in gold and slaves really began to roll in. By 1488, Bartolemeo Dias had made it to the southern tip of Africa, only to be turned back by a mutinous crew.

As this trend progressed, a whole new economy was building in the Atlantic, one based on sugar. Sugar was a luxury in the 1400s and the market was insatiable. Sugar produced for sale in Europe came mostly from Cyprus and Sicily, so when the Portuguese (and Spanish) came to control islands off Africa they naturally considered their new possessions as suitable to cultivate some of that sweet business. And by 1490, the Portuguese and Spanish were importing more sugar to Europe than anyone else. Disputes between Portugal and Spain over these island conquests resulted in the treaty of Alcáçovas in 1479. The treaty granted the Spanish permanent control of the Canaries but recognized Portuguese control over all other Atlantic islands and *any other islands or discoveries south of the Canaries.* The long-term repercussions of that treaty were tremendous.

## Columbus

Columbus

Columbus is the perfect character to bring together all the threads of this chapter. He grew up in the first European generation to live in a world of mass-produced books. The invention of moveable type had stimulated an information revolution on the same scale as the Internet in our own time. The total number of books in circulation virtually exploded in Columbus' lifetime. He carted his favorite books around with him wherever he went. These included Ptolemy's *Geography*, Marco Polo's travelogue, and Zacuto's almanac of astronomic tables. But although Columbus read voraciously on these new modern topics, he still kept one foot in the past. If we may believe his own words on the matter, he imagined that the wealth of the Asian trade he schemed to take over would become instrumental in asserting a Christian dominion of the world. He would be right, in a sense, because European traders would eventually dominate and subvert political and economic systems in virtually every part of the globe.

The more one looks at Columbus, the more space seems evident between substance of Columbus and the image he cultivated. With respect to his reputation as "the Great Navigator," for example, scholars credit him for being highly competent in the art of dead reckoning,* but the evidence suggests that he never learned to take sun sights, the most advanced method of his time. It seems that Columbus was never a man to be bothered by inconvenient details. If a fact wasn't congenial to his plans, he either substituted one of his own making, or just left it out, so to speak. One might say he *imagined* himself a great man, and then the imagined Columbus consumed the real one. His own writings suggest a life of high drama although modern scholars suspect much of it is...*enhanced*. His first trip through the Straits of Gibraltar was supposedly as a seaman in a fleet of Genoese ships bound for Lisbon. By his account, the fleet was attacked by pirates, the ship on which he worked was sunk, and Columbus swam six miles to the Portuguese shore; it is a great story, but one of dubious veracity. It was 1476, Columbus was a twenty-five year-old dreamer, and he was dreaming great things.

Columbus partnered with his brother in Lisbon and together they ran a shop updating and selling navigation charts. It was a bustling and exciting place to be. There were lots of experienced Italian seamen and merchants in Lisbon with whom Columbus could network; this put him in a strong position to keep abreast of new discoveries and technical developments. He worked on Portuguese ships going north and south on the Atlantic, sailing as far north as Iceland and as far south as Guinea. Chance references here and there in his writings suggest that he gained a fairly sophisticated understanding not only of geography, but also of business. He learned

---

* *Dead reckoning*: the art of using a previously known position on a map to plot a current position by means of estimating speed and direction over the time since that known position was established.

navigation by dead reckoning and he made note of the wind patterns that obstructed or facilitated navigation east and west. Columbus also took note of flotsam born eastward that hinted at land being much closer than the supposed distance to China; plus, he paid careful attention to all the legends of travelers purported to have already been to Asia by western travel.

Sometime after he arrived in Lisbon, Columbus heard that an Italian mathematician and astronomer, Paulo Toscanelli, had written to the king of Portugal in 1474 encouraging him to sail west to China; with this letter came a map indicating that China was *much* closer than anyone had previously argued. Columbus wrote to Toscanelli, who was happy to repeat the details of his earlier missive and also sent Columbus a copy of his map. From this moment, Columbus was seized with the desire to be the one to make that voyage. But Toscanelli was wrong in his geographic assumptions, all of which ran contrary to what was actually a fairly accurate conventional wisdom on the size of the planet and the distance to China. Even so, Columbus was convinced that Toscanelli was right despite any arguments or evidence to the contrary. But Toscanelli was not the only source for Columbus' mistake.

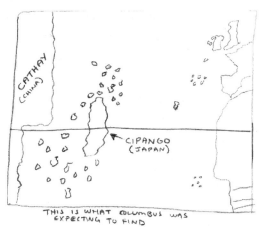

We know that Columbus had acquired a copy of Pierre D'Ailly's *Imago Mundi* (published between 1480 and 1483) and this book also underestimated the size of the earth while over-estimating the size of Asia. Notations that Columbus made in the margins of his copy indicate the main basis of the miscalculation: confusion over the size of the earth. Columbus used every opportunity of interpretation to argue that the world was substantially smaller than it actually is, while at the same time arguing that all estimates of the size of Asia were too small. His tortured calculations put the unknown land that Marco Polo called Cipango (Japan) at about the distance that

Columbus actually covered on his first voyage, except it did not turn out to be Japan (or Cipango), but islands in the Bahamas. It was ironic that Columbus ended up being so right about how far it was to land, but so wrong about what land it was!

In 1484, Columbus put his scheme to the king of Portugal who, after consulting with his own geography experts, concluded that Columbus was a crackpot. Furthermore, since Portuguese efforts to explore and exploit Africa were going quite nicely, there was no reason to throw away ships on such a crazy scheme. But we also know that the Portuguese king did sponsor *other* trips westward from Portugal, so Columbus was not the only would-be explorer importuning royal patrons. One can easily argue that, had Columbus not made his famous voyage, someone else would have done it within just a few decades.

One theory for Columbus' failure with the Portuguese king was an unfortunate association, through the family of his mother-in-law, with certain conspiracies against the king. But whatever the basis of the refusal, Columbus did not skip a beat. He took his proposal to Spain. He traveled to Seville, where he sought the approval and influence of a Spanish friar and astronomer, Antonio de Marchena. Scholars think there might be some family connection at work here, but the evidence is not clear. In any case, de Marchena did provide Columbus' an entre to the Spanish court. Despite this well-placed connection, Columbus was forced to wait for his plan to be reviewed by technical advisors who, on behalf of Ferdinand and Isabella, eventually gave a thumbs-down to the plan. Undeterred, Columbus got by those advisors and gained an actual interview with the monarchs early in 1486. Again he was turned down, but this time the monarchs put him on a modest retainer to keep him around.

Columbus was nothing if not persistent. In 1487, when his royal retainer seems to have run out, Columbus produced a letter he had from the king of Portugal inviting him back to Lisbon to talk about his proposal. Unfortunately, his timing could not have been worse. Shortly after his arrival in Lisbon in 1488, Bartolomeo Dias returned to Portugal after having reached the tip of Africa. Although Dias' trip was cut short by a mutiny of his crew, his successful return to Lisbon nevertheless made it clear that Portuguese ships would soon be sailing in the Indian ocean, the first European ships to do so since the fall of the ancient Roman empire. Columbus was in Lisbon to witness Dias' triumphant return. In all the excitement, the king of Portugal forgot all about Columbus, who went back to Spain.

The next year, the Spanish royal couple, Isabella and Ferdinand, awarded Columbus another allowance to keep him on a leash while they continued their campaign to take the last Muslim fortress in Spain. At the very least, they took him seriously enough to prevent others from gaining by his proposal, but not seriously enough to spend the money necessary to sponsor him, a least for the moment. Columbus never stopped pushing. He approached a number of businessmen in Spain, some Italian and some Spanish but, although he did put together some support, in the end he could not proceed without the permission of the royal couple. In January of 1492, Columbus was invited back to pitch his proposal again and yet again he failed. Meanwhile, the surrender of last Muslim city, Granada, had taken place (January 2, 1492). Thinking his options finally at an end in Spain, Columbus determined to try his luck in France where his brother Bartolomeo had already been making some inquiries. This was the critical moment. Upon hearing of Columbus's plans to depart for France, the royal couple promptly changed their mind. One suspects that Ferdinand and Isabella were less concerned with losing Columbus than they were with keeping him away from the French.

There was still the problem of finances, however, and the royal couple was not prepared to pay for the whole expedition. Their successful campaign to take Granada had exhausted the royal treasury and the job still wasn't quite finished. This had been a crusade after all, and there was the problem of all those pesky Jews and Moslems—they had to go. On March 31, the couple issued the decree of Alhambra giving all Jews exactly three months to convert or leave; some scholars estimate that well over 100,000 Jews chose to leave, mostly for Portugal. Those choosing to leave were barred from taking any gold or silver with them. This tried and true policy toward the Jews had always provided a dependable source of cash for medieval monarchs pinched for cash. The timing synchronized nicely with the royal negotiations with Columbus. These were completed in April and Columbus' actual departure for the new world actually coincided with the departure of the last Jews from Spain. But even with a cash infusion provided by the fleeing Jews, royal financing of Columbus' adventure was lukewarm at best. About half the financing for the expedition was private. The largest of the three ships Columbus used was a rental and the other two had been confiscated in a smuggling dispute. All three were too small for the trip and in questionable condition. Even the crew was a little sketchy. Three convicted murderers were released from jail to fill out the roster. This obviously lukewarm support was offset somewhat by sweeping promises of wealth and position if the voyage were in fact successful. The combination of the weak royal commitment to financing the expedition and the impressive generosity of the terms assuming its success suggests that the royals didn't really expect Columbus to return.

The motives of the Spanish crown were complicated. The combination of Dias' successful turning of the African cape meant that Portugal was about to become Europe's most important trade empire. The Spanish, keenly aware of their neighbor's imminent success, were nonetheless prevented from simply following the Portuguese around Africa by the treaty they had signed only a few years earlier, the treaty of Alcáçovas, in which Spain yielded to Portugal all islands and future discoveries to the south of the Canary islands. That treaty had been brokered by the papacy in 1479 and their very close relationship with the papacy made it problematic for Spain to break that treaty. Giving Columbus a green light to sail west represented a gamble with huge potential rewards yet with little actual cost. What was the worst thing that could happen? If he didn't come back, Columbus would not be pestering them any longer. If he made it? Woohoo!! And of course the bet paid off. The expedition left Palos in Spain on August 3, refitted in the Canaries, and left there for parts unknown on September 6, 1492. On October 11th, Columbus' little fleet reduced sail after sighting land in what we now call the Bahamas. Wary of hidden rocks and shoals, they spent the night tacking back and forth and made landfall on the next day. It was a fateful day for the world.

And so, by having arrived at this place, we have also come to the end of this little volume. The discovery of the new world, its strange peoples, and the incredible quantities of loot waiting to be plundered merely hastened all the political, economic and intellectual trends well under way in the Renaissance era. New overseas empires helped fund the efforts of monarchs to control their nobles and provided a boost to their bona fides as great leaders. The relentless rise of a new economic order combined with the enormously lucrative global trade in spices accelerated the creation and evolution of sophisticated financial institutions. An unceasing parade of discoveries diluted the vestiges of that old medieval idea, "God Wills It," although the notion never died altogether. And as Europe physically shrank on published maps of the world, so also did the sun soon displace the earth from the center of the universe. The Middle Ages were over. The Ancient World was a distant memory. The Modern Age had begun.

# Index